Issues of
National Security
in the 1970's

Colonel George A. Lincoln

Issues of National Security in the 1970's

Essays Presented to Colonel George A. Lincoln on His Sixtieth Birthday

EDITED BY

Colonel Amos A. Jordan, Jr.

FREDERICK A. PRAEGER, Publishers
New York · Washington · London

FREDERICK A. PRAEGER, PUBLISHERS
111 Fourth Avenue, New York, N.Y. 10003, U.S.A.
77–79 Charlotte Street, London W.1, England

Published in the United States of America in 1967
by Frederick A. Praeger, Inc., Publishers

© 1967 by Frederick A. Praeger, Inc.

Library of Congress Catalog Card Number: 67–20483

Printed in the United States of America

Preface

When I first broached to a group of colleagues the idea of a collection of essays in honor of Colonel Lincoln, I found that I had far more volunteer authors than one volume could possibly accommodate. Lincoln's lifelong devotion to the problems of national security made especially attractive the notion of a *Festschrift* devoted to analyzing the security challenges of the future.

The topics covered by the essays in this volume have been selected both because of their pertinence to defense policy in the decade of the 1970's and because they represent the fields in which Colonel Lincoln's contribution over the past forty years has been particularly significant. The authors of the essays are all colleagues of Lincoln who have worked with him on these matters, either in actually making policy or in teaching about it.

Essentially, the authors represent two generations: those who shared with him the tasks of planning the optimum use of American military power during World War II and the immediate postwar years, and those younger colleagues who taught under him in the Department of Social Sciences at West Point about the range of politico-military issues confronting the United States in the 1950's and 1960's. They represent both the military and the civilian elements of our national security and educational processes, as is fitting in a tribute to a man who has been a bridge between the civilian and military worlds in both the policy-making process and education.

Many of the individuals who would have liked to participate in the authorship of this volume have instead offered their thoughts and editorial pens to the authors of the essays. So many have helped that it is not feasible to list their names. Nevertheless, the quality of the volume owes a great deal to them.

Those of the authors who are members of the government have written, not in their capacity as officials, but as students and citizens facing the common problems of defining and meeting the challenges to American security in the decade ahead. Their views are their own and do not necessarily represent those of the United States Government.

COLONEL AMOS A. JORDAN, JR., USA

Contents

Issues of
National Security
in the 1970's

George A. Lincoln:
Architect in National Security

LIEUTENANT COLONEL ROGER H. NYE

The United States Military Academy has rarely been accused of raiding sister schools for its professors. It has preferred to lure them from within the Army's far-flung fortresses and occasionally from inside the Pentagon. Never was this brand of professornapping more successful than just after World War II, when a number of distinguished senior officers were persuaded to leave the line of the Army to become officer-professors. George Arthur ("Abe") Lincoln was in the 1947 draft.

He was not easily shanghaied. He had grown accustomed to heavy responsibilities, had retained his Brigadier General's stars through the postwar cutbacks, and was poised for the command positions that were promised if he stayed in the line. But on September 1, 1947, he became Colonel G. A. Lincoln, Professor and Deputy Head of the Department of Social Sciences, U.S. Military Academy.

His Pentagon boss sent him a letter of farewell, which said, in part:

As you leave the War Department I must express my warm appreciation for the great contributions you have made to our

3

victory in World War II and to the national security of the
United States. . . . I attribute in very great part to you a noticeable growth in the soundness and clarity of military policy pertaining to U.S. security. . . . I personally have leaned heavily
on your advice since my arrival here, confident that your solutions would be the best that hard work, outstanding intelligence,
integrity and devotion to duty could provide. . . .

(s) Dwight D. Eisenhower

The Planner

Chief of Staff Eisenhower did not mention how Professor
Lincoln had become the American Army's chief planner in
those critical years that ushered out the greatest hot war of all
time and ushered in a new "cold" one. Lincoln's career as a
planner had begun in the G-4 (logistics) division of Maj.
Gen. John C. H. Lee's London headquarters. In May, 1943,
he was juggling a headful of statistics about landing craft
and invasion logistics when a visitor, Maj. Gen. Thomas T.
Handy, head of General George Marshall's Operations Division (OPD), noticed him and recalled the Chief of Staff's
policy of recruiting officers from the field. Lee argued that
Lincoln, with his Oxford background, was needed to help
communicate between the British and the Americans. Handy
conceded the point, and suggested that such competence
could be better used to draft cables for Mr. Roosevelt to send
to Mr. Churchill.

Back in Washington shortly thereafter, General Marshall
asked Lincoln to comment on a paragraph he was dictating
about the European theater. Lincoln corrected some errors of
fact, and Marshall dictated it a second time. Lincoln inter-
rupted for further improvement; Marshall gave up and proceeded to other work piled before him. Handy later introduced the new boy around OPD as the only man who
corrected Marshall twice in a given day and still had a job at
sundown. The consensus favored an explanation of beginner's

luck, but most knew that Marshall had no time or tolerance for ceremony; he kept only those people who, regardless of rank, spoke up—and were also right.

The Marshall school was tough and satisfying for Lincoln. As a member of the Joint Staff Planners, he saw the war in an Army-Navy context, and, with the Combined Staff Planners, he lived it with the British. He was military adviser to Assistant Secretary of War John J. McCloy in the latter's role as a member of the State-War-Navy Coordinating Committee. As Chief of the Strategy and Policy Group of OPD, Lincoln's work included not only the military planning but also the meshing of military and political strategies. This put him on the action end of the military messages flowing from Churchill to Roosevelt, to Admiral Leahy, and then informally to Marshall, and on to OPD. Lincoln sent drafts of replies back up the line. Once a draft came back with a note from Marshall: "Rewrite; the PM does not like anyone to opt his style. GCM." The OPD assignment also put Lincoln on the conference circuit. Since General Marshall and the chiefs of OPD traveled light, Lincoln was sometimes a one-man staff division with all the problems in his head and one briefcase. On the circuit were Quebec, Yalta, and Potsdam. He later mused that he had attended most of the "wrong" meetings since Calvary.

Toward the war's end, Lincoln was as involved militarily in deploying American troops from Europe to the Pacific as he was politically in forestalling their usefulness through drafting and processing a surrender formula for the Japanese. In pinning the Distinguished Service Medal on him, Marshall cited General Lincoln for tenacity in planning and negotiating the operations of the global war and for wisdom in integrating logistical and strategic factors of that war.

When peace overtook the simple national objective of "unconditional surrender," the tasks of OPD divided and multiplied. Lincoln, foreseeing the expansion, requested a 50 per cent increase in OPD personnel, was rejected by disbelievers, then got the personnel six months later as the sobering requirements of the American power position pressed on the military chiefs. While dealing with the chores of disestablishing giant military forces at home and in the nations of former enemies, the planners were scratching the surface of such mysteries as the international control of nuclear and other weapons, United Nations security forces, the reconstruction of war-torn continents, and the obstreperous conduct of a Russian ally.

Lincoln started having a weekly informal lunch with George Kennan, head of the new State Department Policy Planning Staff. Seeing the military in a role of greater scope than was traditional, he proposed "National Security" as the title of the new department, which was finally named "Defense," after the Department of State rightly indicated that it, too, was in the security business. Lincoln saw that the emerging "peacetime" world was unlike that known to earlier generations of Americans, but he also saw that the citizenry was responding as if nothing new had taken place. There was a task for teachers in the offing.

The Professor

By 1947, Lincoln had served for four years at the center of the decision-making complex of the world's most powerful nation. Having been promoted to Brigadier General at age thirty-eight, he could expect to hold critical positions of military responsibility for two decades. He had been seasoned in the OPD "school for strategists," and he had watched at close hand the successful methods of a broad spectrum of civilian and military officials in the field of national security affairs. His decision to apply this experience and knowledge as an educator was appraised in later years by West Point's first postwar Superintendent, Maj. Gen. Maxwell D. Taylor: "Colonel George A. Lincoln was one of the bright stars who came to the permanent faculty at this time. . . . While his loss to the Army as a whole may be regretted, I would say that his influence upon many generations of cadets probably constitutes in the aggregate a greater contribution to national defense than that made by most general officers of the line."

At West Point, Lincoln reported to Colonel Herman Beukema, the imaginative and courageous artilleryman who, since 1930, had forged the courses in social sciences in the fire of good scholarship, interdisciplinary realism, and enthusiastic devotion to the national need.

Lincoln's first major contribution as a scholar was his writing up his wartime "research." OPD had been an academy for strategists and statesmen, but it also had great potential— as do most governmental agencies—as a school for scholars. Lincoln's research was eminently practical, for he had written many of the documents himself, had worked with those writing others, and had, at the conference table and committee room, experienced a thoroughly candid research seminar.

In his writing, Lincoln saw his task as one of analysis and exposition, rather than of creating a new synthesis of theoretical conceptions in international relations and national security matters. He had earlier published *Background of Our War*, a 250-page collection of lectures developed under his direction as the Army's first attempt at a modern troop information program. His first postwar book (1948), *International Realities*, was an explication of recent trends in the international political scene and was addressed to the down-to-earth education of the citizenry. Foremost in his mind was the education of cadets for national service; this objective dominated the writing of this and all his subsequent books.

In search of ways to encourage the next generation's leaders to learn how to control and conduct foreign policy after World War II, Lincoln began a career of speaking at universities and colleges, such as the Mount Holyoke College Institute on the United Nations, where he talked on "International Control of Atomic Energy" in 1948 and "Germany's Place in the Search for Security" in 1949. In the same years, he talked "reality" to the officer-students of the nation's higher military schools, beginning with "Planning for War" at the National War College in 1947, and concentrating thereafter on the lessons to be drawn from the Allies' effort to find and implement a winning strategy in World War II.

The Practicing Researcher

The man who dedicates his life to explaining reality in a changing world cannot allow his conception of that reality to atrophy, lest he mislead those he hopes to guide. Within a little more than a year after reporting to the Academy, Lincoln was given his first opportunity to renew his on-the-job research when he was ordered to Washington for five months to fill a key executive position in the Pentagon. He served as deputy to Undersecretary of the Army William H. Draper, Jr., who devoted full time to devising the first unified-services budget and passed the normal undersecretarial tasks to Lincoln.

In 1949, after little more than a year back at the Academy, Lincoln was once again drafted, this time to become a special assistant to the Secretary of Defense, charged with representing the Department in molding the Mutual Security Program. He was not new to the subject of overseas assistance; he had once appeared with Dean Acheson and Admiral Forrest Sherman as witnesses before the Senate Foreign Relations Committee on the Greek-Turkish Aid Program. In 1950, Ambassador Averell Harriman, the U.S. Representative and Chairman of the Temporary Council Committee for NATO, called on this expertise once again. The Ambassador later recalled:

> As soon as I was appointed Chairman, I immediately turned to Abe Lincoln, and asked him to join me as my military advisor. . . . The assignment of this Committee, nicknamed the "Three Wise Men," was of wide significance. Its task was to analyze "the issues involved in reconciling, on the one hand, the re-

quirements of external security, in particular of fulfilling a militarily acceptable NATO plan for the defense of Western Europe with, on the other hand, the realistic political-economic capabilities of member countries. . . ." In dealing with the analysis of each country, the Ministers of Finance and Defense appeared before our Committee to clarify the information submitted and to discuss policy. I looked to Abe to help me reconcile every factor.

During the intense work of the Committee, all of Colonel Lincoln's wisdom and experience was brought into play. I had known him during the war as one of the ablest planners. I had met him on a number of occasions on my trips home from Moscow. His penetrating questions made me realize his deep understanding of the political as well as military aspects of the war and the postwar period. He understood that war was not an operation detached from the political life of a nation. It was, in fact, an expression of essential political objectives, and therefore, had to be conducted with political aims in mind.

Without in any way belittling the contribution of my other American associates on the TCC staff, or the very able group that served on the British and French staffs, I can say unqualifiedly that none had a deeper comprehension than Abe Lincoln of all aspects of the problems of NATO and its member countries as related to our mutual security and defense. . . .

While contributing to these operations, Lincoln was also translating the changing world he had seen into lessons for cadets and others to study. By 1950, he had led thirteen Associates in the Social Sciences in the writing of *Economics of National Security*, a volume that explained the governmental apparatus that copes with national security and the nature of the problems confronted by that apparatus—from budgeting, through manpower allocations, to transportation and foreign aid. The 1954 revision of the book carried the meaningful subtitle, "Managing America's Resources for Defense." The text was the foundation for a course required for all cadets; its use spread through other colleges and government schools and was staple diet for novices in the field until,

more than a decade later, scholarship in defense economics
began to interest other economists and political scientists.

The Lincoln explication of international reality found
many additional outlets in the 1950's. He lectured at Case
Institute on "National Security and Military Geography," and
contributed a chapter entitled "Conflicts Among Nations" to
Global Geography. The subject of a 1953 lecture at Wayne
State University was "Military and Strategic Aspects of Contemporary American Foreign Policy"; a later one at the
Fletcher School of Law and Diplomacy was "Strategic Problems Presented by the Soviet Bloc." With two colleagues, he
provided a unique chapter on "Mobilization and War" in
Seymour Harris' *American Economic History.*

These fragments helped pave the way for a more complete
exposition of Lincoln's theses. Finding that their views, draft
writings, and teaching requirements were substantially alike,
he and Norman Padelford, of the Massachusetts Institute of
Technology, in 1952 joined in a fifteen-year writing association unmarred by any unmanageable disagreement. The first
fruit of their collaboration, *International Politics,* a college
text, was published in 1954. While the book was successful
from the publisher's standpoint, the authors were not satisfied
that they had made their points adequately. In six years, they
began improving and updating their work. The result of their
revisions, *The Dynamics of International Politics* (1961), was
a new book even more widely used, and the rewritten version,
published in 1967, was an improved, even more impressive
volume.

The exposition of one's views is magnified arithmetically
when incorporated by other writers and speakers, and expo-
nentially when incorporated by other teachers, researchers,
and policy makers into their programs. It is, therefore, not
surprising that Lincoln accepted a variety of invitations to
join other scholars and statesmen in the pursuit of joint study
efforts. His association with the Brookings Institution began
in 1949, and through the 1950's he frequently joined in the

discussions of the Council on Foreign Relations and in Professor Frank Tannenbaum's Seminar on War and Peace at Columbia University. He was a consultant of Ohio State's Mershon Institute for its seminars on the teaching of military history for officers assigned to the ROTC. He reviewed manuscript drafts for Masland and Radway's *Soldiers and Scholars* and for Hitch and McKean's *The Economics of Defense in the Nuclear Age*. He aided the Ford Foundation studies on leadership in public affairs in 1955, and later became a member of the Social Science Research Council Committee on National Security Policy Research.

The Lincoln input to these convenings of good minds was substantive, gleaned from experience both as a federal servant and a scholar. Many thought, too, that his hard work and knack for good management helped a discussion group make progress. In late 1957, he was a panel member on the Rockefeller Brothers Fund Study on "International Security: The Military Aspect." He sent off a draft on one topic to Nelson Rockefeller; the reply was to the point: "Dear Abe: I think the Lincoln report is superb in its succinctness. . . . Sincerely, Nelson."

The Consultant and Executive

The Rockefeller studies on mid-century America were only one of the items that marked 1957 as a year of change for Lincoln. He had completed a decade of professorial duties, and, in many ways, had outrun his original mission. The school of reality in defense and foreign policy matters was now accepted by a host of present and future leaders, and scholarly tomes on security were flowing from the university presses and mass media.

In 1956, Lincoln had narrowly escaped an extended tour in Washington. Secretary of State John Foster Dulles and President Eisenhower had asked him to fill the vacant position of

Head of the State Department's Policy Planning Council. To Lincoln's point that he was "not good enough," Eisenhower replied, "Of course not. Nobody is good enough to be President either, but somebody has to do it." As it turned out, the Chairman of the Senate Foreign Relations Committee objected to a professional military man in the job.

In the spring of 1957, the President asked Rowan Gaither, Chairman of the Board of the Ford Foundation, to head a study group that was to make recommendations on "active and passive measures for the defense of the United States." Lincoln joined this group, a distinguished gathering whose "Gaither Report" to the National Security Council endorsed new directions in security policy that had been spurred by rapid technological change. Nearly a decade afterward, former committee member James A. Perkins, now President of Cornell University, recalled Lincoln's role:

> On this, as on other occasions, one remembers with gratitude the presence of Abe Lincoln. His common sense based on wide experience was an indispensable ingredient in a running discourse sometimes dominated by "amateur experts." If the report was both timely and tough (as this witness believes it was), Abe Lincoln, and other wise men who worked hard that summer, can take a special bow.

The work of the Gaither Committee was controversial, according to press speculation, and was kept secret, except for some of the thought that may have entered the Rockefeller studies. The work of the Draper Committee, convened by the President in the following year to study the Military Assistance Program, was equally controversial, but fully in the public eye. William Draper chaired a distinguished group of civilian and military figures in the task. The White House asked West Point for Lincoln's release to perform the tasks of executive officer of the committee. When the final report was published in August, 1959, President Eisenhower wrote Lincoln, in part: "Bill Draper has told me that without you the job could not have been done with the outstanding result that was achieved."

When Lincoln turned to other consultative roles after the Draper Committee, his clients extended across a broadened spectrum of the government, reflecting the new scope of security considerations. William C. Foster and John J. McCloy saw that he joined the consultative group of the new U.S. Arms Control and Disarmament Agency. He continued to share ideas with Allen Dulles and his colleagues at the Central Intelligence Agency. When Senator Henry M. Jackson undertook leadership of the Senate Subcommittee on National Security Machinery, he sought Lincoln's advice, and Lincoln's presentation on military professionalism was published in 1964. As consultant, he could perform many tasks, sometimes little more than commenting on the manuscripts or staff papers of others, more often arming the clients with new facts and ideas—"new ways of going," in Lincoln parlance.

In 1964, Lincoln took sabbatical leave from West Point to embark on his most extensive job of consulting as Special Adviser to the Administrator (David Bell) of the Agency for International Development. In response to Bell's injunction to find ways of appraising foreign aid operations to improve their efficiency, Lincoln focused on the U.S. AID missions in a number of Latin American countries. His report was printed in October, 1965, as "Improving A.I.D. Program Evaluation."

The Head of Department

Lincoln's primary interest in education was, and is, in providing dedicated and well-educated men for service in the variety of government personnel systems. When he became Head of West Point's Department of Social Sciences on Herman Beukema's retirement in 1954, he also added his voice and vote to the Academic Board, the Academy's policy-formulating agency. In subsequent years, his teaching faculty expanded, as West Point itself grew, from thirty-five to more than fifty members, and the number of student enrollments in department courses doubled, to some 2,600 per semester as of 1966–67. New subjects entered the cadet curriculum: Political philosophy, histories of Russia, the Middle East, and American diplomacy, and, not surprisingly, a course entitled "National Security Problems." Economics received new stress, with the introduction, first, of a comparative economic systems course and, more recently, of the essentials of computerized cost-effectiveness analysis. Another significant innovation was the comparative study of developing nations. Asian studies were expanded.

Lincoln's philosophy of officer development went beyond the formally curricular. He stressed that cadet interest is a paramount element in education, and that any "solid" intellectual activity for which a cadet volunteers is likely to be worth supporting. He championed the research and argumentation techniques associated with student debating. These activities grew in great part from Lincoln's efforts to open up West Point's "windows on the world," an objective he also pursued by importing eminent and talented guest speakers on public and international affairs, and by arranging a vastly increased interchange between cadets and their college contemporaries.

In Lincoln's view, his most important task was the selection, acquisition, graduate education, and guidance of his department faculty. He wanted outstanding teachers, whom he believed could generally be found among the best professional officers. For preparation, he arranged short tours of practical experience in Washington, participation in civilian conferences and overseas assignments, as well as two or more years of graduate schooling. Furthermore, Lincoln encouraged latitude and initiative, so much so that his instructors were often reminded of Marshall's staff officer who brought to the chief an obviously valid recommendation and received one comment: "Why haven't you done it already?"

In 1966, Gen. Maxwell D. Taylor, former Chairman of the Joint Chiefs of Staff and United States Ambassador to Viet-Nam, wrote of the "unusual results" of Lincoln's work with his military faculty in the Department of Social Sciences:

> The Department expanded in many fields and began to attract increasing numbers of brilliant young officers into the ranks of its instructors. . . . Gradually they formed in the Officer Corps a group of officers with the Lincoln stamp and his outlook toward the basic issues of national defense. In his Department, Lincoln had taught them the necessity of blending together military and non-military components to form a national strategy of maximum effectiveness. They had acquired from him an understanding of the many facets of national power and the need for flexibility in its application. Such men have become a national asset in preparing the Armed Forces to meet the challenges of the evolving world relationships as typified by the complex situation in Viet-Nam.

> In the course of training officers of this type, Colonel Lincoln has been largely responsible for projecting a new image of West Point throughout the nation. West Point is no longer viewed as a military monastery set back far from the stream of national life. As Colonel Lincoln himself has moved easily back and forth from academic to public life, graduates trained in his model have been conspicuously active in both military and non-military fields. If Clemenceau is correctly quoted as saying that "War is too serious a business to be left to the generals," one may say with equal cogency today that peace is too serious a business to be left entirely to civilians. Officers patterned after Lincoln are the kind needed to work closely with civilian leadership in creating and fostering the conditions most favorable to the maintenance of peace.

Educator-At-Large

It is one of the strange facts of bureaucratic life that the Lincoln talent for linking the military community with higher education has been tapped less by the Army than by the other military services and the nation's great civilian universities, who better recognized the need for counsel in understanding the educational needs of the nation at mid-century. While he was consulted continually on the development of the National War College in 1947, for example, his efforts to reconstitute the Army War College were derailed. When he was asked to comment on the Army's Reserve Officer Training Corps, it was not by the Department of the Army, but by President John Sloan Dickey of Dartmouth College, who convened a distinguished study group on the ROTC in 1958. Writers on military education—John Masland, Laurence Radway, Gene Lyons, Morris Janowitz, Samuel Huntington—found Lincoln's experience valuable in their research. He had less to say to men who conceived of officer schooling as limited to indoctrination and training, without adequate foundations of collegiate and graduate education.

Lincoln's experience in fathoming an appropriate balance among the competing claims at West Point was important to the Air Force leaders responsible for establishing the new Academy in Colorado Springs. In 1954, Colonel (now Brigadier General) Robert F. McDermott went directly from the Department of Social Sciences at West Point to the Air Force Academy where he became the first permanent Professor and first permanent Dean of Faculty. He observed:

> Our best educational concepts, both old and new, can be traced to the seminal influence of Abe Lincoln, through his disciples, who have included besides myself, one Superintendent and four department heads during the formative years. Moreover, the pervasive influence of the great teacher over his disciples was reinforced annually by Colonel Lincoln's visits to the Academy as a consultant. It was during these visits that Abe stimulated our thinking on the realities of developing modern military professionals.

While devoted to the service academies, Lincoln saw them as serving a special purpose, to be achieved at the four-year undergraduate level, not to be diverted into graduate schools nor to provide a model to be copied in the education of other than military officers. As a consultant for the Carnegie Corporation's Study in 1955, and later when serving as a member of President Kennedy's Advisory Panel on a National Academy of Foreign Affairs, he advised against the creation of an academy for Foreign Service Officers. Believing in the liberal undergraduate college as the appropriate preparatory school for public servants, he became a member of the Board of Overseers' Visiting Committee of Harvard's Department of History. Believing also in the interdisciplinary graduate school for qualified military and civilian candidates for positions of great public trust, he has been a consultant to Princeton's Woodrow Wilson School of Public and International Affairs.

Don K. Price, Dean of Harvard's John F. Kennedy School of Government, one of the nation's prominent educators, who views Lincoln as an important builder of bridges between the civilian and military communities, wrote:

Abe Lincoln's combination of scholarly ability and operational experience enabled him to play a rare role in American higher education. He not only built the social sciences at the Military Academy into a close cooperative relationship with civilian universities but he brought his exceptional experience to bear as an adviser to those who were seeking to develop the capacity of those universities to meet their public service responsibilities.

He had a major share in the success of West Point in becoming a vital part of the nation's general system of higher education, without sacrificing its primary role as the training ground for military leadership. His experience with the diplomatic and economic aspects of national security made him an invaluable adviser whenever the Federal government sought to expand its advanced training programs for the civilian departments in ways that could take advantage of the much more extensive experience of the armed services. Few public servants have combined so skillfully the thoughtfulness of the scholar with the effective achievements of the man of action.

The Architect

Abe Lincoln came to West Point in 1925 from a farm near Harbor Beach, Michigan. Since the farm was not an economic venture, he had earned his cadet uniform deposit by working for forty-five cents an hour as a surveyor's helper. He graduated first in mathematics, and was a company commander in the Corps. His tactical officer thought him excellent at handling men but only satisfactory as an instructor. He did the usual thing for a young soldier of academic promise in those days by becoming a lieutenant of the Corps of Engineers, and then, having won a Rhodes Scholarship, departed for three years in Europe, where his travels acquainted him with the area that became so important to his World War II planning. Returning from Oxford in 1932, he commanded a company of the Second Engineer regiment near Denver, where he built camps for the Civilian Conservation Corps. The combined experiences of Michigan, the Military Academy, and Magdalen College were blended with troop experience and the practical school of the construction engineer. The consequent meld was somehow suited to the operation and explication of national security policy in the mid-century revolution in American affairs.

John J. McCloy thought the touchstone of this meld lay within the man's character and integrity. He observed that General Marshall held Lincoln "in high admiration" and that Lincoln was courteous, but forceful and definite in expressing his point of view: "These qualities together with his fairness in argument bespoke his own integrity, and his modesty removed any suggestion of personal bias from his opinion. The reliance on his judgment was always encouraged by the knowledge of this officer's fine character."

In Lincoln's makeup, the pragmatist is more apparent than the philosophical idealist. He views national security problems as operational problems; he sees them with the eyes of the empiricist who construes men's policies from observation of their deeds, and with the eyes of the realist, who prefers to make progress by tailoring the present situation rather than grasping for idealized futures. In the Lincoln meld, there is the historically-conscious activist, who seeks trends and evolutionary processes, in order to channel and hasten the probable future. The result is an action-oriented architect, designing for utility and efficiency, more than the theorist, searching for new intellectual conceptions.

In the design for national security, the Lincoln style has guided growth at all levels—in the policies of national administrations, in the operations and programs manufactured to carry forward these policies, and in the organizations and procedures needed to assure success of the programs. In particular, he has been an architect of the educational and personnel systems that are indispensable to the flow of competent men into the leadership of national security enterprises. As the architect becomes ultimately a teacher of builders, Lincoln also became a teacher of statesmen.

In the crisis of the Viet-Nam conflict, a busy Secretary of State paused in his chores to sum up:

> It has been my privilege to look at "Abe" Lincoln from different vantage points. I knew him first as a fellow Rhodes Scholar. I knew him most intimately when he was my chief in the Operations Division of the War Department General Staff during World War Two. I saw his work as a professor at the Military Academy when I was in a private foundation and deeply interested in the examination of foreign policy questions in our colleges and universities. I was the direct beneficiary of his advisory work on foreign aid. Finally, I have known him and his family as friends.
>
> When one thinks of "Abe" Lincoln, one begins with an appreciation of the personal qualities of integrity and devotion to public service. Such well-worn words should not be carelessly used because they represent simple virtues which are not as common as many believe. But "Abe" Lincoln was cast in the

mold of a George Marshall and those who know him best value such simple virtues most highly.

Having watched Colonel Lincoln from "below" and from "above," I must also note the breadth of his view, the sweep of his imagination, and the daring of his readiness to look at issues or answers which would cause the timid to pale. Perhaps this derives from the breadth and depth of his education and insatiable curiosity, perhaps from his responsible involvement at an early age in some of the largest questions affecting the life and death of nations. The chapters in this book testify to the range of his interests and of his contributions. His approach to serious questions has been infused by a deep understanding of the difference between an opinion and a decision—which is at the heart of the notion of responsibility. There is a very long list of men who have looked to "Abe" Lincoln as their teacher, and I am honored to be counted among them.

In these words, Dean Rusk speaks for a host of grateful men.

1. *The International Environment: Possibilities, Perils, and Promises**

COLONEL ROBERT N. GINSBURGH

The primary purpose of our arms is peace, not war—to make certain that they will never have to be used—to deter all wars, general or limited, nuclear or conventional, large or small—to convince all aggressors that any attack would be futile—to provide backing for diplomatic settlement of disputes—to insure the adequacy of our bargaining power for an end to the arms race. . . . Our military posture must be sufficiently flexible and under control to be consistent with our efforts to explore all possibilities and to take every step to lessen tensions, to obtain peaceful solutions and to secure arms limitations.

> —President John F. Kennedy
> March 28, 1961
> *Recommendations Relating to*
> *Our Defense Budget*

In the decade ahead there is a wide range of possibilities for both war and peace. If we are to achieve the primary purpose of our arms, we must first have some notion of this range of possibilities.

We should not attempt precise prediction, for the future of

---

* The views expressed in this essay are the author's own and do not necessarily represent those of the United States Government.

human events is not predetermined, and in the very act of projecting the future we give ourselves the opportunity of changing its shape. We need, however, to be aware of the possibilities confronting us, both of the perils and of the promises.

Looking back over the last decade or two, it would be easy to become discouraged, because the bright promises of the Declaration of the United Nations remain unfulfilled. On the other hand, the oft-predicted peril of inevitable nuclear holocaust is also unfulfilled—despite a manifold nuclear proliferation.

The next ten years offer similar possibilities of peril and promise. It is reasonable to expect that neither the worst of the perils nor the best of the promises will materialize. The extent to which we can avoid the perils and fulfill the promises will depend in large measure on our ability to perceive these possibilities, to grasp the opportunities they present, and to develop and execute our policies accordingly.

Each perceived peril may, in fact, contain the seeds of promise, the two thus interacting in a Hegelian thesis and antithesis and eventually producing a new synthesis. In just such a way, the stark peril of the Cuban missile crisis raised a promise of détente between the Soviet Union and the United States, even though there was no objective change in comparative nuclear power positions. This détente, on the one hand, opens up the possibility of expanding cooperation in areas of interest to both parties, while, on the other, it raises possible dangers such as delusions about the depth and range of mutual interests between the United States and the Soviet Union.

In a similar process, the threat of Soviet invasion of Western Europe prompted wide acceptance of the vision of a United Europe. As the threat receded, the vision gave way to a resurgence of European nationalism and its accompanying strains in the North Atlantic Alliance.

Possibilities and Perils

As a base for surveying the various possible international environments of the future, it is useful to identify the forces that might be expected to have a major influence on the shape of the future. In international affairs, as in physics, for every action there is a reaction (but not necessarily "opposite" and "equal"). By identifying, observing, interpreting, and evaluating these opposing forces we can approach a general appreciation of the environmental parameters within which our national security policies must be developed.

Four major sets of opposing considerations or forces warrant our attention: Nuclear proliferation versus arms control, confrontation versus détente, nationalism versus internationalism, and the aspirations versus the achievements of the underdeveloped nations. Within the decade, we should expect that other sets of significant forces, as yet unperceived or only dimly seen, will emerge. In any event, these four sets will be central to the kind of environment that will prevail.

Nuclear Proliferation or Arms Control. For the last twenty years, one of the major determinants of the international environment has been the existence of nuclear weapons and the associated delivery capability. On some occasions, as in the Cuban missile crisis, the implications of nuclear weaponry have dominated the world stage. At others, they have receded to the background, while other more pressing matters have attracted our attention. Regardless of variation in emphasis, the implicit danger of nuclear weapons has been ever present as an important component of our consciousness of the total international environment.

Since the very beginning of the nuclear age, concern about the control of nuclear weapons has been a major problem in international politics. Nevertheless, the world has watched impotently while nuclear weapons have spread from one state to—presently—five. Even now, we recognize that many more nation-states have a nuclear capability almost within their grasp, should they choose to seek it. We might anticipate that, within the next ten years, at least three or four more nations would exercise this option. It is no longer a question of whether or not they could choose to develop such weapons, but whether they will consider it worthwhile to do so in terms of their interpretations of their own national interests.

Although the world community during this time period might arrive at agreements that could effectively halt further nuclear proliferation, the forces for proliferation may well overbalance the forces for control of such arms. Our national security policy and programs must, therefore, be prepared to cope with the security problems that would confront us within an international environment of either arms control or nuclear proliferation (or even elements of both, as at present).

The full implications of either possibility are difficult to estimate. It is not clear, for example, what the impact on U.S. national security interests might be in an arms-controlled world where we would share nuclear weapons in various degrees with our allies in NATO or in other parts of the world. While the U.S. has from the first been opposed to the proliferation of nuclear weapons, it is not clear that—from the time the Soviet Union broke our nuclear monopoly up to the present—the U.S. has really been made less secure because of proliferation. The penalties for major political blunders or miscalculations are obviously greater as the number of nuclear powers rises; but, in the case of the Soviets, at least, it seems that their realization of the full implications of nuclear weaponry has induced a greater sense of responsibility and a policy of self-restraint. Their greater understanding of the perils of nuclear warfare has, on the one hand, contributed to an apparent reduction in the threat (although not the capability) of invasion of Western Europe—but, on the other, has led to their recent emphasis on "wars of national liberation."

For those who see a causal relationship between increased power and a heightened sense of responsibility, there is hope that, as the Chinese Communists move from a token nuclear capability to a more meaningful military nuclear capability, they too will evolve a more responsible and more restrained foreign policy. This is certainly not a development on which we can count, but we should be alert to such a possibility and the opportunities it may offer. In any event, amelioration of current Chinese Communist goals and policies is an objective we should seek.

For all their aggressive talk, the Chinese Communists' actions have generally fallen short of their words. Successful containment of Chinese military adventures, mounting problems of internal development, the succession of younger leaders, and the prospect of admission to the family of responsible nations could mitigate the dangers inherent in their expanding nuclear capability.

Nevertheless, if the Chinese Communists develop their nuclear potential as fully as possible in the next ten years, they will constitute a threat to U.S. security second only to that posed by the Soviet Union. During this period, they will not be able to threaten our immediate survival, but they could directly threaten the continental United States with major damage and erode the confidence others place in the value of American commitments. They will also be in a better position to attempt nuclear blackmail directly on their Asian neighbors, which could have profound effects on U.S. security arrangements in the Far East itself.

The development of a nuclear capability by any of the other potential nuclear powers does not pose a direct threat to American security in terms of ability to inflict serious damage on the continental U.S. Our major concern with the spread of nuclear weapons to lesser powers is in the possibility of catalytic nuclear war. The outbreak of hostilities anywhere in the world has become a matter of concern to us, and the possible use of nuclear weapons in such cases intensifies that concern.

From an optimistic viewpoint, it is conceivable that a multipolar balance of nuclear power could result from further nuclear proliferation. Theoretically, such a balance of power could lead to a greater degree of international stability, even though the balance was precarious, for the penalties for upsetting the balance would be more severe. Paradoxically, however, to the extent that nations perceive this possibility and its dangers, they may be dissuaded from proliferating in the first place. Paradoxically, too, it is possible that a world in which nuclear arms were controlled would be more unstable than a world in which they simply proliferated without controls. If the chances of provoking nuclear hostilities were lowered, some nations might be encouraged to embark more freely on hostilities at lower levels. The saving grace of such a world would be the hope—and the higher probability—of holding such hostilities to lower intensities of warfare.

Confrontation or Détente. The major factor that has heightened the perils of nuclear developments during the period since World War II has been the confrontation between the United States and the Soviet Union. The state of détente that exists in the late 1960's should not obscure the fact that there has been little or no fundamental philosophical change in the nature of this confrontation. Although we may take some comfort and advantage from the Sino-Soviet split, we ought to recognize that the Sino-Soviet argument is not over whether they should bury us, but how.

We must anticipate that this U.S.–U.S.S.R. confrontation will continue in various forms in the future. The nature of the competition is complicated by the fact that it is not simply a confrontation between states with competing interests, but reaches into the most basic beliefs about man's relations to the universe and his fellow man and about how the world should be ordered. Despite this basic conflict, however, it has been apparent for some time that there is a certain commonality of interests on both sides. Recognition of this overlap of interests has already taken some of the edge off our confrontation with the Soviet Union and the European Communist states. There is a wide range of possibilities for further expansion of the areas of mutual interests among us, and the coming decade will likely see increased realization of these possibilities.

The interaction of the opposing forces of confrontation and of détente based on commonality of interests is complicated and sometimes obscured by several factors. The development of China as a distinct center of Communist power is perhaps the most obvious of these factors, but it has had mixed effects. On the one hand, it has highlighted the mutuality of certain American-Soviet interests as opposed to Sino-Soviet interests. (The Chinese, in fact, seldom lose an opportunity to draw the attention of other Communist nations to this situation in an effort to undercut Soviet leadership of the Communist bloc.) On the other hand, the Soviets are very self-conscious about this situation and are constantly under pressure to compete with the Chinese in risk-taking to promote the spread of Communism.

A more subtle but at least equally troubling problem for Soviet hegemony of the Communist movement has been the general force of polycentrism within the Communist world. The phenomenon of polycentrism has been encouraged and reinforced by a certain amount of bridge-building between East and West, which has opened up the various Communist nations to Western influences.

Among the nations allied with the United States, there has also been a progressive diffusion of power and influence. The resurgence of Western Europe has led Europeans to reassert the independent exercise of national power—political and military, as well as economic. Here also two conflicting forces are at work: The centrifugal force of nationalism, and the centripetal force toward a united or integrated Europe as a locus of power distinct from the United States.

The recent assertions of political and economic independence by the nations of Western Europe, however, have not been accompanied by a proportionate increase in their nuclear or conventional military capability. Thus, U.S. military force is still the main restraint on the overt use of force by Moscow or, for that matter, by Peking. Similarly, polycentrism in the Communist nations has not yet been accompanied by a proportionate diffusion of military power away from Moscow or Peking.

Any analysis of the confrontation between Communism and the West is complicated by Communist emphasis on "wars of national liberation"—and the varying emphases on this technique within the Communist camp. Having achieved reasonable success in containing Communist expansion at higher levels of conflict, the West is faced with the difficult problem of containing or neutralizing the subversive Communist export of arms and men across international frontiers. The West's success or failure in coping with this present and continuing challenge will undoubtedly have a major impact on the shape of its confrontation with Communism in the future.

It is not difficult to construct a logical case for either heightened confrontation or progressive détente. There is, of course, always a tendency to assign a higher probability to the continuation than to the reversal of current trends. On that basis, one could reasonably predict a progressive relaxation of confrontation, a resurgence of nationalism, the spread of polycentrism, and increasing strains on free world alliances. On the other hand, the fundamental conflict between the philosophies of East and West could lead to intensified confrontation.

Thus, our national security policy ought to be based on a continued observation of these forces, alert to changes in the direction and strength of the resultant force; it must provide enough military power to protect, yet be sufficiently flexible to cope in timely fashion, and, if possible, to influence these forces in directions we desire.

Nationalism or Interdependence. In examining confrontation versus détente, we noted that these forces were in turn complicated by the conflicting forces of nationalism and interdependence. The importance of nationalism and interdependence, however, transcends the questions of confrontation, and they deserve consideration as a major set of factors influencing the world environment.

The revolution in weapons technology has dramatized strikingly the heightened interdependence of nations. Nations have at times considered possession of sufficient independent military power to defend their interests to be a prime requisite of national sovereignty. This may at one time have been true of most states, but it is far less so today. Technology has forced all nations into patterns of military interdependence. In a less dramatic sense, economic and political interdependence of nations is equally significant in an assessment of probable future policy developments. This political, economic, and military interdependence, combined with strong psychological and moral aspirations, has made internationalism a significant counterforce to nationalism.

The last half century can be viewed as a continuing struggle between these competing forces. World War I tragically illustrated the inadequacies of an international order based on competitive nationalism. The failure of the League of Nations to preserve international stability again demonstrated the strength of the forces of nationalism. World War II reaffirmed the inadequacies of the nation-state system and gave birth to the United Nations. The strengthening of internationalism represented by the United Nations has, in turn, been increasingly beset by nationalism as well as by the confrontation between the U.S. and the U.S.S.R.

As the prospect of major war has receded—or at least as our perception of the prospect has—individual nations have sought to reassert their right to exercise greater control over their own destinies in the light of their unilateral interpretations of their national interests.

In the Communist world, the lessened sense of danger has contributed to the rise of polycentrism and to the Sino-Soviet split. In the uncommitted areas of the former colonial world, this feeling has given birth to a radical nationalism. In the free world, it has led to major strains in NATO and other alliance systems. (In fact, the conflicts derived from opposing *national* interests have more frequently led to active hostilities than has the basic ideological conflict between Communism and the West.)

Few of these open conflicts have resulted in solutions the competing parties are willing to regard as permanent: Greece and Turkey remain at odds over the future of Cyprus; Kashmir remains a bone of contention between India and Pakistan; and the very existence of Israel is a constant irritant to the Arab world.

Any of these sore spots, or any number of others, could erupt momentarily. There is no reason to predict that the frequency of such eruptions in the next twenty years will be any less than in the last twenty. Yet there is a growing awareness that compromise—tacit or open agreement to "encapsulate conflicts"—can be mutually beneficial, especially if it provides a basis for cooperative attack on other problems of mutual concern that cannot be solved within national boundaries. For example, the 1966 Tashkent Agreement, which halted the Indo-Pakistani conflict, provides the opportunity for both countries to focus on mutual problems of water, trade, and economic development, all of which can best be attacked by collective action. It is not entirely inconceivable that such action could lead eventually to solution of the most emotional and sensitive of the issues between the two nations, namely, Kashmir.

In many other areas of the less developed world, there are hopeful signs that the radical nationalism of the immediate postcolonial period is being transformed into a more mature concern with and sense of responsibility for the fundamental problems of internal political, economic, and social development. As the new nations' leaders turn away from outdated slogans of anticolonialism, they must perforce establish better relations both with their neighbors and with the more highly developed nations upon whom they must depend for assistance in tackling the difficult problems of development.

Thus, it remains to be seen whether the present forces of resurgent nationalism represent the spring of a new year in international affairs or the Indian Summer of a dying era. The obstacles to internationalism are certainly great—not only nationalism and the momentum of the past, but also an aggressive Communism striving for a different kind of international order. These obstacles do not augur well for a peaceful unified world order in the next decade—or even in the next several decades.

On the other hand, the need for collective rather than national patterns of action to deal with urgent human problems will surely result in a continuing and intensifying search for effective international associations—global, free-world, regional, and subregional—as well as functional organizations to meet specific problems.

The Underdeveloped Nations. Nowhere is the need for collective action more pressing than in the less developed areas of the world. Beginning with the industrial revolution, more and more people have come to realize that poverty and want are not necessary and immutable conditions of mankind. During the last quarter century, the explosive impact of the revolution in mass communications technology has created an almost universal demand for higher standards of living. This phenomenon, surely one of the major forces in international affairs, has been widely described as the revolution in rising expectations. It might more aptly be called the "revolution in rising frustrations," for there is a wide gap between the aspirations for higher living standards and the generally disappointing results achieved. If the aspirations are themselves revolutionary, the gap between aspirations and accomplishments must make them more so—especially as the majority of the world's population aspire to overcome in one generation a lead resulting from several generations of rapid growth in the more developed world.

In many respects the gap is widening rather than narrowing. Even within the developed world, there is a widening gap in many areas of activity between the most technologically advanced nations and the nearest competitors. In automation, communications, computer technology, and the aerospace industry, to mention a few examples, the nations of Western Europe—despite dramatic economic progress—are finding it increasingly difficult to compete with the United States.

Similarly, despite great efforts at modernization, many less-developed nations find themselves falling farther behind in comparative terms or, in some cases, even losing ground in absolute terms, as population increases faster than gross national product. In fact, a straight line projection of food and population trends indicates that, for many millions of people, it will not be simply a question of enjoying reduced standards of living in the next ten years but of mass starvation. In many areas, this situation results simply from the fact that increases in population, stemming from advances in public health, have not been matched by compensating progress in food production and population control. The technology for vastly expanded food production and for population control is probably as advanced as for public health measures, but the application of technological know-how to the former has so far been too little and too slow. Furthermore, the agricultural sectors of many underdeveloped countries are so structured that it is virtually impossible for farmers to take advantage of improved methods of food production. Thus, agricultural modernization in many cases would require drastic changes in land tenure, creation of capital for agricultural uses, agricultural credit, training and education, and development of distribution and marketing systems—in short, social and economic revolution.

Equivalent revolutionary actions are required in industry, commerce, science, education, administration, and urban development if these nations are to make the jump from the nineteenth (or earlier) century to the present. Simultaneously, they are faced with the problems of creating and developing modern political and social as well as economic institutions. In the modernization process, they are confronted with pressures to follow Western models, to adopt Communist models, or to create their own new patterns. For many nations, these pressures come at a time when they are just beginning to realize that the successful slogans of anticolonialism are useless in going about the business of modernization.

Clearly, accomplishments will not match aspirations during the next ten to twenty years, but the process of growth and development will certainly be revolutionary. With so many conflicting forces at work, it is impossible to predict which nations will follow which routes, for how long, or how fast. The revolution of rising frustrations is bound to erupt from time to time in violent forms.

Our national security policy must thus concern itself with trying to deter such violence and coping with violence when it does erupt. This does not mean that we should necessarily intervene as policeman of the world. It does mean that as a member of the U.N. Security Council, as the world's leading political, economic, and military power, and as the leader of the free world, our attitudes and our policies will have an important if not decisive impact on the outcome of the revolution of rising frustrations.

Promises

The perils that may beset us in the decade ahead indicate a continuing high level of employment for national security planners. The very nature of the problem of national security indicates that we must be ready to deal with the pessimistic side of the possibilities.

Yet it seems to me that there are considerable grounds for an optimistic—at least cautiously optimistic—view of the decade ahead. Although it is prudent to recognize the high probability of further nuclear proliferation, it is a good bet that not all of the nations that have the potential will decide to "go nuclear." Furthermore, there is a reasonable possibility that such proliferation as occurs will not increase the perils as much as we fear. Finally, the forces tending toward proliferation will surely generate increased impetus in the field of arms control so that arms control measures may well be able to keep pace with, if not ahead of, proliferation.

In a similar vein, an expanded détente makes more sense for all concerned than renewed intensive confrontation. As long as we are prepared to stand up to a confrontation, we can reasonably expect continuation of détente. It will probably not be an uninterrupted détente, however. The Soviets have tested us from time to time in the past, and they may well do so again within the next ten years. We must also expect to be confronted by the Chinese Communists. Détente with the Chinese seems most likely only after we have experienced a Chinese version of the Cuban missile crisis. Crises of confrontation in the decade will require all the wisdom and courage that we can muster to convert such crises into the promise of détente. Again, if rationality prevails, there is hope.

In the conflict between the forces of nationalism and internationalism, the long-run trends favor internationalism. Increased interdependence is an unavoidable accompaniment to the process of modernization, and nations will be forced to enter into broader international associations because there will be no viable alternatives for achieving their political, military, or economic objectives. There will undoubtedly be many painful periods during the decade, but the process of modernization and internationalization seems destined to continue—barring an irrational catastrophe.

Coping with the revolution in rising frustrations seems likely to be the most difficult problem of the coming decade. Success in this endeavor requires not only an imaginative, cooperative, large-scale effort in itself, but perhaps also progress in arms control, extension of détente, and the developing and strengthening of international associations. Despite the great difficulties, we can hope for some progress, because at least the problems have been recognized, the methods of attack are available, and there is a growing appreciation of the importance of tackling the subject in a major way.

This cautiously optimistic view of the coming decade requires full measures of both strength and wisdom. The road ahead will be difficult, but no available detour can lead us to a satisfactory destination. We must persist. In the words of President Johnson, "We must be strong enough to win any war, and we must be wise enough to prevent one."

2. *Employing America's Military Strength in the 1970's**

C O L O N E L A M O S A. J O R D A N , J R.

Paradoxically, as the gap between the military capabilities of strong and weak states has increased in recent decades, the ability of the strong to impose their will upon the weak seems to have diminished. The traditional role of military power as the final arbiter of interstate relations seems somehow to have changed. That traditional role, expressed by Louis XIV on the barrels of his cannon as *Ultima Ratio Regnum* ("the last argument of kings"), was, of course, always more ambiguous than any simple formulation would suggest. The brevity of Louis's particular formulation was perhaps more a consequence of the high cost of engraving cannon than of his simplistic estimate of the uses of military power. Since his time, and especially in the past two decades, the relation between armed might and statecraft has changed sharply with the shifting nature of the international system and the radically expanded technology of warfare.

Determining the relevance and utility of United States military power in the decade of the 1970's involves gauging the military implications of national foreign policy goals, the international and domestic political setting in which those

* The views expressed in this essay are the author's own and do not necessarily represent those of the United States Government.

objectives will be pursued, and the nature of the military means that can be brought to bear to achieve them.

The fundamental foreign policy goals of the United States have remained remarkably stable for more than two decades and seem unlikely to change significantly for at least another one. In the simplest terms, we have two objectives: to protect the United States against any direct assault on its territory or institutions, and to help create and maintain an international order in which the values the American people espouse and the domestic political, economic, and social institutions embodying those values can continue to thrive.

When the United States first set itself the second of these objectives at the close of World War II, the threats to the kind of world order we sought—the order envisaged in the United Nations Charter—seemed clear. A monolithic or apparently monolithic Communist bloc, with demonstrably aggressive aims toward non-Communist neighbors, presented an unambiguous challenge. Under such conditions, it was relatively simple to identify areas which, because of their actual or potential strength and their vulnerability to Soviet power, had to be secured. Among these so-called vital areas, Western Europe and Northeast Asia became primary arenas of confrontation with the Communists. We sought to bolster indigenous defenses through alliances, military and economic assistance, and the deployment of our own forces, and we engaged in actual conflict in Korea. The U.S. linked its security to the security of these areas and explicitly committed its military power to their defense.

The East-West confrontation extended also to other areas which, though not immediately crucial to the over-all power balance were still sufficiently important to us to risk war with the U.S.S.R. and lesser powers and pour out billions of dollars of assistance. These other areas consisted for the most part of less developed countries that faced varied dangers—local insurgencies, intra-regional quarrels, and, where proximity permitted, the threat of external Communist intervention. The

American response to such nations' plight, first enunciated by President Truman, was to promise "to support friendly peoples who are resisting attempted subjugation by armed minorities or by outside pressures."* That support came to include not only military aid and general guarantees but also explicit alliance commitments that, by engaging American prestige and reputation, tended to transform those areas from "non-vital" to "vital." Commitments tended to expand; within the broad umbrella of "containment" there was added to the idea that every case of Communist pressure, intervention, or subversion must be resisted the notion that the loss of any one position could "domino" into the loss of successive positions—which, though perhaps not "vital" individually, were essential collectively.

During the decade of the 1960's, the Communist monolith has lost cohesion and the dynamism of its ideology has waned. The independence of Western Europe is still of key importance to us, but its internal revitalization, the increasing autonomy of the Communist nations of Eastern Europe, and the apparent lessening of the militant Communist expansionist drive of the Soviet Union have all combined to reduce the immediate danger—or at least the sense of danger—in Europe. Similarly, the renaissance of Japan and the Republic of Korea and the normalization of Soviet-Japanese relations have made Northeast Asia seem less vulnerable to Soviet power. The Asian area confronts another danger, however, yet to be measured and countered, in the threat of Red China—now possessing nuclear weapons and displaying radical revolutionary intent. Although some may argue that the improvement of the security situation in these key areas of the world during these past years shows that Americans overestimated earlier dangers, it is at least equally likely that the improved situation stems in large part from the success of our earlier policies.

* Speech before a joint session of Congress, March 12, 1947. *The New York Times*, March 13, 1947, 1:8f.

The security problem with respect to the less developed areas of Latin America, Africa, and Asia and, therefore, to the kind of world order the U.S. seeks, has also changed in recent years. The gradual internal strengthening of many of these states, their disillusionment with Communism's purported answers to their modernization needs, and the splitting of the Communist bloc have combined to shift their and our attention increasingly from the dangers of Communist takeovers to the need for calming intra-regional disputes and for concentrating on the problems of development. These are urgent problems. Moreover, the Communist shift of front to "wars of national liberation" continues to pose a danger, though it is increasingly clear that, by and large, neither Russian nor Chinese prospects are bright for harnessing the political and social revolutions of the less developed world to the wave of a Communist future.

The interplay of this changed and changing international climate with American foreign policy goals and security requirements blurs the earlier, clear guidelines for defense policy. With the waning of ideology, balance of power considerations and relationships in which the U.S. can play a leading but not dominating role loom larger; with the strengthening of friends and allies, comes the opportunity for the U.S. to readjust between unilateral or bilateral security measures on the one hand and regional and international actions on the other; with military and non-military responses having widely varying relevance to the challenges confronting different nations, America's leadership role becomes increasingly difficult and its security requirements less clearly definable.

Pursuing our foreign policy goals in the next decade in such an environment will entail meeting three distinct types of security challenges. First, we must continue to deter direct aggression against the United States proper—aggression which, if it is to represent any real danger, can only be nuclear or thermonuclear in character. Second, in other vital areas such as Western Europe and Japan, we must continue to deter nuclear and non-nuclear aggression (or threat of aggression used for aggressive purpose), and we must help defeat such aggression if deterrence fails. Third, wherever feasible, we should help weak and vulnerable states strengthen themselves against overt or covert aggression, increasing the prospects that inevitable changes in the international system will be peaceful and evolutionary in character. This stabilizing objective includes limiting both the scale and scope of violence—precluding resorts to violence if possible, restraining and confining them if they occur, and preventing their escalation to a confrontation of the nuclear powers.

Succeeding sections deal with the changing nature of these tasks and the various courses of action available to pursue each of them.

Deterring Attack on the United States

Deterring attack on the United States must continue to be a pre-eminent concern in the 1970's, the principal purpose of our nuclear arsenal, and a major recipient of defense resources. Though we need to hedge against uncertainty and miscalculation, the size and sophistication of our arsenal and the advanced state of its technological support suggest that we should be able to maintain that deterrence throughout the decade. No rational opponent will deliberately attack the United States if the certain outcome of that initiative is suicide. Taking even the most generous estimates of Soviet and Chinese Communist offensive capabilities in the 1970's and the most pessimistic figures for our missile, submarine, and bomber survival prospects, we should continue to be able to destroy both the U.S.S.R. and Communist China as viable states should they attack us. Other things remaining equal, our strength should continue to deter.

Things may not, however, remain equal. To the challenges of maintaining an effective, invulnerable nuclear strike force and of locating targets for it—critically important but not new tasks—must in the future be added the problem of dealing with Anti-Ballistic-Missile defenses (ABM's). Both the Soviet Union and the United States command the technology and economic strength to develop and deploy ABM systems in the 1970's. But any sizable deployment of ABM's risks instability by giving fresh impetus on both sides to the race for bigger and better offensive arms. On the other hand, if we make the assumption that the U.S. does not intend to be the aggressor—which seems true beyond doubt—then defenses which tend to deny any would-be nuclear aggressor the prospect of destroying us serves to deter him and tends to be stabilizing. To these considerations must be added the high costs of the ABM's—in the tens of billions of dollars, depending on system sophistication, the number of threatening missiles, and how many targets are to be defended. These costs should, of course, be measured in the perspective of military budget levels; thus viewed, they represent an increment of some 5 to 10 per cent over the periods currently planned for.

If we could be sure of Communist compliance with an arms agreement banning all ABM's, a treaty approach to the problem would make sense. By 1967, the United States seemed to be ready to treat this as its preferred option for dealing with the U.S.S.R. If this attempt at limited arms control fails, due to mutual distrust and the difficulties of enforcement (or if Communist China acquires a significant arsenal of nuclear weapons and will not join the anti-ABM pact), we may well feel compelled to build our own ABM system. Although such a first generation system would almost certainly not be airtight, even a limited defense could, of course, have considerable value. The key question is whether such an improvement would be worth what may become a very sizable cost, and, if so, what alternative defense or non-defense programs, if any, should be sacrificed to pay for it.

Also pertinent to our ABM decisions is that there are an increasing number of sides to the strategic equation. Effective nuclear military power—i.e., ability to hit the United States directly with at least a few weapons—will be progressively dispersed as more nations cross the atomic threshold. Maintaining the balance of terror has been difficult enough in the kind of essentially bilateral situation obtaining between the U.S. and U.S.S.R. up to the late 1960's. In the decade of the 1970's and beyond, the nuclear deterrence problem will become even more difficult as the Red Chinese—and probably others—gain effective atomic weapons. Peking will have the capability to threaten nuclear assaults on America's allies and overseas bases early in the 1970's (or even at the end of the 1960's) and to deliver a small number of nuclear-armed Intercontinental Ballistic Missiles on the United States itself by the mid-1970's.[*] The same weapons will, of course, also threaten Europe, including the Soviet Union.

Since the Chinese arsenal will at first be small and comparatively unsophisticated in terms of its capability to penetrate to its targets, the U.S. and the U.S.S.R. could probably largely cancel out its danger to their homelands—at least into the late 1970's or 1980's—with relatively modest ABM systems, setting aside the question of whether the deployment of such systems would tend to stabilize or destabilize the U.S.-U.S.S.R. nuclear relationship.

Though a limited ABM defense against the threat of Chinese Intercontinental Ballistic Missiles (ICBM's) may later prove desirable, there can be no doubt that a major counter to this danger must be provided during the 1970's by the same means as those used to meet the Soviet threat—that is, the certainty of U.S. retaliation on a scale that would cause tremendous damage. That deterrent should suffice, for though the Chinese' words may be bellicose, their practices have been prudent. In spite of the rural character of their society, they know that they are vulnerable to retaliatory strikes and will be for decades. The extent of their vulnerability is indi-

* Morton Halperin, "China's Nuclear Strategy," *Survival*, III, No. 2 (Nov., 1966), 350.

cated by the statement of the U.S. Defense Department that a limited number of weapons "detonated over fifty Chinese urban centers would destroy half of the urban population (more than 50 million people) and destroy more than half of their industry. Such an attack would also destroy most of the key governmental and managerial personnel and a large proportion of the skilled workers."*

Not only will Communist China's acquisition of a number of effective nuclear weapons gravely complicate the task of stabilizing the nuclear situation, but nuclear proliferation *per se* brings increased dangers. The risk of nuclear war by miscalculation or accident rises—perhaps geometrically—with the number of holders of such weapons. More widely held weapons mean more ambiguities, complexities, possibilities of catalytic nuclear war, and risks of uncontrolled escalation of limited conflicts to nuclear ones. The notion of an n-sided balance leads to a confusion not only of metaphors but also of policy makers.

Halting the spread of such weapons may be beyond the capability of the United States and the Soviet Union, acting singly or together. Theoretically, states now possessing nuclear weapons might deter further proliferation by threatening an aspiring possessor with assault against its atomic facilities if it did not desist. Such a future threat could hardly be credible, however, in view of American and Soviet inaction in the past when faced with the imminent threat of acquisition of such weapons by Communist China—a major nation avowedly hostile to the U.S. and potentially hostile to the U.S.S.R. A non-proliferation treaty, mutually agreed nuclear-free areas, and protective guarantees by those armed with nuclear weapons to those not so armed are more promising checks. Though unlikely by themselves to be decisive, such measures are sufficiently attractive and low-risk to most

* Statement of Secretary of Defense Robert McNamara before the House Subcommittee on Department of Defense Appropriations on FY 1967 Defense Budget, Feb. 14, 1966, p. 49.

states that each may well be negotiated in some form within the next few years.

Ideally, proliferation would be checked by the emergence of a climate of international stability in which the defensive use of such weapons would be unnecessary and their offensive use unthinkable. As long, however, as there are acute dangers of conflict and as long as the nations owning nuclear weapons are themselves unwilling or unable to discard them, we cannot realistically hope that others which have the technological and economic strength to produce such weapons will indefinitely forego their acquisition. Yet, if proliferation can be kept from proceeding too far in the short run, the required climatic change may occur over the long run. Napoleon reportedly said that the one thing any army cannot do with its bayonets is sit on them; the longer the nuclear powers show that the only thing they can and will do with their most awesome weapons is sit on them, the better the chance that wholesale proliferation can be precluded.

It is encouraging in this regard that none of the nuclear powers has thus far found a military role for its nuclear weapons beyond the passive one of deterrence. Although Khrushchev's rocket rattling in 1956 during the Suez crisis might seem to have been an exception, his threats actually had little influence in the situation. Similarly, the United States' so-called nuclear trump in the Cuban missile crisis, in 1962, was not strictly an exception either, for it was the combination of the threat of local application of superior American conventional force and the nuclear deterrent that caused the Soviet Union to retire.

If and as the international security environment is stabilized, internal pressures against proliferation will have the opportunity to work within the states aspiring to become nuclear powers. Such weapons are highly expensive. Even though the nuclear technology of several nations is far advanced and their supply of raw materials plentiful, acquiring a complete nuclear weapons system, including effective delivery means, would add several hundred million dollars to their defense budget for a number of years. Thus, achieving full status as a military nuclear power of strategic significance involves such a high fee that few countries can both pay it and continue to develop and modernize their economies. If the U.S.S.R. and perhaps the U.S. acquire ABM systems, the cost of joining the club will climb even higher since the independent deterrent value vis-à-vis the two super powers of the limited delivery capability other countries could muster would drop sharply.

Summing up, deterring attack on the United States proper over the next decade and laying the basis for the continuance of that deterrence over the longer run will in large part be a matter of technological innovation and of our willingness to spend adequate resources. It will also be a matter of searching for political paths to ease the confrontation between the nuclear powers and to dampen the quarrels among nuclear and non-nuclear states that may lead to proliferation. The diligence with which we conduct this search and the restraint with which our diplomacy leans on our nuclear strength will not only importantly influence the stability of the nuclear relationship itself but the climate in which the other defense challenges have to be met.

Deterring and Defending Against Attacks on Other Vital Areas

Deterring attack on such vital areas as Western Europe and Japan, or helping them defend themselves if deterrence fails, can be accomplished in part with the same resources that deter attack on the United States proper. Since the United States has and will continue to have sufficient nuclear weapons to destroy the Soviet Union and Communist China, it does not face a problem of allocating weapons between deterrent missions. Our missiles pointed at the Soviet Union and Communist China are directed as much against Soviet or Chinese nuclear threats to Western Europe and Japan as they are against similar threats to the United States itself.

The principal difficulty in obtaining this double duty from our nuclear strength has been, and will increasingly be, to convince both skeptical allies and potential aggressors that the United States is as ready to use its nuclear weapons if London or Bonn, for instance, are attacked as if Washington itself is hit. The task in the decade ahead will be to continue to strengthen the identification of the U.S. with Western Europe and Northeast Asia so that the notion of "we and they" becomes simply "we."

Political, cultural, and economic ties, as well as troops and bases, have in the past helped convince the Russians that the United States views its NATO partners as "we." Similarly, although the number of American military men and bases in Japan have not been so large nor the common non-defense ties so intimate, the U.S. interests in and guarantees to Japan have been sufficiently explicit that the Soviet Union has recognized the fact of our nuclear deterrent shield over Japan as well. (Moreover, the U.S. intervention in Korea demonstrated in a way persuasive far beyond words the significance of the U.S. interest in the area.) But with fewer U.S. forces and bases in the area and with the nuclear threat from Communist China growing in the decade ahead, Japan itself may increasingly question the strength of the American commitment, and hence the credibility of our nuclear deterrent. There, as in Western Europe, creating a sense of "we-ness" through increasing political and economic cooperation is a promising route out of this potential difficulty.

But even a highly credible threat of countervailing nuclear power is not a sufficient answer—though a necessary part of the answer—to the range of the military pressures to which our allies may be subjected in the 1970's. In the early 1950's, when the Soviet atomic force was still weak and American nuclear predominance was clear, the U.S. chose to rest deterrence and defense of vital areas essentially on American nuclear strength—the capacity for "massive retaliation." As Soviet nuclear strength increased during the 1950's, and particularly when its missile-delivery capability began to grow in the early 1960's, it became evident, however, that the United States could convince neither friends nor potential enemies that it would direct thermonuclear thunderbolts against all aggression, no matter what the retaliatory consequences for itself. It was clear that the U.S. needed a substantial conventional military capacity in, or deployable to, vital areas in order to complement its nuclear strength and to provide it the option of responding to any level of aggression with a riposte appropriate to the circumstances.

The resulting build-up to a "flexible response" posture, so designated in the early 1960's, involved stationing more than 250,000 American soldiers (along with larger numbers of allied troops) in the countries bordering the Iron Curtain and improved weapons and mobility. These forces made a forward, on-the-ground defense possible, and they also helped deter aggression, both by denying a quick *coup de main* by limited conventional thrusts and by confronting the other side with the probability that a small conflict would escalate into a large one, perhaps into nuclear warfare. The allied garrisons in Berlin, for example, have deterred an East German or Soviet thrust, both because they can fight sufficiently long to make aggression unambiguous and to raise its costs and also because they call up the specter of a conflict in and about that city escalating to nuclear warfare.

Changing conditions, such as French disaffection within NATO, the improvement of East-West relations, and response to economic pressures have combined in the late 1960's to raise anew the question of how best to defend Western Europe. If the major reduction of conventional troop strength in Europe implicit in the combination of developments cited were to occur, a forward strategy with a non-nuclear option could become infeasible in the 1970's. Yet alternative, manpower-conserving strategies—such as using ground troops only to trigger nuclear retaliation or relying exclusively on tactical nuclear weapons—will likely be unpersuasive as deterrents to the full range of dangers and to entail unacceptable damage should deterrence fail and combat occur.

Increased strategic mobility, for example, through the development of long-range, high-capacity transport aircraft such as the C-5A (which the U.S. will begin to have in quantity in the early 1970's), suggests an attractive alternative—namely, a combination of forward deployment of limited numbers of ground forces, pre-stocked equipment, and large, quick-reacting strategic reserves which could move into an actual or threatened battle area within a short time from the recognition of threat. Such an approach could be fitted into the changing climate in Europe, for instance, with minimum sacrifice of the advantages of the flexible response posture. Moreover, though costly, the scheme would result in smaller overseas dollar expenditures for the U.S. than the conventional flexible response approach. It would also afford greater flexibility in operations inasmuch as the centrally held reserve could be shifted about as necessity dictated.

Of course, a drastic thinning of NATO's forward troops might invite limited attacks if the East Germans or Russians proved less tame than hoped. Moreover, over the long range, the alliance itself might be eroded by such an option, for the presence of significant numbers of American troops has come to symbolize the seriousness of the American commitment to Europe's defense. Any major troop thin-out would have to be carefully phased with the availability of the long-range transports (and battle-ready forces to fill them) and with other evidences of American will and capability in order to avert signaling a weakening of that commitment.

In sum, then, contributing to deterrence and defense against attacks on such vital areas as Western Europe and Japan over the next decade will continue to challenge the

U.S., requiring of it substantial resources and considerable flexibility—both in adapting to the changing political climate in Europe and Asia and in exploiting technological advances, such as the C-5A, which permit adjustments in strategies and force levels. Local forces in countries bordering on the Soviet Union, Communist China, or lesser Communist countries will continue to be an important element of deterrence and defense in their areas. U.S. military supply programs, though they may increasingly shift from a grant to a sales basis as recipients gain economic well-being, will continue to be important in providing equipment for these forces. It may be that strengthened local forces will become even more significant in the future, for the further loosening of the Communist bloc may lead to adventurism by lesser Communist powers, overturning the assumption of the past that any aggression by such states would be undertaken only as a part of general bloc aggression. Thus, although the character and level of U.S. troop deployments and supply programs to vital areas will change, the necessity for the alliances and the supportive leadership role of the U.S. behind them will remain.

Despite the demands on imagination and adaptability that such challenges will pose, the outlines of what can and should be done in defense of the vital areas of Europe and Northeast Asia are fairly clear by extrapolation from the past. The most far-reaching and fundamental challenges to American defense policy are likely to occur over the next decade in other areas, largely in the less developed areas. In these areas, where over sixty new countries have been born since World War II, unequivocal answers to questions concerning the United States' security commitments and the appropriate use of its military power are more difficult to formulate.

Strengthening and Stabilizing Other Areas

America's proper role in strengthening vulnerable states in Asia, Latin America, and Africa against overt and covert aggression and in defining and maintaining stability in the evolving interstate system provokes sharp differences of opinion. There are some who believe in an activist, interventionist policy of becoming involved wherever potentially hostile forces threaten; others maintain that an overcommitted U.S. should sharply limit its objectives and especially avoid world power aspirations. Some of these latter critics hold, for example, that since Chinese domination in Asia is inevitable, the U.S. should extricate itself from commitments in the area other than those arising from its indisputably vital interests (such as the continued independence of Japan) and withdraw its forces from the mainland, or even from the Western Pacific. The view of this group is typified in the frequently heard assertion that Southeast Asia is not of vital interest to the United States and that we should not dissipate our power in such peripheral areas, lest the center, presumably Europe, be fatally weakened. (Such criticisms assume, of course, that there is still a single center, Europe or the Atlantic Community, and that when the periphery erodes, the center will be unaffected—an assumption that underestimates both the interdependence of the modern world and the fact that when any given peripheral position disappears it merely leaves a new, closer-in one.)

In contrast to the withdrawal school of thought, the "involvement" school maintains that, unless Communist pressure, whether Soviet or Chinese-backed, is met by American or American-assisted counterpressure, vulnerable areas will be taken over one by one and the balance of power in the world be shifted against us. With respect to Southeast Asia specifically, this school is likely to recall the consequences of the failure to check Hitler's aggressions at Munich. Or, this school may say, with *The Economist*:

> What is happening in and around Southeast Asia in 1966 is exactly what happened in and around Southeast Europe in 1947. When President Truman committed the United States to the

defense of Greece and Turkey in 1947, he achieved two things. He gave the non-Communist forces in the region a center of power to rally around. And he started a fierce argument in the Communist camp between those who wanted to pull back in the face of the American commitment and those who wanted to fight the Greek civil war to a finish. It took 2½ years from the declaration of the Truman doctrine in 1947 for the Greek Communists to accept that they could not take over power in Athens by armed force; but accept it in the end they did.*

Whether the withdrawal or the involvement view will predominate (neither can wholly win out) in the 1970's will depend partly on the character and intensity of the various crises that arise. It may be that the number and intensity of crises will diminish, that the phenomenon of "internal war," which has afflicted the bulk of the new nations, will begin to dry up—as was the case after a few decades with the internal upheavals in Europe that marked the birth and consolidation of the modern European state system in the mid-19th century. But even if this proves to be true in the longer run, revolutionary violence is so endemic in the less-developed areas that insurgency and "internal wars" will likely be widespread through the 1970's.

Furthermore, the tinder of external, intra-regional quarrels will be plentiful in the next decade, and conflicts of varying intensities and susceptibility to outside exploitation or escalation are certain to occur. Neither the Soviet Union nor Communist China is yet a *status quo* power and other regional revolutionary powers may well arise. In the 1970's, the U.S.S.R. will likely exploit these intra-regional troubles through arms aid and advisers and will probably further add to its potential for mischief by acquiring the ability to project limited conventional power into remote areas through increased naval power and by developing its own long-range air transport, equivalent to our C-5A. In the absence of locally available or potentially available countervailing conventional

* *The Economist*, CCXXI, No. 6427 (Oct. 29, 1966), p. 445.

power, in the 1970's the U.S.S.R. could intervene successfully in Africa or the Middle East, for example, in support of a Communist insurgency or on behalf of a client state or ally. Communist China shows even fewer signs of being ready to limit its military reach to its present boundaries. Its claims to the historic marches of Han power has led it to assert its sovereignty over a number of neighboring areas and to resort to arms to enforce its demands, as in the case of the Sino-Indian border conflict in 1962. Chairman Mao Tse-tung's view that "power grows out of a gun" does not augur well for the stability of states within reach of Chinese Communist weapons or other pressure instruments.

Clearly, if the United States is not to abandon altogether the stabilizing role it has played in the less developed areas for the last two decades, namely, its role in strengthening evolutionary forces and in checking conventional aggression, then it must anticipate the likelihood that it will have to intervene in various situations during the 1970's—not because it should police the world but because otherwise dangerous upheavals would result. But unilateral intervention, even if sparingly and grudgingly entered into, generates clamor and evokes misgivings; it calls forth images of colonialism, punitive expeditions, and gunboat diplomacy, all anathema to the spirit of the times.

The Siberian expedition of 1919–21, afforded an early example of another prime difficulty with intervention. General Graves, the American commander, was instructed to stabilize the situation in Siberia, but to stay out of politics. When he was called home, he reported as follows:

> "Some might have liked us more if we had intervened less; some might have disliked us less had we intervened more; but having concluded that we intended to intervene no more nor no less than we actually did, nobody had any use for us at all."*

An apolitical intervention is a contradiction in terms.

* George Kennan, *Russia and the West Under Lenin and Stalin* (Boston: Little, Brown, 1961), p. 112.

Though necessity may be the mother of intervention, the prospect of sending even small American expeditionary forces to other lands is not an inviting one. Even initially limited involvements may well grow into much larger ones. The American engagement in South Viet-Nam can be cited as a case in point: what began in 1954 as a small U.S. military training group had become in 1963 a large training and helicopter support group, which in turn had grown by the end of 1966 into a combat force of over 400,000 men. This story of escalation is the more noteworthy for having occurred in spite of long-standing American reluctance to commit land forces to combat on the Asian mainland—a reluctance that was fortified by the losses and unhappy memories of the Korean War. (On the other hand, we need to ask ourselves what kind of Asia we might be confronting in the 1970's had we not involved ourselves in the struggles in South Korea and South Viet-Nam in the 1950's and 1960's.)

The range of difficulties—concern about escalation, pressures from other governments, ambiguities in the situations being confronted, and domestic fears of burgeoning dangers and costs—combine to make it less likely that in the future we will intervene unilaterally except in cases of major and immediate danger to critically important American interests. Some of these difficulties can be averted if we make common cause with others whose interests are also affected by the various crises. Participation in multilateral arrangements will have its own difficulties, but it will enable us to bring others into a partnership in providing resources and in furnishing wisdom about what needs to be done and how to do it. Adlai Stevenson once said, "Our power and our will to use it remain the underpinning of worldwide freedom. But we should seek to mediate its application through the international institutions which seek to express the general judgments of mankind." Intervention will increasingly need the sanction of international legitimacy.

At the same time experience shows the value of acquiring the views and support of others, it also underlines the wisdom of speed and boldness in action, once the need for intervention is clear. The will to use appropriate power when needed is the primary pillar of deterrence and may often be the overriding consideration. Although critics may disagree that American action was necessary in the Dominican Republic in 1965, it is clear that the speed and strength of the American deployment there forestalled imminent civil war, made multilateral intervention practical, and laid the basis for the subsequent political settlement. Not only do such rapid and massive concentrations of military power have an immediate psychological value, but if combat is involved they also save lives and make possible battlefield decisions that a slower and more measured reaction might preclude.

If situations develop in which competitive intervention occurs, such as in Korea or Viet-Nam, nuclear blows could theoretically be threatened to induce the other side not to continue its intervention. But threatening nuclear escalation runs counter to the strong inhibitions on the use of nuclear weapons already discussed. Similarly, interdicting the other side's build-up by hitting directly at bases in supporting countries has but limited promise. Nuclear interdiction is insufficiently selective and is likely to be interpreted as unrestricted nuclear warfare; conventional interdiction, on the other hand, is both expensive and of less-than-total effectiveness if carried out by air power alone—and even more expensive and dangerously escalatory if carried out by land forces. Taken in conjunction with attrition warfare in the contested area, interdiction of supply areas and routes can play an important role, but it is unlikely to be decisive.

The foregoing analysis suggests that if competitive intervention leads to combat, success is likely to fall to the side that can move to the battlefield "fustest with the mostest." While hardly new, this strategic equivalent to the classic formula for tactical success has a special relevance for the

United States in the years ahead. In view of the already-discussed constraints on the use of our massive nuclear and strategic air power, ground forces—supported by tactical air forces and helicopter mobility—will undoubtedly bear the brunt of future combat. Such forces need to be specially tailored, trained, and equipped and sufficiently mobile to acquire battlefield superiority quickly in order to bring early favorable results.

Though never popular anywhere or anytime, wars of attrition have at least seemed bearable to the masses of people during modern total wars, when the stakes were apparently survival and when nationalistic passions ran high. The public of a democratic state is not likely, however, to support long, indecisive, and costly struggles for what it deems to be relatively limited stakes. It is probably no coincidence that the seventeenth and eighteenth century heyday of limited war—the period toward which all the theorists of "diplomacy through violence" from Clausewitz to the present have looked for inspiration—predated modern democracy. The French Revolution not only ushered in the era of mass political participation; it also ushered out the era of carefully limited wars—of wars as "diplomacy somewhat intensified, a more forceful way of negotiating, in which battles and sieges were the diplomatic notes."* Thus, as modern technology has ruled out general war as a rational policy instrument, so modern participatory politics have made limited war as an instrument of policy impracticable, except when a state is *in extremis* or its truly vital interests are at stake—or conceivably when such a conflict is under a multilateral banner. Viet-Nam may prove to be the last large-scale intervention of its type by the United States.

These considerations underline the importance of our defining our "vital" interests moderately and in ways which preserve freedom of decision to meet changing times. This

* Clausewitz, *On War*, Book VIII, Chapter III (Washington, D.C.: Combat Forces Press, 1953), p. 580.

does not imply that the U.S. can or should repudiate commitments it is now pledged to honor. The nuclear guarantee to Europe, the mutual defense pact with the Republic of China, and the Japanese-American Mutual Security Treaty are examples of previously made commitments that have become symbols of American integrity and responsibility. Thomas Schelling has rightly observed, "Face is . . . the interdependence of a country's commitments; it is a country's reputation for action, the expectations other countries have about its behaviour"; it is one of the few things "worth fighting for."*

What is in question is the wisdom of defining further "vital interests" in areas of the world where not-yet-stabilized political and social forces indicate that the decades ahead will witness a high state of flux in relationships between the U.S. and the nations involved, among the developing nations themselves, and within the political systems of each of them. In such an environment, the U.S. must reserve to itself the ability to interpret its interests as changing circumstances dictate.

The difficulties surrounding commitments and interventions underline the desirability of forehanded preventive action in the less developed world to avert insurgency and to deter aggression. The international community, or at least those members of it whose important interests are involved in the various danger spots, must be brought to greater effectiveness in these preventive and deterrent tasks. For its part the United States should increasingly focus its diplomacy and economic resources on galvanizing such forehanded efforts. Similarly, America's military resources should increasingly be brought to bear on the same problem; U.S. training, doctrine, materiel and organization should be directed toward preparing American and friendly forces for the kinds of challenges confronting the vulnerable developing nations. (See Chapter 6.)

* Thomas Schelling, *Arms and Influence* (New Haven: Yale University Press, 1966), p. 124.

In sum, in the future the U.S. seems less likely to involve itself in others' quarrels throughout the world, more likely to seek international support when involvement appears unavoidable. Though this approach may result in American forces being engaged in combat less frequently, the certainty that future crises will occur and the premium on rapid, large-scale deployment when they occur make it essential that the U.S. have quick-reacting, well-trained forces available for intervention. These forces will have to be flexible enough to be adaptable to pre-insurgency situations or to post-aggression combat in conjunction with other national or international forces.

Concluding Reflections

This essay began by noting the decreasing political utility of increasing military strength, a paradox which applies not only to the nuclear-armed nations in their relations with each other and with third parties, but even to situations where direct confrontation of nuclear nations is unlikely. Yet, despite the narrowing political limits on the uses of armed force, military power is far from irrelevant to the great foreign policy and security issues which will confront the U.S. in the decade of the 1970's (See Chapter 1.) Whether confrontation or détente will characterize relations between the U.S. and the U.S.S.R., for instance, will depend in large part on the United States' continued ability to stand up to confrontation. The roots of the present détente lie in the military strength that we and our allies built in order to counterbalance Soviet power; if that sustaining military strength withers, so, too, may the apparent reasonability of the Soviet Union.

Similarly, though awareness of the danger and wastefulness of excessive military strength impels us and others to seek arms limitations, we can hope for meaningful arms control only if our military power covers the spectrum of threats and is sufficient at each point on the spectrum to give us negotiating positions. Only if we can meet security challenges at every level of conflict can we contemplate limits on our arms suitable for clashes at any level—otherwise conflict will merely shift to levels left uncovered.

So, too, is it the availability of the military power of the U.S. and other responsible nations that makes it possible to limit the claims of aggressors, to curb expansionist nationalism, and to permit international cooperation to grow. The sheer physical power of the U.S., demonstrated by the rapidity and strength of the American buildup in Viet-Nam—not only of combat forces, but of logistical facilities, ports, and airfields—cannot but impress friends and potential foes alike. Though many will argue whether we should be in Viet-Nam or not, the reputation for effectiveness which the success of American arms there has won is a major asset for the future, one that we cannot afford to dissipate.

Our power, in terms of the strength and reach of our military forces, will likely continue to grow over the next decade. As it does so, restraint in its use will become ever more important, for building a stable international order compatible with our values and purposes is a matter of how we conduct ourselves as well as the wisdom of our policy. Secretary of Defense McNamara expressed this same point when he said, "The decisive factor for a powerful nation—already adequately armed—is the character of its relationships with the world."*

By using our power responsibly, we can help mankind avert a choice between the stark alternatives of a world state or planetary desolation—of conformity or catastrophe. Men have been stumbling toward other solutions in the quarter-century since the nuclear age dawned, a stumbling that has sometimes brought them to the precipice and that has frightened many into reaching for absolute solutions. Thus

---

* Robert S. McNamara, Speech before the American Society of Newspaper Editors in Montreal, Canada, May 18, 1966, *The New York Times*, May 19, 1966, p. 11.

far, we have succeeded in turning away from the brink, and each time we have turned away, the goal of a stable international order has come that much closer. Only the visionary believes that violence can be extirpated, but responsible men can legitimately hope that it can be contained and its incidence and scale gradually reduced. That is challenge enough for the next decade.

3. The Meaning of National Military Power Today and Tomorrow*

GENERAL C. H. BONESTEEL, III

I have long since come to the conclusion that one of the greatest difficulties all of us have in coping with the world of today, and will have even more with the world of tomorrow, is that, parallel with the vastly increasing complexities of our societies there has been a growth in the number of a certain type of expert who strives to take the already complex and make it even more complicated. I believe that what our world needs most is wisdom, even above expertise—wisdom in the classical sense, which can take the very complicated and reduce it to its component verities. Unfortunately, the process of trying to reduce problems to their more simple factors is sometimes frowned on today, and one who tries to do so is more often than not accused of dangerous oversimplification.

However that may be, I have tried to state my points simply in what follows, but at the same time have attempted not to be guilty of oversimplification. At least, the issues on which I have, wisely or unwisely, tried to speak are among the more fundamental ones that any person seriously considering the meaning of power today should first sort out to his own

* The views expressed in this essay are the author's own and do not necessarily represent those of the United States Government.

basic satisfaction, lest he commit himself prematurely on the mere sophistications of the subject.

The Concept of Power

Before one can put the subject of this essay in full perspective, one should ruminate on the many divergent views on power, in its broadest sense, and on the application of power, that exist today. It is also wise to examine these different views against the harsher realities of the real world as well as in the more abstract sense.

Perhaps the simplest definition of "power" is "the ability to do, act, or influence." "Powerful" can be defined as "having great power or influence over." "Powerless" means "without power; wholly unable." Power in the sense that it enables man or groups of men to "do, act, or influence" derives primarily from a combination of physical, mental, moral, and emotional forces. The effective application of power is conditioned by the environment in which it is used and the power that opposes it.

In some quarters today, there appears to be a feeling that power *per se* is immoral, wrong, perhaps evil. It is hard to find the rationale for this thinking. If men or groups of men were each and all wholly without the ability to "do, act, or influence," human society would surely be moribund, either utterly flaccid or totally anarchical. Certainly it could not long survive.

Perhaps the rationale that power is intrinsically evil rests on the observation that the groups that have power range from very strong to very weak. A power adequate to provide balance between very strong groups can permit the strong to coerce, as contrasted with influence, the weak. But this must be seen as a condemnation not of power *per se* but of its use or potential use. Alternatively, such a view might rest on the observation that power has frequently been misused in the past and the conclusion that it will necessarily be misused in the future.

Not only is this faulty logic, it may also be bad history. If one generalizes from the concept of the good for a particular group or society to the concept of the good for mankind as a whole, it is difficult to judge the rightness or wrongness of a particular use of power. The Indo-European conquest of the Indus Valley and the Tigris and Euphrates cultures produced change, but not clearly good or evil. The same can be said of the Norman Conquest. Although a clear majority might concede Genghis Khan to have been a villain, it is not clear that all of the consequences of his use of power were bad.

Power, then, must be at worst amoral. It is to the human somewhat like sound: is there "sound" if there is no ear to hear it? Power can be judged moral or immoral in its application, in its threat of application, or in the context or the consequences or motives of its application, but history would indicate that such judgments are hardly self-evident truths on which everyone can agree. Lord Acton's famous words, "Power tends to corrupt; absolute power corrupts absolutely," must therefore be a comment not on power in itself, but on the foibles of the humans who wield extraordinary power.

The world of today is torn by many active and often violent quests for change. The ferment, frustrations, impatience, and resorts to violence deriving from them bid fair to continue for a long time to come. The ferment derives largely from the many searches for a different and hopefully better life for individuals, for groups, and for nations. These quests have been given the broadly descriptive title, the revolution of rising expectations.

Spurring the search for change are the varied economic, political, and ideological motivations and objectives of individuals, of a whole range of movements, and of nations. Some extend this search to one for a supranational government. These motivations, aims, and objectives cover a broad spectrum, from the constructively altruistic to the destructively selfish.

The gradation of motives and aims within the spectrum is

frequently pictured as a broad arc, curving from a violently reactionary "far right" through the constructively reasonable center to the violently radical "far left." This visualization seems both unsound and, more importantly, unhelpful. A clearer understanding might be gained by looking at the spectrum as a straight line, not curving back on itself, but beginning at one end with those movements that responsibly espouse and work toward a destiny for the human race in which freedom, with its concomitant and inescapable responsibilities, recognition of the dignity and sensitive conscience of each individual, and the growth of human knowledge and wisdom are all fitted to a social structure that both supports the growth of these fundamental values and protects them from the deliberate or capricious use of coercion or violence to pervert or destroy them. At the other end of the spectrum are the movements controlled by the destructive and cynical zealots—it matters not whether they be of the "far right" or "far left"—who have no real faith or hope in mankind, and who see the fulfillment of human destiny as only the creation of a structure in which the vast majority is organized, ruled, and manipulated "for its own good," by dictators or oligarchies. Between the ends of the spectrum lie many gradations and mixtures of aims and methods.

Thus, our simplified spectrum presents at one end those who have both hope and faith in the ordinary man and at the other end those who, however much they protest to the contrary, have neither. To oversimplify: Democracy stands at one end, totalitarianism at the other—the open society at one end, the closed society at the other.

The methods and techniques used to reach the respective objectives within the spectrum vary from the affirmative appeal to reason, through passive or active combinations of moral, political, emotional, and physical force, to the subtle or unsubtle use of confusion, subversion, coercion, terror, and violence. They all, however, involve real power of one or another or a combination of sorts.

Change—whether quiet or drastic, constructive or destructive, revolutionary or evolutionary—is the order of the day, and the value judgments involved in determining what part of this change represents "progress" for the human race are just as fiercely and violently argued as are some of the aims and actions themselves.

It is within this context that one should examine the meaning of national military power today and speculate on the roles it may play in the future.

Conditions Affecting Power

There are many paradoxical factors—psychological, sociological, scientific, and economic—influencing both the meaning and the applicability of national military power. Each impinges upon the others, and none can be neatly categorized. For the sake of simplicity, however, we may examine them within the general areas of the military, the political, and the ideological considerations.*

Not all of us have looked deeply enough into the intrinsic changes that have taken place in military capabilities over the last century to understand how profoundly the meaning and utility of military force has changed. Nearly all recognize, of course, the contradiction that the availability of nuclear weapons—weapons which, in some versions, can be of unbelievable if not nearly total destructiveness—has imposed on the meaning of war as Clausewitz defined it over a century ago: "the mere continuation of policy [Politik] by other means."

No rational nation will attempt to continue its policy by initiating nuclear war of near-total destruction against another

---

* I must say, here, that I am writing in the environment of the open society. The open society developed because its members came to understand that, if each wished to enjoy its benefits, he had to learn that it was his responsibility to restrain his own personal use of power or force for capricious or selfish ends. I explain my own stand lest some readers think the adjectives I use subsequently are proscriptive rather than, as I see them, descriptive.

nation, if that other nation has and keeps up an assured capability to retaliate in kind. Self-destruction is not, and never has been, an objective of any nation's policies. The maintenance, then, as an element of national military power, of a nuclear capability that deters the initiation of all-out nuclear warfare by some aggressively motivated nation is a simple example of how the constraint of violence, rather than the so-called Clausewitzian exercise of violence, has come to be a necessary and proper use of national military power.

What has not been so widely understood is that the perfection of the machine gun, of rapid-firing, accurate artillery, and of tanks, and the conventional military application of the airplane, both as a weapons carrier and as a means of general transportation, were leading toward the same conclusion well before the advent of nuclear weapons. Since the American Civil War, there have been awesome improvements, measured in orders of magnitude, in firepower, in mobility, and in communications as applied to war. Furthermore, the airplane opened all of a nation to attack rather than only its front lines.

However, even after two world wars that caused tens of millions of military casualties and, directly or indirectly, even greater civilian deaths and destruction,* there are still aggressive dictatorial cliques today that think a resort to force can serve as the continuation of their selfish objectives. Because such unenlightened or opportunistic national leadership still exists, nations that treasure their freedom and independence must maintain and use, when necessary, national military forces, or some credible substitute, to restrain the conventional military or paramilitary power of the aggressively-oriented nations.

To go back a moment to the nuclear stalemate—the condition of so-called mutual deterrence. This *de facto* state of affairs is less absolute than many might wish, and we must be careful neither to assume its permanence nor to permit it to

* Some sources indicate these wars accounted for 65 million casualties.

obscure all else. For one thing, the restricted use of small-yield weapons is not unimaginable. In spite of what should be the incentive produced by man's new inventiveness in military destructiveness, the basic nature of man has not changed perceptibly, particularly in regard to his predilection to resolve disputes by force. One might wonder, in this regard, how our children's children will view the validity of the solution to this difficulty advanced by a microscopically small minority of anti-historicists, who suggest the rather degrading concept that free men should be "reasonable" and, in exchange for animal survival, surrender their souls, their faith, and their convictions.

At any rate, aggressiveness in man and the tendency or need to resort to force to settle disputes on all levels are still with us. In fact, pessimists claim to detect an increasing rather than decreasing resort to anarchical violence in all aspects of human conflict—not only in crime and local disputes, but also in international and ideological disputes—while they note, too, one hopes, that this violence exists well below the level of the exchange of nuclear weapons.

What may be happening is that the pragmatic common sense aspect of the mutual deterrent to the use of the ultimate in destructive weapons, with its accompanying fears of the escalation of lesser conflicts, is being misunderstood in the international arena by some disciples of the aggressive use of lesser violence or terror. They may be interpreting the situation to mean that all uses of power to restrain irresponsible or opportunistic acts are now severely inhibited by the nuclear deterrent. They seem to be developing a potentially dangerous feeling that as long as they can claim that their anarchical use of force is a "family affair" or can, if necessary, involve the interests of opposing nuclear powers, they will be able, literally, to get away with murder.

The growing number of examples of capricious, low-level resorts to violence, whether in the form of externally supported insurgency or in the form of aggressions against neighbors, highlights the requirement for the existence and sensible use of national military power to restrain destructive power, particularly in the newly emerging nations, which are struggling to grow while preserving their independence and integrity. Such nations, if powerless in themselves, are unfortunately at the mercy of other nations or movements that control a significant degree of organized power. An emerging nation's only realistic alternatives for survival are to build its own adequate power for defense and security, a course it frequently has not the resources to follow, or to make some arrangement to obtain the help of another nation in support of its integrity. It may look for this help from supranational sources such as the "power of world public opinion" or the United Nations, or from these plus alliances or sympathetic friendly nations.

The dilemma of how the newly emerging nations can protect their integrity, as well as the dilemma of nuclear weapons, explains in part why an increasing number of world leaders and a greater number of the idealistic are so seriously pursuing the search for wider peace and security through some sort of an international rule of law or rule of reason. The United Nations is, perhaps, the most dramatic manifestation of this search. The current difficulties, however, in the U.N. approach are exemplified by the fact that the sanction of power available to the U.N. for the enforcement of a world rule of law or to punish those who selfishly transgress a rule of reason is severely limited. The pressure of world opinion carries weight, it is true, if it can be defined, but there remains the real-life fact that peace-keeping or enforcement actions by the U.N. have taken place only when not one or more of the major powers believed its interests so adversely affected by the U.N. action that it at least did not forcefully and directly oppose it.

On this basis, the U.N. has intervened in about a dozen cases where significant violence and conflict had begun or were imminent. These actions have made an important contribution to the search for a more peaceful world, but are not, certainly as yet, the basis on which to assume that a major solution has been found. One must view the U.N.'s record against the hundred or more significant resorts to violence or armed conflict in internal, ideological, or international disputes among opposing groups or nations that have taken place since the end of World War II. In the vast majority of these events, it has not been supranational power but other types of organized power, mostly military or paramilitary, that have been the prime factor in resolving the issue or temporarily subduing one faction or the other.

One little remembered but illuminating drama bearing on the two faces of power and stressing the need for the responsible exercise of power to contain irresponsible power occurred after World War I. In the 1920's, an argument developed between those who, on the one hand, believed that peace could be preserved best by disarmament agreements based largely on faith between those nations sincerely searching for peace and their evasive potential enemies, and those who, on the other hand, felt that the maintenance of adequate military power was essential to convince potential enemies that war in the Clausewitzian sense did not pay. The broad concept of disarmament without adequate safeguards prevailed. As a result, history records that the evasive potential enemies of those days, later to be the Axis powers, precipitated and finally lost another world war, involving over 30 million casualties, before they learned that Clausewitz' view of war did not, in fact, pay off.

The arguments pro and con on disarmament were, of course, much more sophisticated than my simple story and (quite properly considering the true meaning of that much overworked word "sophisticated") involved some sophistries and misleading assertions. What apparently was not adequately understood, however, was that disarmament based on faith and not also on safeguards left, in the end, the faithful nations weak and the perfidious nations strong. Thus, Lord Acton's point was proved again.

This point remains to be fully understood by many today. No matter how much we may hope for and approve of the concept of peace through the rule of law or through the rule of reason, this hope will remain utopian—and can be danger-ous—in the real world of today and tomorrow. Man remains a subjective being, as much or more motivated by emotion and pragmatism as by objective reason. Not until all, and not just part, of the human race is convinced of the dangers of unconstrained power, particularly military power, in the hands of opportunists or zealots who believe they can use it for their own ends without challenge can we hope for law and reason to bring lasting peace. If the point needs greater clarity, think of it only in respect to the increases of crime and lawlessness on our own city streets. Law can survive only in an ordered society, and, therefore, still requires the sanction of force to maintain order amongst the selfish, the irresponsible, or the lawless. It is in this area of consideration—the possible use of national military power, in the absence of other real-istic alternatives, as a localized or substitute sanction support-ing an international rule of law—that we move to the political part of our discussion.

The sophisticated critic of the value of national military power may well admit the validity of the existence of such power if it is used only as a sanction of the law to restrain or to deter the selfish or irresponsible resort to violence by others. But he then may introduce the sophistry of a half-truth. "How can anyone," he will say, "be sure that country 'A' is qualified to judge whether another country's use of military power is irresponsible, selfish, or morally wrong?" The argument may seem to have superficial merit, but it cannot be considered without the other half of the truth. Suppose no power, either supranational or national, exists to restrain the devotee of selfish and irresponsible power. In such a case, there remains no moral or political judgment to be made, because the results are foreordained—"Might will make the right."

Furthermore, we must recognize that one cannot generalize on the attributes of nations, because these vary almost as widely as do the attributes of individuals. To assert that the United States, as an example, has not done its best to exercise its military power responsibly rather than opportunistically, selfishly, and irresponsibly is to deny the anguish of decision that wracked our country before we committed our power in both world wars, in Korea, and in Viet-Nam. In not one of these decisions have we sought territorial gain or subjugation of others. We decided, and the mass of the country's manhood fought and many died, on the simple basis that it is morally important as well as physically necessary to defend the concepts of Liberty and the Dignity of Man and to resist the tyranny of unconstrained power. Of course, the reasons and motivations for our fighting were more complicated and, in some cases, not so clear. But the basic convictions involved in the defense of freedom against aggression were what the mass of the country was fighting for in the two world wars, Korea, and Viet-Nam. This, in itself, cannot be brushed away as an unmeaningful or immoral motivation.

The sophisticate, however, may argue on. By what right, he may ask, could the United States, as a major power, feel itself justified in intervening in other people's conflicts, for whatever purpose, even though it has been asked for help? Why do we not practice the peaceful concept of "live and let live"? This argument must first be examined to see if it is being used as a red herring to distract from the fundamental issue involving the value of the freedom and dignity of man. Without prejudice to the issue of freedom, however, the answer to the sophisticate's question is simply that it takes both sides to apply the principle of live and let live. In Viet-Nam, where this argument has been applied so often, one need only look at the situation long before American forces supported the cause of freedom there. The local villagers were then quite ready to live and let live, but not the Viet-Cong. The Viet-Cong infiltrated villages, where they coerced and terrorized citizens who would not cooperate. The murder of powerless village chiefs, of local wise men, of constructively helpful agricultural and other experts, and of any who acted independently was not the practice of "live and let live" on the part of the wielders of unrestrained power. A simple fact is that at the Communist level of action, the matter appears in a different light. "Those who are not with us are against us."

Now we have come to ideological considerations.

Can we, in the context of today's world, sensibly afford to trust that, for instance, the Communist Chinese leaders will live and let live, when they so emphatically reiterated only last year the words of Mao Tse-tung: "Political power grows out of the barrel of a gun."* Characteristically, in their devoted support of Mao's teachings, the Chinese Communist leaders have engaged repeatedly in ruthless purges of their own intellectuals and, interestingly enough, of many of their military. If no power exists to deter the internationally aggressive use of Communist China's power in support of Mao's words, is it then clear that the Chinese will not so use it? The existence of power to restrain China's power need not be used to intervene in China's own internal affairs. A restraining power can coexist with a self-contained China and at the same time remain capable of convincing the Communist Chinese rulers that the same policy would also be wisest for them to practice vis-à-vis their own neighbors and "all other countries."

I am aware that it may affront the sensibilities of some to bring a discussion of ideological conflict into an abstract discussion of the meaning of power. There is, however, no other way to illuminate all real-life aspects of power. Power cannot be considered comprehensively by theoretical standards alone. The reason for this is simple. Man develops and applies power. Man is a curious mélange of the objective and

---

* From a 1938 speech, "Problems of War and Strategy," cited in Mao Tse-tung, *Selected Works* (New York: International Publishers, 1954), II, 272.

the subjective. Power is meaningful, therefore, only when placed in the real world as well as the mental world, in the subjective as well as the objective context.

The profound conflict between totalitarian and free societies is an inescapable aspect of today's world. Hence, we cannot presume to have discussed power in its present-day context without looking at it in the light of ideology. As the most successful totalitarian form, Communism is based on the subjugation of the individual to the all-wise party and the state and on the warping or destruction of the sensitive conscience of the individual as a technique in this subjugation. Despite the schisms in Communist ranks, the operative concepts of Communism are linked with the massive and technologically advanced military power of the Soviet Union and the lesser power of Communist China and the other Communist nations.

Communist use of this military power or the threat of the use of this power is directly correlated with Communist techniques of propaganda, agitation, and subversion. These multiple facets of the use or the threat of power and violence are, in the eyes of anyone who has convictions on the importance of freedom, clearly a corrupting use of power. Also, the pattern of the anarchical use of violence so widespread in the world today is, all too often, incited, exploited, and supported by Communism. The Communists' design, over the years, has been clearly to break down and destroy order with the intent of building the totalitarianism of its oligarchy on the ruins and debris of the past. Communism's efficacy depends on the linking of its half-truths with the tremendous, and frequently valid, pressures for change that derive from the much deeper ferment of the revolution of rising expectations. The essence of its techniques is based not on a reasoned effort to rectify the causes of discontent in nations trying to throw off "the shackles of the past," but on the psychological manipulation, through a tight organization of conspirators, of the human foible that when the *status quo* seems no longer acceptable, any violent change appears better than a slower but more constructive evolutionary progress.

On the other hand, the concepts of liberty, freedom, and the responsibility and dignity of the individual, supported by the power of the free world alliances with the United States as their strongest and most modern military focus, try to operate to constrain aggressive violence and to prevent coercion by violence. Sometimes this necessitates the application of counterviolence.

The Ecumenical Council Document of December 7, 1965, "The Church in the Modern World," contains this interesting paragraph:

> As long as the danger of war remains and there is no competent and sufficiently powerful authority at the International level, Government cannot be denied the right to legitimate defense once every means of settlement has been exhausted. Therefore, Government authorities who share public responsibility have the duty to protect the welfare of the people entrusted to their care and to conduct such grave matters soberly.

In this context, the use of military or paramilitary power to coerce or to threaten others in the furtherance of Communist objectives brings one directly to the clash of convictions.

This situation has required a loose coalition of free nations and the many struggling new nations that wish to work out their own destinies free of external coercion, to develop and maintain their own national power and alliances to an end that is quite opposed to much in the nineteenth-century concept of the use of national military forces. Today, the military forces of the free world and in much of the emerging world are built toward the purpose of containing violence. We believe that the end objective is right—irresponsible power must be controlled if the human race and its national subdivisions are to evolve on a basis of reason and law. The threat of nuclear war must be contained and countered by at least equal nuclear capabilities. The containment of lower levels of aggressive violence—by counterviolence if necessary —is equally essential, not only because we must prevent the build-up of successive lesser conflicts to the level where, deliberately or inadvertently, the weapons of ultimate destruction are brought to bear, but also because the current stage of the social evolution of the human race requires it and this is an even more important reason.

The main drive of my argument has, perhaps, been easy to detect. It has not been that power is amoral—that should be self-evident—but that the immorality or morality of its use is essentially a matter of the convictions and beliefs of its users. Comprehension of this fact is the most important of all. Power cannot meaningfully be discussed in the abstract. The existence of real power requires of those who can apply it a real and inescapable responsibility. They must have convictions. If power is to be used responsibly in the service of all mankind, as we in the free and open society of the United States believe we are doing, then our society must have convictions. If we lose these convictions, we shall eventually become powerless and shall turn the defense of freedom over to those willing to use their power to achieve their totalitarian ends. We would then, in effect, resign ourselves to a world of unconstrained power in the hands of others where might will always be right. History can rightly be our judge and it may judge us right or wrong. But history cannot relieve us now of our responsibility. Power is a matter of morally vital importance to the free world. It is vital to our country within the free world. And in our country its use should, and does, reflect the wise consensus of our citizenry. It is too important to be condemned by those who wish to ignore responsibility, history, or present reality.

4. *Security of the North Atlantic Alliance**

General Robert J. Wood (Ret.)

Since World War II, the United States has unstintingly joined in the development and defense of the North Atlantic area.† It has maintained substantial military forces in Europe, fostered the area's economic recovery and growth, rebuilt damaged or destroyed military power, promoted political stability under conditions of free democracy, and helped both friend and defeated enemy. Through these efforts, the United States has provided a bulwark against the military power that supported the crusade of international Communism. In short, it has worn the mantle of Western leadership, uncomfortable though the fit has been to many.

Now, in the late-1960's, though heavily engaged in other parts of the world, the United States continues to find that it cannot neglect its leadership responsibilities in the North Atlantic area—even if collective action in support of common interests is questioned in some quarters.

What does the future hold for the nations of the North

---

* The views expressed in this essay are the author's own and do not necessarily represent those of the United States Government.

† The term is used to include all the members of the North Atlantic Treaty Organization (NATO), even those nations distant from the Atlantic Ocean, such as Italy, Greece, and Turkey, as well as Spain, even though it is not a member of NATO.

Atlantic area? What problems will they face in the next decade? How can they deal with such problems? What policy should the United States adopt to secure its interests in this area, in view of the changes time and circumstance have wrought?

The Threat

In the late 1960's, there is no doubt that the Russians, whose aggressive actions in Eastern Europe called NATO into being, have been much less belligerent—in Europe, at least. No Khrushchev rattles his rockets or beats his shoe on a desk in the United Nations. No Czech foreign ministers "fall" out of windows. No tanks rumble through the streets of Budapest or Poznan. Berlin is not blockaded. Nevertheless, a wall separates East and West Berlin, and, despite easement in travel restrictions, an Iron Curtain still divides Europe.

The Russians now busy themselves largely with bettering their own economic conditions and with "peaceful" competition in outer space. Moreover, they have increasingly difficult problems with the Red Chinese. In the Eastern European satellites, individuals and national leaders publicly express nationalistic sentiments that, in the past, would have been good for a firing squad or at least disappearance behind prison walls. In short, the formerly monolithic structure of world Communism seems fractured beyond repair. If one can depend on one's own estimate of *rational* Soviet intentions, then the European states of the Atlantic Alliance can justify their desire to relax their guard.

To a military professional, however, it is obvious that Soviet *capabilities* remain strong. The Russians have kept their arms and equipment up to date. They have a formidable ballistic missile thermonuclear delivery force. They are deploying an anti-missile system. Their submarine strength is great. Their conventional forces still threaten to overrun Europe. And, as

American Ambassador Charles E. Bohlen remarked at a hearing conducted by a House Foreign Affairs subcommittee on March 17, 1966, " . . . all you would need to have is another change of leadership [in Moscow] and you could have another Berlin crisis on your hands."*

Western Europe relaxes partly because of a hopeful estimate of Soviet *intentions*, but more because it knows that if there is any single overriding reason why the Russians appear to breathe sweetness and light, it is the strategic nuclear capability of the United States. In my own view, the Soviet Union's possession of and experimentation with nuclear devices has matured its leaders' judgment, restrained their recklessness, and cooled their passions for adventure. The Kremlin leaders have a stake in Russia's future and are pragmatic realists, not interested in national suicide. As matters now stand, they can hardly foresee a conflict with America, the winning of which would be so important to Soviet interests as to justify a nuclear exchange. But when their anti-missile system is deployed and creates a favorable balance of power with respect to the United States, they may again become more adventurous. Governments can change quickly in the Soviet Union. A future Khrushchev may become another rocket rattler. Finally, the uncertain Asian situation contains the potential for generating dangerous possibilities in Europe and elsewhere.

On balance, I think most Western military men would say that current Soviet intentions and tactics seem favorable to the West, but that there is no apparent change in basic Communist ideology or in the urge to remake the world in the Communist image. The military capability remains. Thus, the threat to the West, however quiescent at the moment, remains, and adequate NATO forces, backed by American nuclear power, are still needed to deter Communist aggression.

* *The Washington Post*, April 24, 1966, p. N3.

The New Europe

In his article, "Old Nations, New Europe," Raymond Aron writes:

> . . . sooner or later Europeans would have come, in one way or another, to ask those questions of principle whose resolution they have been leaving to time and experience. What kind of Europe do they wish? Do they wish a federated Europe capable of defending itself and limited to states willing to sacrifice their sovereignty? Do they wish a Europe which will be a great power dealing with the Soviet Union and the United States as an equal? Do they wish an enlarged Europe, including Great Britain, Denmark, and Norway, which will leave the main responsibility for defense with the United States? In short, are the old nations, theoretically not opposed to a common diplomacy, capable of having one? In other words, do they have the same image of the world, or their goals and their interests?*

The answer to the last question (which provides a key to the questions that precede it) is clearly, "No." One has only to think quickly of France, Germany, The Netherlands, Turkey, Norway, and Greece to realize that the differences among European states are striking. As Cyrus Sulzberger asks, ". . . is it not possible that Communist Rumania is closer to Italy than Norway is to Portugal?"†

Remembering that American strategic nuclear power has been the North Atlantic umbrella since World War II, Henry Ehrmann maintains that, "Most European nations are willing to concede that the United States is entitled to ask its allies to abandon their freedom of action in the military field for the sake of a centralized military strategy. But in return they ask

---

* Raymond Aron, "Old Nations, New Europe," *Daedelus*, Journal of the American Academy of Arts and Sciences, XCIII, No. 1 (Winter, 1964).

† Cyrus L. Sulzberger, "Europe or Atlantica—The West's Biggest Problem," address to the Second Annual Orvil E. Dryfoos Conference on Public Affairs, May 22–23, 1965. See Conference Report, "European Views of America" (Hanover, N.H.: Public Affairs Center, Dartmouth College, October, 1965), p. 7.

that they be given a reasonable amount of participation in common political decision-making."*

While Ehrmann's assertion may well present the essence of the claims the United States and its European allies have made upon each other, the premises implicit in his statement go to the heart of the matter. Timothy Stanley points out that, on its side, the United States has pursued an inconsistent policy toward its North Atlantic allies, urging European union (without the United States) for economic purposes, but fostering an *Atlantic* alliance for defense purposes—not *European* union.† As for the Europeans, Henry Kissinger reminds us that, "Our penchant for treating the Atlantic Area as if it were a single unit runs counter to the fact that the Alliance is still composed of sovereign states."‡

As long as the United States remains in NATO and its nuclear striking power and mobile reserves serve as a backstop to Europe's defense, then America's embroilments world wide have implications for the Alliance's security. On the other hand, many of these American involvements are remote to Europe, and Alliance interests and national interests can and do conflict, creating dilemmas for "centralized military strategy" and "common political decision-making." The Atlantic Alliance must sail between a Scylla of local and regional interests and a Charybdis of world-wide involvements, all affecting its security in varying degrees.

Nevertheless, it seems to me that fundamental European security interests will parallel those of the United States *in the North Atlantic area* for at least another decade and possibly longer. The European states, while their problems and outlooks differ, have a common security problem posed

---

* Henry W. Ehrmann, "European Views of the Atlantic Alliance," at the Second Annual Orvil E. Dryfoos Conference on Public Affairs, May 22–23, 1965. See Conference Report, cited above.

† Timothy W. Stanley, *NATO in Transition—The Future of the Atlantic Alliance* (New York: Frederick A. Praeger, 1965), p. 417.

‡ Henry A. Kissinger, *The Troubled Partnership—A Reappraisal of the Atlantic Alliance* (New York: McGraw-Hill Book Co., 1965), p. 21.

by Soviet military power. The European states also have in common a desire for peace and stability, for economic progress, and for low military budgets. They most emphatically do not want war or Communist subversion. They cherish their freedom and have high hopes for a bright economic future. But they are apprehensive of a peace built on entangling alliances and requiring heavy defense expenditures, for which they must sacrifice at least a degree of their independence and economic progress.

If this summation projects a picture of trying to have one's cake and eat it too, then the image is correct. The Western European states would gain this utopia by keeping America "interested" and American power always available. American forces on European soil are important as an indication of American intent; their size and number can be reduced, however. Western Europe's desired participation in political and military decision-making will vary from country to country. Individual national problems and interests temper the unity of purpose and effectiveness of effort possible within the Alliance structure. It is to these problems and interests that we now turn briefly.

The North Atlantic Nations

The French people have taken up the task of bearing what Winston Churchill reportedly once called his "heaviest cross —the cross of Lorraine." By all odds, the French appear willing to bear the weight indefinitely. Sure of national support, President de Gaulle has ordered NATO and Allied national forces to leave France. Their continued presence, he feels, humbles the honor of France and detracts from that glory, grandeur, and sovereign independence he has pledged himself to restore. This motivation is common to the French nuclear *force de frappe*, the *Concorde* super transport, French intransigence within the Common Market, the obsession for

American gold, and de Gaulle's visit to Moscow in June, 1966.

Is it possible that President de Gaulle is thinking of anchoring European security to a Franco-Russian *entente?* Perhaps a nonaggression pact incorporating an understanding regarding Germany? A nuclear *cordon sanitaire?* German unification? Nonalignment? All these things are *possibilities,* for de Gaulle has repeatedly made major tactical shifts in pursuit of his enigmatic long-term goals. First, however, de Gaulle must convince the Russians—who still respect only power—that he is the Westerner to deal with, rather than the Americans. Secondly, the Germans just might want to do the talking about their future themselves; otherwise, they could conceivably revert to the strident nationalism that many European nations still remember with fear.

France is the most obvious example of determination to have one's cake and eat it, too. France wishes to remain on the North Atlantic Council and thus participate in policy decisions involving the Alliance, but wishes no part in the integrated organization and command of NATO military forces. In fact, France apparently wishes to return to the ancient system of separate national forces held together only by international staff coordination—subject to final national approval—a system that broke down in preparing for two world wars and that could not be expected to function in a future conflict in which those not ready to fight at H-Hour on D-Day probably will not get to fight. So, to a major extent, the problems and interests peculiar to France, at least at the beginning of the next decade, are embodied in one word— "de Gaulle."

The problems of Germany are of a different nature. A divided country, with its former capital surrounded by Communist territory, German security problems stem from its forward position vis-à-vis Soviet power, its lack of geographical depth, the nuclear and other arms restrictions of the Western European Union Treaty, and its need for firm friends. Reunification is the supreme national goal, but this the Soviets will not permit, and NATO cannot achieve. As long as Germany is bound by the post–World War II treaties, its security requires NATO. But if the German problem is ever to be resolved—if reunification is ever to be achieved peacefully—then Germany and NATO probably must part company.

One can, I think, treat the Benelux countries as a group. Many of their internal problems are similar. Both Belgium and The Netherlands have lost their major overseas possessions. Both have been made uncomfortable by their royalty. Both are preoccupied with internal social and economic problems that tempt them to reduce their defense costs. They are interested in an effective Atlantic Alliance, but think their limited military potential justifies letting bigger nations carry the load. Each is anxious that the other's token share be "fair" relative to its own. They have a common fear that they are submerged by their great power allies and have lost their freedom of action. Hence these nations are anxious to support proposals for East-West détente, especially if there are prospects for a neutralized Germany.

The Scandinavian countries of Norway and Denmark have been uncertain members of NATO—although Norway, with its common border with the Soviet Union, has been more aware of the value of Allied support. Neither country contributes major forces to NATO. Their value to the alliance is largely geographic, and both would need outside help, as also would Iceland, to defend their territory. Meanwhile, both countries refuse to have nuclear weapons on their soil, feeling that such action would create an unnecessary problem with their mighty Russian neighbor. Both are fearful of German power and limit their intra-Alliance cooperation with German forces. Neutralist trends and overemphasis of any signs of East-West détente are evident. Scandinavian neutrality may look attractive as an alternative to NATO if the cohesion of the Alliance seems to weaken.

Italy is a staunch member of NATO, with apparently no intention of terminating the agreement that permits American elements of the Southern European Task Force (a missile command) to be stationed in the Po Valley, nor of issuing movement orders to the Allied headquarters in Naples. Indeed, it has welcomed transfer of the NATO Defense College from Paris to Rome. But Italy has never been completely happy with its part in the NATO military structure. It would have liked to have been a member of the American-British-French military Standing Group (abolished July 1, 1966), and has long sought an arrangement whereby an Italian officer could be selected to command NATO naval forces in the Mediterranean. Italy has actively participated in NATO's Special Nuclear Committee. In sum, it is unlikely, even if its government should go farther left, that Italy will abandon its ties to and faith in the Atlantic Alliance.

Portugal is quite a different story. It would not take much provocation for this country to quit the Atlantic Alliance and to deny the United States use of the Azores bases. The base rights agreement expired in 1963 and has never been renewed, the Portuguese saying simply that, when they get around to discussing the bases, they will let us know. They are irked by our anticolonial position in the United Nations and by Britain's attitude toward South Africa and Rhodesia. They feel it is desirable to maintain good relations with France, which may help in United Nations debates on Angola and Mozambique. They have also been willing to allow Germany to set up a training and logistics installation in Portugal. Neither of these friendships, however, *requires* NATO. In fact, the Portuguese seem to feel that NATO has been of no particular value to them.

Spain, though not a member of NATO, has shown a willingness to join, if asked; but Northern European members have not been keen on admitting Generalissimo Franco to the Alliance because of the Fascist taint of his regime. Spain's dispute with Britain over Gibraltar is another obstacle to be overcome. However, the flagging of French cooperation in the Alliance may make Spanish membership look more attractive to the other NATO partners. Although United States forces not committed to NATO do have access to military facilities on Spanish soil, their need for bomber bases has decreased with technological progress. The Spanish have taken over the bases' air defense, to which the United States once made a major contribution. While the bases still house a number of U.S. fighters and some aerial refueling capability, this activity will inevitably decline. The utility of these facilities in connection with Middle Eastern or African contingency deployments remains, as does the very valuable capability for use in post-strike recovery for nuclear bombers. The Rota naval base is particularly valuable for the provisioning and maintenance of Polaris-type submarines stationed in the Mediterranean and Eastern Atlantic. While Spain's economy has boomed, like that of all Western European states, Spain nevertheless still looks to America for its external security needs. Finally, both Spain and Portugal share France's governmental problem—that of a powerful but aging leader with no obvious successor in view.

Greece and Turkey pose special problems for NATO. They occupy an exposed position on the Alliance's southern flank. Economically, they are still, at best, "developing" nations. They are heavily dependent on the United States for arms and other military support, although they have earnestly sought assistance from other NATO countries. They are sensitive to their geographic isolation from their Alliance partners and their proximity to traditional enemies, including each other. Unlike other NATO members, these two countries are vulnerable to subversion, conventional warfare, or guerrilla insurgency. All these factors generate a feeling that they have special defense problems that are not sufficiently appreciated by their prosperous and remote allies. Furthermore, the Greek-Turkish differences over Cyprus are still unresolved. While they have several times come close to fighting, their membership in NATO and their ties to the United States have been restraining influences. Both countries, while they have no particular reason to love each other, recognize the value of their NATO membership and the friendship of the United States. Both Greece and Turkey should eventually agree on some way of telling Archbishop Makarios that they have had enough of his dither in a demitasse. Hopefully, too, eventual economic prosperity will help both to solve their internal governmental crises.

Great Britain is a special case. One of the originators of NATO and of the earlier Brussels Treaty (now Western European Union), Britain in recent years has shown little stomach for the hard efforts needed to maintain effective British forces in Europe. Its original determination to be one of the leaders in post–World War II Europe has been repeatedly dampened and often blocked by the conflicting ambition to lead a vast Commonwealth. While the Commonwealth dream has faded over the years and Britain has moved slowly toward "joining Europe," a lagging economy, repeated balance of payments crises, and internal political uncertainties over nuclear weapons and the "special relationship" with the United States have all prevented the adoption of any clear policy regarding Britain's role in world affairs. Meanwhile, NATO has suffered from a slow decline in British attention and contributions.

Canada has a special internal problem with French-speaking Quebec, which conditions its relations with one ally— France. More important is its sensitive relationship with the United States. Canadian economic prosperity is heavily dependent upon its business with the United States and the influx of American capital. Geography makes the hemispheric defense of Canada and the United States a single military task. There are those who say that Canada would be just as happy to withdraw its forces from Europe, make a bilateral arrangement with the United States for the handling of Western Hemisphere and Pacific problems, and make its forces available to the United Nations for "peace-keeping" functions. It is in this last area that Canada sees for itself a unique role and opportunity for world leadership, an attitude also espoused by the Scandinavian allies and some neutrals. Furthermore, the roles of intermediary and U.N. "peace-keeper" offset Canada's discomfort over its junior-partner status relative to the United States and salves the Canadian consciousness of its sovereignty. As for NATO, John W. Holmes, Director-General of the Canadian Institute of International Affairs, pointed out that, "The Alliance is in a period when the nature of our relations among ourselves, with our antagonists and with the rest of the world are in flux, and we must grope for new or at least adjusted concepts."* This attitude was reiterated by Prime Minister Lester Pearson on June 12, 1966, in a speech at Springfield, Illinois. Thus, the Canadians had urged that the *démarche* in NATO prompted by President de Gaulle's ultimatum of March, 1966, represented an opportunity for re-thinking the organization and goals of the Alliance, rather than preserving the *status* quo at a new location in Belgium.

It seems clear that *all* of the NATO countries still count on American military power in any possible conflict with the Soviet Union. All, except France, want to be certain of retaining an effective American military presence on the Continent and will compromise their particular national interests and sovereignty to some extent to be assured of the American commitment. All want to continue NATO, even without active French participation—though the Fourteen (the NATO members less France) vary as between "hard-liners" toward France and "leaving the door open" for negotiation on future French re-integration. Each member, however, has some reservations in the areas of safeguarding its political

* John W. Holmes, "The Atlantic Community—Unity and Reality," speech delivered in Ottawa, September 15, 1964, to the Atlantic Treaty Association, and reprinted by the U.S. Senate Subcommittee on National Security and International Operations (Washington, D.C.: U.S. Government Printing Office, 1966).

sovereignty, maintaining economic progress, and avoiding increasing defense expenditures. Even among the Fourteen, there are differences of emphasis on such matters as nuclear armaments, force structure, the approaches to a détente in East-West relations, and, most important of all, the viability and purpose of NATO itself.

Western European Security

We commonly say that the underdeveloped countries need at least a minimum of military forces in order to provide the internal security without which economic progress and political stability are impossible. Even the sophisticated states of the North Atlantic area, however, have felt it necessary to maintain military forces at least partly for internal security as well as for purposes of expressing national power and prestige. But both the Communist ideological threat against internal security and the Communist military threat against external security have seemed to decline, and the nations of Western Europe have felt it less and less important to handicap their economic well-being by relatively heavy defense expenditures.

Despite paying lip service to "agreed" NATO force goals, none of the European members of the Atlantic Alliance has ever really felt that a major war in Europe could remain conventional. Thus, they have consoled themselves with modest conventional forces, which hopefully would be large enough to give the Soviet Union and the Eastern European states pause before embarking on combat, would require assembly and deployment of forces of a size that could not remain unnoticed, and, in short, would make Soviet intentions unambiguous. Furthermore, such a build-up of enemy forces would take enough time to give the Alliance time for consultations, mobilization, and for bringing pressures to bear on the aggressor to cease and desist. Then, on the assumptions that the U.S. nuclear deterrent is credible and that a thermonuclear holocaust is unthinkable to the enemy, the war threat will subside. This thesis permeates Western European defense thinking so effectively that it has become the essence of "strategy."

Since World War II, no single Western European country has ever been militarily strong enough to provide adequate forces for either deterrence or successful combat. Nor have all of them *together* possessed either adequate conventional forces for the screening function or sufficient nuclear forces for deterrence or combat. If France deserts the Alliance, the situation does not improve; but, in terms of power, it is not much worse, either.

Thus, to the Western European countries, the advantage of having the United States as a member of the Alliance is at least two-fold: First, by having forces physically in Europe, the Americans would be involved at H-Hour on D-Day in any European conflict; second, American strategic nuclear power is the most effective deterrent possessed by the West and, should the deterrent fail, the most effective force to combat the enemy. Western Europeans have tended to polarize the alternatives as no war or all-out thermonuclear war in which Europe would be destroyed and in which the West's modest conventional ground forces in Europe would be irrelevant. American palliatives, such as "prepositioned stocks" and "mobile strategic reserves," are unassuring to the Europeans, particularly as they see the growing U.S. force commitment to Viet-Nam.

To the possibility that war in Europe could take the form of "limited conventional" warfare, the Europeans point to the seeming horde of Soviet and Eastern satellite ground forces in comparison to the few dozen Western divisions. A conventional war of attrition simply does not add up to Western victory. Further, there is the danger of "escalation," with nuclear warfare at the end of the escalator. In crowded Western Europe, as in other parts of the world, the distinction between "tactical" and "strategic" thermonuclear yields is rather moot. Thus, to the Western European mind, any European war resolves itself to nuclear war.

The credibility of the possibility of a limited or conventional war in Europe is further lessened by President Johnson's October, 1966, overtures for inclusion of European troop reductions among measures for an easement of East-West tensions. Any U.S. force withdrawal would have to be from the Continent. NATO's conventional forces would lose one of their most modern components, the U.S. Seventh Army in Germany. It is not likely that the withdrawn U.S. forces would be immediately available to return in a crisis—especially if they were committed in Viet-Nam, as seems possible. The upshot is that a nuclear defense of Europe increasingly becomes the only viable alternative, at least to European thinking.

Since a nuclear arms race seems out of the question economically and politically for Europe, and since so many hopes are pinned on eventual nuclear disarmament or non-proliferation treaties, Europe is forced to rely on the existing American deterrent and to eschew any defensive build-up that might be provocative and spike cherished hopes for an East-West détente. Hence, a combination of European realism about the present and optimism for the future militates against any substantial build-up of NATO's defensive forces in Europe. This, in turn, generates a certain reluctance even to spend the money to modernize existing forces, especially since "modernity" today implies at least "tactical" nuclear weapons. Therefore, U.S. pleas for the European allies to build up and modernize their conventional forces, while leaving the nuclear defense to the United States, frequently fall on deaf ears. Furthermore, such a U.S. approach clearly subordinates the defense of Europe to the United States, which alone possesses the necessary nuclear sanction to make the Alliance's defense effective. As a consequence, many West Europeans feel helpless to defend themselves, yet resentful of the manner and means by which their defense is underwritten by the United

States through NATO. What are the prospects, then, for the Atlantic Alliance?

The Future of NATO

The principal short-run problem confronting the North Atlantic nations, looming like the Eiffel Tower above lesser problems, is France's Charles de Gaulle. His March, 1966, notice to NATO that its military headquarters must vacate France, that foreign forces must withdraw or come under French command, that the remaining French air and ground forces committed to NATO would revert to national control, and that all bases and logistical facilities in France must pass under French command have shaken the Alliance into a fundamental review of its position. By this initiative, the French President has not only knocked over the military applecart but has also shaken the whole NATO fruit stand, including the side displays.

Many of the problems raised by de Gaulle are of a continuing nature. For France, some may be "solved" by his formula in the short term, but then will have to be "re-solved" later, when he disappears from the scene. In any event, America's military and foreign policies in Western Europe have been so long associated with NATO that de Gaulle's threat to its vitality forces a re-examination of those policies and their future viability.

By 1966, NATO, which had remained largely unchanged since the North Atlantic Treaty was signed in 1949, undoubtedly needed "modernization" or "reform." I was among those who helped put together its military headquarters, Supreme Headquarters Allied Powers Europe (SHAPE), in the early days of 1951. Surely the peril we who were engaged in that enterprise were convinced we faced at that time—the threat of imminent Soviet military attack, not *whether*, but *where* and *when*—has passed. So, too, has passed the American hegemony under which it became customary for the United

States to formulate and announce its plans, while the other members of NATO restricted themselves largely to commenting on American proposals—if, indeed, they were given the time and opportunity to do even that.

Nevertheless, our partners seemed generally happy with that situation. Though they made minor noises from time to time, mostly of a procedural nature, they were delighted with the opportunity to concentrate their attention on economic and political recovery from World War II. Except for France in the years since 1958, they have by and large been willing to continue the Alliance essentially unchanged—until, perhaps, now. One major reason for this attitude has clearly been the knowledge that deterrence of aggression in the area rests on American strategic nuclear power. Not only has de Gaulle understood this, but he has undoubtedly based his effort to recapture French independence of action on the realization that the U.S. deterrent can still be counted upon.

It is clear in retrospect that when the community of interest in the North Atlantic area, as strong as the threat itself in the early 1950's, began to weaken with the apparently diminishing threat, we should have been alert to the change. Our sensitivity to the altered circumstances may have been dulled by the fact that, simultaneously, American interests were increasingly engaged on a broadening stage—in Lebanon, Cuba, Cyprus, the Congo, Pakistan and India, the Dominican Republic, and South Viet-Nam. Our European allies, who were formerly colonial powers, were generally less and less interested in world-wide matters, as decolonization became more and more the norm. (Those allies still possessing colonies in the 1960's, such as Portugal, became less friendly, as American representatives deplored colonization in world forums.)

De Gaulle began hinting his intentions with a memorandum of September 24, 1958, to the British Prime Minister and the American President, suggesting a "Standing Group" in the political field so that France, Britain, and the United

States would have a forum in which to deal with world-wide political and strategic problems. This Western "troika," he visualized, would deal with the employment of nuclear weapons as well. His proposal, and the implication that France would become less cooperative if his suggestion were not heeded, fell on deaf ears. The "troika" idea was rejected as undercutting the basic principle of NATO as an alliance of equal partners—but it may also have been judged an unwelcome assertion of French interest and influence beyond Europe. In any event, the United States should have been more alert as de Gaulle proceeded to pursue a systematically independent course culminating in his dénouement of March, 1966.

By 1966, it was time indeed for President Johnson to indicate, as he did in a television broadcast on March 23 (two weeks after de Gaulle's notes to the allies spelling out his demands for NATO "reform"), that there was no particular righteousness in immobility, and that NATO must grow and adapt. He added that the Alliance shared one common danger —division—and one common strength—union. The irony is that it took so long for an American President to make such a statement, and then not as a matter of initiative but of response.

NATO is basically a military alliance. It was constituted to counter a threat, and its current "disarray" is due to de Gaulle's feeling (shared in varying degrees by many others) that either the threat has changed or it can be handled by other means. Nevertheless, the physical threat to Western Europe remains, and there is no certainty that changing to the French horse from the American one will provide adequate security. I judge the likelihood of major war in Europe in the next decade to be slight, but only if the Russians continue to confront a force-in-being that will make any military effort on their part one of quickly diminishing returns. I believe that Western Europe still wants the United States to maintain its interest in Europe and, above all, wants American strategic nuclear power committed as a counter-threat (deterrent)— and as a combat force, if required.

The problems created by the loss of France to NATO's integrated command and force structure are not easy, but neither are they insoluble. The major military contribution of France to the Alliance has been the militarily important geographical position that it occupies, not the forces made available.

NATO will organize itself without France. For our part, we could play down the "flexible response" concept and pledge the use of American strategic forces should Russia attack. ("Flexible response" is a genteel strategic notion, but hardly credible when one looks at the scanty "hardware" capability in position to implement it vis-à-vis the manifest capability of the potential aggressor. If our allies themselves challenge the realism of the strategy, then surely the enemy discounts it, too.) We can reduce to "trip wire" status our ground and air forces permanently stationed in Europe, use less real estate and fewer bases, require less supplies, and incidentally reduce our balance-of-payments burden. We would, of course, need to maintain adequate conventional power to oppose Soviet pressure on Berlin.

Thus, NATO could remain integrated, but brought "up-to-date." It should, of course, continue to encourage full participation by France. In the interim, participation in control of military matters should be restricted to those members of the Alliance that maintain and contribute forces or facilities to NATO's integrated commands.

More is called for than organizational changes, relocation of headquarters and facilities, and possible force manipulations. Walter Lippmann stated the problem succinctly:

> The criterion of an acceptable compromise is not whether joint planning can be made as effective as integrated planning, whether in time of peace the liaison staff officers can do approximately as well as integrated staff officers. Virtually nobody thinks that the defense of Western Europe against the Red Army is a

sufficient purpose of NATO today. There is virtually no one who does not believe that if Western Europe needs to be defended by armies, the principal weapon will be the unintegrated American Strategic Air Command.

The importance of NATO is now political. That is to say, the NATO forces give weight and authority to the diplomatic posture of the Western nations. They would have little influence on East-West relations and on the future of Germany if they became sharply divided. . . .

The real problem is that the original purpose of NATO no longer provides a mainspring for the Alliance. The original purpose is no longer relevant as it was fifteen years ago . . . to preserve the Alliance as a vigorous influence in the affairs of the European continent, it needs a new purpose. Whereas its purpose has been the defense of the West, its purpose should now be the healing of the division between Western Europe and Eastern Europe and a settlement of the European Cold War. . . .*

How to transform a defensive alliance into a political organization for the coordination of foreign policy is not at all clear. Will the goal of détente provide the same stimulus as fear of a common enemy? Will France subordinate its cherished independence to achieve an *Atlantic* foreign policy? An affirmative answer hinges on the resolution of another critical issue—German reunification. This issue is at the heart of the future of NATO, the future of Europe, and the future of East-West relations.

The German Dilemma

As long as Germany remains divided between an alliance of free Western democracies and an alliance of Eastern Communist states tied to Russia through the Warsaw Pact, the security problems of countervailing power create circumstances that make further détente remote. Hanson Baldwin

---

* Walter Lippmann, "A New Direction in Europe," *The Washington Post,* April 21, 1966, p. 7.

aptly described the problem this situation creates within the Atlantic Alliance:

> The real problem is not only—and not so much—military, as it is political. A primary military problem still exists, it is true—the maintenance of an allied capability to react with less than nuclear power to renewed Soviet pressure on West Berlin. But the major problem of the future alliance is how to integrate Western Germany. . . . How can one give renascent Germany an equal-member status without allowing Germany control over her own nuclear weapons, while the United States, Britain and France have them? How can one maintain German military power without encouraging dangerous German irredentism? And what effect would the reduction—few think in terms of complete withdrawal—of U.S. troops in Europe have upon: (a) German politics and psychology, keyed to reunification and to fear of Russia; and (b) Eastern European satellites like Poland, whose peoples (as distinct from their governments) welcome U.S. troops in Europe as a form of leverage against their Russian masters?*

NATO has given West Germany a climate and context in which to grow economically and politically, to avoid an overburdening and overbearing military establishment, and to pursue a low-key approach to eventual reunification. West Germany has recovered from the ravages of World War II, as have its former enemies. Today the German army is the largest NATO land force in Western Europe. Economically, the German "miracle" has produced the strongest economy in Europe west of the Soviet Union. On the face of it, Germany would appear to be having its cake and eating it, too—vast economic bounty relatively unburdened by defense expenditure, and security through NATO under the umbrella of U.S. strategic nuclear power. But nagging the German national consciousness are the desires for equality with its allies and restoration as a whole nation of Germans. The implications of

---

* Hanson Baldwin, *The New York Times*, March 13, 1966, p. E3.

these desires are contradictory, and they squarely pose the issues for the future of Europe.

The *sine qua non* of "great power equality" today is the possession of nuclear weapons, however few. At least Britain and France trade on this criterion. A Germany armed with nuclear weapons raises fearful spectres on both sides of the Iron Curtain. The Russians will not tolerate a nuclear Germany. U.S. forces stationed in Germany with nuclear weapons are an entirely different matter. The Russians know whose finger is on the trigger, and they know the parameters of any nuclear confrontation with the United States. The United States is also unwilling to provide Germany with a "hardware solution" to the latter's nuclear dilemma. It would be contrary to U.S. interests in nuclear disarmament or at least nuclear non-proliferation. More important, a nuclear-armed Germany would shift the East-West power balance, and would probably spark an arms race that would make a détente even more remote. Finally, a nuclear-armed Federal Republic of Germany might be tempted to declare its independence of the West in search of a "final solution" for a peace treaty and reunification, a situation with high explosive potential.

A reunited Germany—even without nuclear weapons—also poses severe tests for the East and West in Europe. The Soviets will not agree to a united Germany remaining in NATO; and the United States, with equal vigor, will not allow a unified Germany allied to the Warsaw Pact. Very simply, German reunification can come about only under some variety of neutrality, which certainly means the end of NATO as we have known it. With the independence of a neutral Germany, the U.S. presence in Europe has no place to go, unless France changes its attitude—and well it might under the circumstances. The effect on the Warsaw Pact is less certain, but with Eastern European nationalism and independence of the Soviet Union on the rise, the implications for the Pact are not favorable to Soviet interests. Disbanding NATO could involve a similar action by the Warsaw Pact nations. Finally, it must be recognized that some Western European nations are not keen on the creation of a united Germany in the heart of Europe without firm security guarantees or a supervised neutrality.

Even a reunified, independent, non-nuclear, neutral Germany is not necessarily a stable solution. Yet, a viable solution to the problem of German reunification is at the heart of the quest for an East-West détente. What is troubling is that the quest cannot be postponed interminably. In the meantime, the more immediate NATO problem of German participation in the nuclear defense of the Alliance persists. Compounding the difficulty is that the resolution of the near-term defense problem must not be such as to preclude peaceful resolution of the long-term reunification issue.

Summarizing, it would seem that the principal objectives of the Western European nations for the next decade include European and internal political stability, economic progress, and military security. Progress has been made in all three areas in the two decades since World War II. That progress has been achieved by farsighted individuals who placed collective action above narrow nationalism. Indeed, I believe it can be shown that each Western European nation has achieved a greater degree of nationalistic objectives by operating within the framework of collective agreements than it would have achieved on its own. This is particularly true in the economic and security fields, which may well be worth any political sacrifices involved.

If Western Europe wishes to become a separate power center comparable to the United States or Russia, it must have nuclear strength of its own. Assuming that France would be willing to join (and I think it would if it thought it could be the leader), the French and British could form the nucleus of a Western European nuclear force. The Alliance could agree that all members would own and control the nuclear force jointly, thus technically retaining inviolate the atomic restrictions on Germany. This would, of course, toss the Geneva non-proliferation discussion into a cocked hat, and might even cause the Soviet Union to assume a more warlike posture. Fear of such reaction, however, should not be the determining factor if other signs point to success as a deterrent force. Western Europe could hardly be a separate power center without France. American encouragement and aid also would appear essential, initially at least. A concomitant is probably American leadership, but it is just this leadership ("hegemony") that de Gaulle rejects.

It would seem unwise, if not, indeed, foolish, for any of the Western European nations to abandon successful *principles* and fly to ills they do not know. Improvement in Alliance organization is certainly possible. Good management recognizes the need of organizations to grow and to find new ways of doing things. It would seem desirable for the Western European nations to continue in the forthcoming decade their economic organizations and the Atlantic Alliance. Both should achieve as high a degree of collective political action as may be possible, keeping in mind the fact that France apparently is schizophrenic in these two areas—seemingly willing to continue to support collective action (with some reservations) in the economic field, but unwilling to do so in the field of security.

The next decade should see closer economic relations with the nations of Eastern Europe, and between East and West Germany. Western Europe knows that it must someday contemplate the reunification of Germany, and that it cannot exclude the possibility from its thinking. But it is difficult to reconcile such an event with a meaningful NATO. It will require careful consideration of the security situation before it can come to pass.

Most important in the next decade, NATO should be more of a political forum and the United States should not neglect to consult therein—not only on matters affecting the North Atlantic area but also with respect to those having world-wide implications. I believe that Timothy Stanley's view that the Atlantic Alliance is in transition from a regional security mission to the task of providing leadership in building a viable world order is worth considering.* But the Alliance's security aspects cannot be neglected. Western Europe still wants NATO for its collective military power potential (including American strategic nuclear power), and hopes that it can have this security with minimum interference in its own political arrangements.

The American Interest and Policy

What does the United States want in Europe? I think we desire, first, to keep Western Europe from being organized against us by an unfriendly power; second, to protect our right to a major voice in any settlement of World War II and the future of Germany; and third, to maintain some measure of American influence in Europe. To accomplish these objectives, we need a diplomatic and military posture in Europe that is alert to and capable of resisting Soviet political or territorial encroachment. An American presence in Europe also serves to remind our allies that we do not intend to abandon our European interests.

Do our objectives mean continuation of the present search for détente with Russia? I think that they do not imply any sudden reversal of our current policy, but neither, I submit, is this policy essential to our objectives; it may, indeed, inhibit their full accomplishment. It is clear, for example, that the more successful the détente appears to be (and I say "appears to be" because I cannot bring myself to place full faith and confidence in the Kremlin), the more nations like de Gaulle's France can act independently, and the more a lack of confidence in American intentions can be engendered in nations like West Germany. In the latter case, the quest for détente involves compromises of policy and abandonment of old

* Stanley, op. cit., p. 395.

shibboleths. Necessary as these shifts may be, they shake the confidence of weaker nations that have come to anchor their own hopes and security on the fixity of American policies.

We are in this seeming détente primarily because the Soviet Union has finally learned that its threatening moves serve only to consolidate NATO determination and cohesion in resistance. On our side, there are many who think that by encouraging détente we decrease the threat of nuclear war and create an atmosphere in which progress might be made toward disarmament. We have been misleading ourselves on both points. Even in the Cuban missile crisis, and certainly since then, there has been no overt threat of the use of nuclear weapons. The "threshold" of such employment has risen, not because of any policy of détente, but because both the United States and the Soviet Union have learned they can tolerate threats to their interests without recourse to devastating each other. The nuclear weapon itself has been the primary cause of the détente, such as it is; the détente has not ruled out the necessity for the weapon. Indeed, the détente posture requires as much strength and alertness on the part of the West as any other defensive posture.

As we look forward to the next decade, the interests of the United States in Europe will be best served by a policy of flexibility rather than rigidity. America is still interested in a greater measure of independence for the Eastern European states and should lose no opportunity to encourage such independence. This does not mean inflammatory speeches or rocket rattling; rather, it means an alertness to capitalize on propitious situations as they present themselves and the creation of "openings to the West" that permit such situations to develop. To visualize the possibility of eventual reunification of Germany, we must face the need for considering confederation or federalism. This will require some sort of Western recognition of the existence of East Germany. We should not hesitate to face these possibilities, and should take the lead in educating others to face such prospects without fear.

To achieve our objective of no further Soviet territorial or political encroachment, we need some sort of agreement with like-minded nations. I think that a modified NATO is still the best starting point for the forthcoming decade.

If the keynote of American policy for this period is to be "flexibility," we need to visualize movement toward a loose association of states rather than a rigid alliance. The timing must be governed by the events of the period. The decade we are facing is more likely to be characterized by change than by immobility. To exert leadership on the international scene, America must free itself from the bondage of the past, cast a jaundiced eye over its policies, and be prepared with a wider range of options than it enjoyed during the heyday of rigid "containment."

Conclusion

The community of interest between the United States and Western Europe will be no less strong in the next decade than it has been in the past two. The United States wants for Western Europe those things that Western Europe wants for itself. It is in the United States' own self-interest to see Western Europe politically stable, economically prosperous, and militarily secure.

It is in the United States' own self-interest to use its military power to help Western Europe achieve security, though it would be preferable economically (and in some cases politically) to eliminate its overseas deployments and depend on a combination of greater indigenous strength and its own strategic mobility and nuclear power to provide both the deterrent and the combat potential required. There is also a requirement either to find a way within existing law and treaties to increase the nuclear potential of the European allies, or amend the law itself and reconsider the treaties being discussed affecting nuclear weapons in order to permit the controlled build-up of this strength.

I think there are limits to American ability to make NATO a strong collective power in the political arena, but I have no objection to attempts at moving toward that end. The United States cannot force such an outcome. But it can make consultation with its allies a fundamental precept of policy instead of the hit-or-miss approach it has used in the past.

It can and should take the position in the next decade that NATO, with or without full French participation, is a major U.S. concern, recognizing that the interests of its highly sophisticated members are world-wide—though in varying degrees, and not simply regional—and require some reasonable accommodation.

It must adjust to the French *démarche* and proceed with reorganizing and revitalizing the Alliance. But it should not attempt to exile France from NATO; rather, it should seek to make those compromises that are in the best interests of the Alliance as a whole and hope that these will induce a renewal of French participation.

It can and should enunciate the thesis that NATO has the necessary power for peace, that it is a proper forum for discussing and developing courses of action directed toward reduction of tensions, disarmament, collective security, and the post—World War II settlement of Europe that has never been completed.

Above all, Americans should realize that there is no single non-Communist nation or group of nations competent to lead other than themselves. They should be prepared to use their power, both political and military, restrainedly but effectively to achieve their purposes. They should evaluate their existing world commitments from a viewpoint of enlightened self-interest, and face the next decade with a wider range of options in solving international problems than they have had in the recent past.

5. *National Security Policy and the Asian Area**

LIEUTENANT COLONEL GEORGE K. OSBORN, III

Security policy in the Asian area† in the decade of the 1970's will be concerned with five sets of problems: Those generated by the existence of a nuclear-armed Communist China; those arising from the possibility of local conventional wars; those related to the vulnerability of much of the area to subversion and internal war; those connected with Taiwan and the question of what government legitimately represents China on the international stage; and those deriving from Japan's changing security role in Asia. Each of these, in turn, must be examined from the viewpoint of three states or groups of states: Communist China—the People's Republic of China; the other Asian states, individually and collectively; and the non-Asian states, principally the United States and the Soviet Union. If these problems of the 1970's are to be dealt with rationally, serious consideration must be given to them now.

---

* The views expressed in this essay are the author's own and do not necessarily represent those of the United States Government.

† For the purposes of this paper, the Asian area includes the Far East and South and Southeast Asia; it excludes Southwest Asia, which has more in common with the Near East and North Africa than with the rest of Asia. The U.S.S.R. is treated as a non-Asian state with interests in Asia.

A Nuclear-Armed China

The existence of a nuclear-armed Communist China will be the dominant problem of the next decade because the solution to almost any security problem will have to take into account Chinese nuclear strength and responses to it by other states. For purposes of analysis, it is convenient to approach the problems generated by the existence of this new member of the nuclear club in two ways: Through analysis of its capabilities, and through examination of its possible strategies.

Capabilities should be discussed in terms of two time phases. During Phase I, beginning in the late 1960's and running well into the 1970's, Communist China will probably have a limited number of nuclear weapons and a delivery capability restricted to mainland Asia, including Asiatic U.S.S.R., Japan, the Ryukyus, Taiwan, the Philippines, and parts of Indonesia. The P.R.C. is likely to develop a thermonuclear device during Phase I, and could succeed in producing a thermonuclear weapons system late in this phase. During Phase II, beginning in the mid-1970's and continuing into the early or mid-1980's, Communist China should have not only more of the shorter-range weapons systems, armed with both nuclear and thermonuclear warheads, but also some intercontinental delivery capability. At some time, probably in the early 1970's, Communist China could also deploy a number of submarines equipped with cruise missiles and low-yield atomic warheads.

In Phase I, the major concern of China's neighbors and of the U.S. and U.S.S.R. will be deterrence of the limited Chinese nuclear threat, and this will mean—among other things—facing up to the problem of further proliferation of nuclear weapons. Asian states will have to decide whether to attempt weapons production themselves—such as in the cases of India and Japan—whether to enter the world market to buy or borrow weapons, or whether to seek guarantees from non-Asian nuclear powers. The other members of the nuclear club (U.S., U.S.S.R., U.K., and France) will have to re-evaluate their positions on proliferation to cope with these Asian choices.

If the three powers that presently oppose proliferation (U.S., U.S.S.R., U.K.) choose to continue their opposition, certain options would be open to them. They might attempt, singly or collectively, to bring Communist China into meaningful nuclear and/or general arms limitation or disarmament negotiations to head off arms races and to allay fears of the other Asian nations.* They might attempt to block proliferation by providing guarantees—unilateral, bilateral, or multilateral—to the Asian states, or they might simply use pressure or economic inducements to prevent proliferation without providing any sort of guarantee and in the absence of successful disarmament or arms limitation negotiations with China. Such pressure might be effective in the case of some Asian states, but it probably would be relatively ineffective (or politically very costly) against India or Japan, if either or both of those countries found it in their own national interest to arm themselves with nuclear weapons.† If it became necessary to apply pressure greater than diplomatic and minor economic sanctions, some general agreement within the non-Asian nuclear club—especially between the U.S. and the U.S.S.R., but also including France—would be required.

* Admittedly, this would be difficult, since the Chinese might well be in no mood for such negotiations just when they see themselves on the threshold of at least relative nuclear parity with the other major powers. However, at the extreme end of the spectrum of inducement for the Chinese to negotiate lies the possibility of the United States and/or the Soviet Union mounting an exemplary disarming attack on selected elements of Chinese nuclear installations. More realistic inducements might include holding out the possibility of economic benefits from an arms-race slowdown, offering nonaggression pacts, etc.

† India might be susceptible to economic pressure at a relatively low level, but political risks involved in the economic collapse of India undoubtedly would deter friendly powers from applying such pressure. Japan could resist low-level pressure once the domestic political decision was taken.

Alternatively, the powers that presently oppose nuclear proliferation could decide to withdraw their opposition. This would require implicit acceptance of the argument that they cannot prevent such proliferation by acceptable means or that stability rather than instability might actually be the result of proliferation.* Again, a number of alternative policies are open to them once they accept proliferation. States capable of producing their own weapons systems within a relatively short time—India and Japan—could be left to make their own decisions, technical assistance could be made available to them, or production of both weapons and delivery systems could be directly or indirectly subsidized, or actual hardware could be made available on an interim or permanent basis, and so forth. Similarly, Pakistan and Indonesia might be left to embark on individual development programs, although both would require a longer lead time. Since other Asian states would find it very difficult to embark on nuclear weapons development on their own, this whole line of policy may lead to a new factor in the armaments market—the nuclear salesman.†

A decision to accept proliferation would also raise the problem of whether the present nuclear powers would attempt to control or influence the direction of the proliferation within Asia, or whether they would permit the indiscriminate development of possibly second-rate—and therefore doubly dangerous—weapons systems there. Such influence or control might be accomplished through selective availability of hardware and technology, but it would require close agreement among all the non-Asian nuclear powers to assure this. Even then, there is the possibility that Communist China itself

---

* In other words, that the "price" of preventing proliferation might be too high or that the possession of nuclear weapons by a substantial number of states would actually deter rather than encourage usage.

† With many states capable of producing nuclear weapons—India, Japan, Israel, Federal Republic of Germany, Sweden, Switzerland, to name a few— the smaller Asian states might shop around, and the states with the capability might be willing to enter into sales agreements and into competition with each other, perhaps to help defray the costs of developing their own weapons.

would become an uncontrolled "salesman," or source of nuclear weapons, for Asian nations facing rivals other than China (e.g., Pakistan with its concern with India rather than with Communist China).

Finally, during Phase I, decisions must be made regarding the Chinese nuclear threat during Phase II. Asian states choosing to counter Communist China's Phase I capabilities will have to continue (and even accelerate) their efforts in Phase II or reconcile themselves to living without hole cards in an extremely dangerous poker game. Or they might resort to indecision until late in Phase I if they believe that others, i.e., the non-Asian great powers, can be compelled to make decisions and choices for them. In this regard, the non-Asian nuclear powers also have options. Conceivably, they could threaten—or actually mount—an exemplary disarming attack on Chinese nuclear facilities to force the Chinese into disarmament or arms limitation negotiations. More productive marginally, and more feasible politically, they could devote increased investment to Anti-Ballistic-Missile systems that would counter the threat of direct Chinese attack on them during Phase II.

Since the establishment of the People's Republic of China in October, 1949, Peking has consistently pursued a strategy of caution. Low nuclear capability and high vulnerability to nuclear attack during Phase I indicates continuation of this approach into the 1970's.* At least two neighbors (Japan and India) could initiate crash programs to catch up with Communist China, and either the U.S. or the U.S.S.R. could destroy or severely damage the Chinese nuclear capability by applying comparatively little force. This suggests, then, a Chinese strategy of probing and subtle nuclear blackmail, rather than blatant nuclear sabre rattling or actual weapons use. Such a strategy of caution might have a variety of related,

---

* Space does not permit full development of the historical background here. For an excellent summary treatment, see Davis Bobrow's article, "Peking's Military Calculus," in *World Politics*, XVI, No. 2 (January, 1964), 287–301.

sometimes contradictory goals: To convince all Asians that Chinese possession of nuclear weapons is, in reality, no threat to their security, that Chinese nuclear weapons are for defense only and especially for the defense of the weak and non-nuclear states against the "nuclear bullies" (the U.S. and U.S.S.R.); to convince India and Japan that Communist China is so far ahead in research and development that they would be wasting time and resources in attempting to catch up; to prevent or preclude the establishment of new U.S. bases on the periphery of Asia and to gain the removal of existing bases if possible; to keep the U.S.S.R. from undertaking a massive build-up in the Mongolian People's Republic or along the Sino-Soviet frontier; and to attempt to determine, without undue risk, the precise threshold of U.S.–U.S.S.R. nuclear action.*

Communist China's strategy well into Phase II is unlikely to change substantially. By then both the U.S. and U.S.S.R., if they make the necessary decisions, should be capable of deploying Anti-Ballistic-Missile (ABM) systems to cope with any direct Chinese threat against them. This does not, however, preclude a Chinese aggressive blackmail strategy in Asia to undercut American or Soviet influence there. For example, China might attempt to force Thailand to abandon ties with the U.S. and to accept a neutralist coalition using a complex nuclear blackmail strategy—a war of nerves, in which the Peking-sponsored Thai Patriotic Front would be permitted to rattle Chinese nuclear sabres.

Some Asian states—e.g., Indonesia, India, Japan, the Philippines, and Thailand—seem likely to reject the idea that Chinese possession of nuclear weapons is not a threat to their security or that they exist in part to protect non-nuclear Asian states; none of them, except possibly Pakistan, is likely to welcome the potential protection of Peking's nuclear um-

---

* In other words, at what point will the U.S.–U.S.S.R. be moved to prevent or pre-empt; within what parameters can Communist China act freely without running a high risk of a nuclear response?

brella. Further, it is unlikely that either India or Japan could be convinced that China is too far ahead of them to attempt to catch up or pass. Feasible options for Asian states resisting Chinese nuclear blackmail appear to be: Unilateral nuclear deterrent forces for India and Japan; a multilateral Asian deterrent; a number of bilateral deterrents, involving Asian and non-Asian states or a New Delhi-Tokyo axis; multilateral deterrents involving Asian and non-Asian states; and appeasement of Communist China by some Asian states in the hope that at some point non-Asians will be forced to intervene. In theory, the most attractive choice for Asian states, excluding perhaps Pakistan, would seem to be a multilateral Asian deterrent, based on Indian and Japanese nuclear forces initially, because this could deter Communist China without involving Asians in great-power politics, i.e., an Asian deterrent under Asian control. In practice, it is doubtful that these Asian states would be more successful at constructing a multilateral force than was NATO in the early 1960's. A more likely Asian choice would be to seek bilateral or multilateral agreements— some involving both Asian (Indian, Japanese, possibly Pakistani) and non-Asian forces, some involving non-Asian guarantees to Asian states.*

Communist China's ability to blackmail and to probe successfully is likely to depend mainly on the reaction of the U.S. and its allies and the U.S.S.R. to probes. To thwart Chinese aggression, the U.S. and U.S.S.R. must pursue a strategy of deterrence, both by conventional and nuclear means, and of maintaining the capability to threaten the destruction of Peking's limited nuclear forces and installations.† They can do this singly in their own spheres, in tandem on an informal

---

* The U.S.S.R. might provide guarantees to North Korea, North Viet-Nam, and the Mongolian Peoples' Republic, while the U.S. guarantees Japan, South Korea, the Philippines, Taiwan, Thailand, and possibly Indonesia, India, and Malaysia.

† To use Herman Kahn's terminology: deterrence and denial plus counterforce, as developed in his *On Thermonuclear War* (Princeton, N.J.: Princeton University Press, 1960).

basis, or conceivably even in formal cooperation. The possibilities for cooperation between the U.S. and U.S.S.R., both implicit and explicit, in dealing with a Chinese nuclear threat will most likely increase. Certainly, both would have to deploy ABM systems against Chinese nuclear weapons, although the requirement will exist earlier for the U.S.S.R. to do so because of its geographic location. Both should be prepared, also, to deploy conventional forces to deter Communist China below the nuclear threshold and to keep that threshold relatively high. Both should have a clear idea of the internal structure of their respective escalation ladder *vis-à-vis* Communist China; and both must find ways to apprise Communist China of the nuclear threshold without drawing the line so high or so explicitly that it permits Peking freedom to blackmail below that line.*

Local Conventional War

International conflict in Asia below the nuclear threshold— i.e. local conventional war—will remain a possibility in the next decade, because the basic causes of conflict between various Asian states are not likely to be eliminated. This could be complicated by an intra-Asian nuclear proliferation, "local conventional war" even coming to include limited nuclear exchanges. Local wars in Asia might involve: India and Pakistan at war over Kashmir and other questions; Cambodia and Thailand at war over disputed border provinces; Cambodia and Viet-Nam at war over disputed frontiers; and Communist China in limited, perhaps ambiguous, conflict with India, Burma, Laos, and Thailand. Further, Thailand and North Viet-Nam might become involved in a war in or because of Laos.† Other conflicts, less likely to escalate above the raid

---

* See Herman Kahn, *On Escalation: Metaphors and Scenarios,* for a discussion of escalation ladders. (New York: Frederick A. Praeger, 1965).

† The pre-French history of Laos reveals a history of internal war among factions supported by Thailand and Viet-Nam. Hence, Laos is included here both as a potential catalyst in a Thailand–Viet-Nam war and as a likely candidate for continued internal war.

level, might involve Burma and Thailand, Indonesia and Malaysia, Indonesia and the Philippines, and North Korea and South Korea.

The principal danger arising from such wars is that they could result in the economic or political collapse of one or all of the antagonists. Such collapse could lead to discontent, internal war, and intervention by outside powers, with a subsequent widening of the conflict well beyond the interests of the original protagonists.

It seems clear that, in general, the long-term interests of the present Asian states will not be served by the economic and subsequent political collapse of any one of them, although short-term interests might well be. For example, an extended war between India and Pakistan might end in the economic collapse of India and a political disintegration of its union into independent linguistic states. In such a milieu, Pakistan might gain a temporarily favorable settlement of the Kashmir question. Internal war in India, however, might lead to outside intervention and, conceivably, to the emergence of a Communist-controlled India on Pakistan's flanks, or it might lead to a blood bath for India's Muslims and the reunification of India under a Hindu nationalist regime bent on revenge. In such cases, long-term risks appear to outweigh short-term gains; there is no guarantee, however, that the individual states concerned will see it that way.

It also seems clear that the interests of the U.S., U.K., Australia, and New Zealand would be served best if Asian conflicts were kept somewhere below the level of local war. Past experience suggests that this will not in every case be possible, however, and the interest of the powers mentioned would then be in limiting or controlling conflict at a level that will not end in the collapse of one or more of the protagonists —even if this meant pursuing strategies of active intervention.

The interest of the U.S.S.R. in the case of local Asian wars is not altogether clear. Certainly, at the ends of the Asian arc, in the Indian subcontinent and in Northeast Asia, the Soviet interest coincides with that of the U.S. and its allies—keeping conflict somewhere below the level of local war. Conflict in these areas of geographic propinquity directly affects the security of the U.S.S.R. and could lead to problems of multiple intervention and U.S.–U.S.S.R. confrontation. In other areas, specifically in Southeast Asia, Soviet interests are ambiguous. As the U.S.S.R. sees it, conflict in Southeast Asia might be attractive either because it could serve as a vehicle on which local Communists could ride to power or as a means of diverting Chinese attention from the long land frontier with the U.S.S.R. On the other hand, conflict in Southeast Asia might lead to the expansion of Chinese power in the region and/or to a direct Sino–U.S. confrontation—forcing the U.S.S.R. to make unpalatable policy decisions about an area in which there is little disposable Soviet power. It would seem to be in the American interest to attempt to eliminate Soviet ambiguity, convincing the U.S.S.R. that its interests are best served by opposing local wars in Southeast Asia.

Communist China, on the other hand, appears to have an interest in stimulating conflict—local war—throughout the Asian area, with the limitation that such conflict should not lead to the development of any major American presence in the areas immediately contiguous to China's frontiers or to a concentration of Soviet forces in Asia. This indicates that Peking will probably continue to pursue a cautious and conservative course in its border regions, at least until it can effect an American withdrawal from the area, meanwhile attempting to stir up trouble elsewhere. The collapse of governments in India, Burma, Thailand, the Philippines, and Malaysia normally might be expected to serve Chinese interests by offering an opportunity for exploitation through support of local pro-Peking Communists, encouragement of neutralist (and weak) coalition governments, or the raising of Chinese territorial claims.

The foregoing analysis leads to the general conclusion that conflict in the Asian area will probably be endemic in the decade of the 1970's, and that some of this conflict could result in local war. In such a milieu, some states may be willing to trade off possible long-term losses for probable short-term gains. The U.S. and its allies will likely pursue policies of active intervention of some type and degree in order to limit and control conflict—sometimes in cooperation with, or parallel to, sometimes in opposition to, the U.S.S.R., and almost always in opposition to Communist China.

Subversion and Internal War*

The third set of problems stems from the vulnerability of the area to subversion and internal war, a phenomenon that includes but is not restricted to Communist subversion or to internal war between a legitimate government and a Communist-led or Communist-dominated alternate.

Vulnerability to internal war and subversion is a highly complex matter. In attempting to derive some idea of the area's susceptibility, a number of factors must be considered. In brief, those used in the following discussion are: The ability of a government to communicate and to enforce its decisions; the pace and nature of economic development; the attitude of the intelligentsia; type and stability of social structure; strength and content of ideology; character of revolutionary parties and leaders; the existence of potential revolutionary military base areas; revolutionary armed forces; existing or potential alternate governments; and external factors influencing internal stability.

Obviously, these factors are not independent variables. Further, not all of them need be operationally effective at any

---

* This section was written at a time when the military outcome of the war in South Viet-Nam appeared reasonably clear, but the political outcome was very much in doubt. The underlying assumptions were: North Viet-Nam would not be invaded and destroyed by U.S. and South Vietnamese ground forces; second, a neutral South Viet-Nam might emerge; third, U.S. commitments in Southeast Asia would be stepped up if (a) a neutralization agreement for South Viet-Nam were negotiated and/or (b) the Hanoi government ultimately attained control over the south.

single point in time. However, most, if not all of them, will affect any single situation if destructive discontent is to develop and revolutionary internal war is to prosper. A brief explanation of each factor may lead to a better understanding of the hypotheses that follow.

Governments must be able to communicate and be communicated with, and they must be able to enforce their writ throughout the territory over which they claim sovereignty. Where such conditions do not obtain, opposition can coalesce. Frequently, where governments cannot enforce their writ—i.e., cannot collect taxes, police, hold periodic courts—other power centers grow. A closely related phenomenon appears to be the presence or lack of an institutionalized framework for the transfer of power—from government to government or from clique to clique—for succession squabbles may reduce communications and administration to the point where power vacuums occur.

In the area of economic development, there are a number of critical relationships. First is the relation between economic and population growth. If the rate of economic growth does not substantially exceed that of population growth, for example, by a factor of two or more, instability and discontent are likely. Second are the relationships of specific economic groups to each other in producing and consuming the fruits of economic development; if there is an economic elite that is growing in wealth at the same time that other groups are in chronic economic distress, discontent will develop and intensify. Third is the relationship between total work force and employment. If the numbers of unemployed or underemployed are substantial and the trend is rising, a pool of potential revolutionary manpower is created.

The intelligentsia constitutes a special group of great importance in a developing or transitional society.* The active support of all the intelligentsia is not required for stability,

* Transitional, here, is broadly interpreted to include all of the societies in East, South, and Southeast Asia.

but, if large numbers of or groups within the intelligentsia are disenchanted with the existing order, they form a peculiarly potent source of discontent and revolutionary leadership. However, the intelligentsia may form a reservoir of talent capable of assisting governments exposed to the threat of subversion and internal war.

Social structure is significant in a number of ways. A highly rigidified social structure is inherently unstable in the long term, however stable it may be in the short term. Further, a social structure that does not correspond to the political and economic structures is dysfunctional in the long term and may be so in the short term as well. If a society contains large, self-conscious ethnic or other minorities, the resultant structural complexity and rigidity do not augur well for internal stability.

The *sine qua non* for the conversion of destructive discontent into internal war is a revolutionary ideology. Such an ideology must have a view of the present—objective reality; a view of what should be (present or future)—subjective reality; a perception of a gap between objective and subjective; and, finally, an action program designed to eliminate the gap. It must be truly revolutionary—i.e., it must assume *a priori* that compromise is unacceptable if not impossible. Further, the ideology must be susceptible to adaptation from theoretical principle to practical reality—to the combination of theory and practice.

To convert ideological prescription into revolutionary action requires a revolutionary elite and party. The elite must be capable of interpreting and manipulating the ideology in such a fashion that it gains the active support of, first, a group of followers (the party), who will work to implement the ideological prescriptions and, second, a larger group of individuals (the mass base), who know or understand little of the formal ideology, but will support the elite and the party for their own reasons.

Judging from precedent, the revolutionary elite and party

must, at some point in time, have access to a relatively secure military base area, from which operations can be directed. Any area in which a government is unable or unwilling to govern on a continuing basis—be it within the capital city or in the remotest mountain fastness—constitutes a potential base. Further, a revolutionary military base may be external to the state threatened by revolution, if the revolutionary movement has direct and continuing access to it, e.g. across an open border.

Revolutionary armed forces constitute the vehicle for the destruction of the existing political power and the security and extension of the political power of the revolutionary elite. When fully developed, these armed forces consist of a regular army, guerrilla forces, local militia, and an underground. Clearly, any assessment of the strength of revolutionary armed forces is most difficult when only an underground organization exists, and it becomes easier as more conventional armed forces are organized.

If a revolutionary movement is to take over state power, it must in due course form an alternate government with sovereignty over part or all of the territory claimed by the existing legitimate government. This may take place very early in the internal war, as with the formation of the Chinese Soviet Republic in 1931 or with the acknowledged claim of dual power by the Petrograd Soviet in 1917, or it may not take place until the revolutionary internal war is visible—the local government of an area not under control of a central authority is but one example.

Finally, among the factors to be considered in gauging the likelihood of subversion and internal war occurring in a state are those external to the state that may influence its internal stability. In the context of Asia in the 1970's, the most important external factor will probably be outside support for revolutionary forces (or for the existing government, for that matter).

Application of the foregoing factors to the states in the

Asian area in the decade of the 1970's leads to some generalized hypotheses. First, the potential for subversion and internal war appears to be more likely to rise than to fall throughout the decade, as problems of economic and political development become more and more pressing. Second, uncoordinated actions by Asian states and by outside interventionists might well increase the potential and real levels of internal conflict rather than reduce them, as interests of Asians and outsiders conflict. Third, because internal war is the result both of complex interactions within a society and of external influences, highly sophisticated and articulated programs are required to reduce the potential and eliminate the reality of internal war. Fourth, the susceptibility of the various Asian states to internal war ranges all the way from the acutely vulnerable nations of Burma, Indonesia, and Laos to Japan, which has a limited subversion problem and a very low potential for internal war.

Many of the implications for security policy in these circumstances are evident, but it is useful to summarize them here. First, if the leaders of Asian states wish to combat subversion and reduce or eliminate the possibility of internal war, they will have to implement large-scale prophylactic programs to eradicate or ameliorate the causes of internal discontent. At the same time, they might have to maintain substantial internal security forces. To do these things, they are likely to require and seek large-scale assistance from the outside. Such assistance and intervention may be political, economic, and military in nature.

Second, the U.S. and its allies must continually reassess their interests, state by state, and come to new decisions on the amounts of assistance they could make available and on the degree and type of intervention they could usefully attempt. In the narrower sphere of military policy, the U.S. might have to make some difficult decisions about the allocation of resources, especially manpower, to internal war intervention.

Third, the U.S.S.R. must make similar reassessments and decide how to accomplish four goals: protect its vital interests, especially in the Indian subcontinent; prevent the extension of Chinese power or control along common border areas and in Southeast Asia; advance the cause of world Communism through the rise of Communist governments in non-Communist Asia; forestall the retreat of world Communism by preventing the destruction of existing Communist governments in Asia.

Fourth, Communist China must determine how to encourage subversion and internal war in the non-Communist states, how to control the process of subversion and internal war to the end that pro-Chinese or Chinese-dominated regimes emerge, and at the same time to preclude the establishment of new U.S. bases or of regimes favorable to the U.S. in the areas contiguous to Communist China.

Taiwan

Nikita Khrushchev is reported to have said that West Berlin was like a bone sticking in his throat. Taiwan, or the Republic of China, is a bone sticking in the individual throats of many states and statesmen. For the Republic of China, and for the mainland Chinese on the island, it remains a temporary home in exile, but one that becomes more and more permanent with the passage of time. For Communist China, it represents imperialist invasion of China's territory and the existence of a potential alternative government of China. Admittedly the potential is low, but the Republic of China is Chinese, it does control Chinese territory, and it does compete for the loyalties of Chinese people, especially the overseas Chinese. For the U.S., it is an important link in the security of U.S. interests in the Western Pacific, but it is also a major obstacle to American–Communist Chinese accommodation (by no means the only one) and an impediment to improvement of U.S. relations with some other states. For some

Asian states, it is an irritating obstacle to the admission of Communist China to the United Nations; for others, it is welcome proof of the credibility of American intent to contain Communist China. For some Taiwanese, it represents domination by a group of carpetbaggers from the mainland, who deprive Taiwan of any opportunity to be truly independent.

Many members of the U.N. are likely to continue to seek a formula within which Communist China can take a seat—the permanent seat of China—in the world organization. This might be justified on two grounds: That the United Nations has a weak claim to be a world peace-keeping organization if the largest single population in the world is not represented; and that Communist China will behave responsibly only if treated responsibly.* The formula might include some provision for including the Republic of China as a member of the U.N., representing only Taiwan. Both Peking and Taipeh reject such a solution—two Chinas—in advance, but neither has been faced with the reality of making a decision. It is plausible that either or both could change their attitude in time.

For the United States, as for the Republic of China, the most serious problems are likely to arise with the passing of Chiang Kai-shek. The new leadership of the Republic of China will presumably have four choices: to attempt to maintain the *status quo*, but at the same time accept the fact that a return of the Republic of China to control over the mainland grows more and more unlikely with the passage of time; to attempt to force the U.S. into supporting an invasion of the mainland, perhaps by threatening to surrender to Communist China if support is not forthcoming; to negotiate a *modus vivendi* with Communist China under which the Republic of China gives up any claim to the government of

---

* It is a fact, however, that few individuals favor inviting criminals into their homes or businesses on the ground that this would convert them into responsible members of society.

China and becomes the government of an autonomous province or region within Communist China; and simply to surrender to Communist China.

The United States must be alert to avoid being placed in a position in which any change in U.N. status or change in the relationship between the two Chinas can be interpreted, domestically or internationally, as a major defeat for U.S. policy. This requires serious consideration of alternate policies or fall-back positions to ameliorate the effects of apparent defeat. For example, the U.S. could withdraw, quietly, its opposition to a resolution to admit Communist China to the General Assembly as long as the U.N. guaranteed some kind of representation for the government in Taiwan. Even in this unlikely event, the problem of China's permanent seat on the Security Council would still remain to plague U.S. policy-makers.

The Japanese Security Role

If the actual timing of other important decisions on Asian security problems, such as the Chinese nuclear threat, are still necessarily vague, the question of Japan's security role is almost certain to be essentially settled by 1970—when the American-Japanese Mutual Security Treaty first becomes susceptible to revision. This will be a political and security watershed for more than Japan itself, because it will have to choose, basically, between continued reliance on outside (mainly U.S.) protection or new and independent arrangements for its own defense. Either choice has serious ramifications for the security policy of other Asian and non-Asian powers alike.

To Communist China, Japan represents the main Asian counterweight to Chinese ambitions and pretensions. Japan's industrial strength, its latent military capacity, and its actual and potential influence in the East and Southeast Asian states on China's periphery are permanent factors with which Communist China must contend, regardless of which basic choice the Japanese make on defense policy. Communist China undoubtedly prefers to have Japan's ties with the U.S. severed in 1970 (or sooner), for this would serve immediate Chinese security interests by reducing the pressure of U.S. "containment." Even if this does occur, however, Communist China could scarcely expect a permanently cowed, harmless, and "neutral" Japan as a result. On the contrary, the independent arrangements Japan would need to make for its own defense —such as significantly increased conventional armament and probably nuclear arms development as well—would constitute a new and perhaps equally dangerous longer-run threat to China. Thus, the implications of the Japanese choice in 1970 may be somewhat more ambiguous for China than they appear at first glance.

The U.S., of course, faces at least the possibility of a drastic realignment in its security arrangements in East Asia. A Japanese choice to sever or to revise drastically its defense ties with the U.S. would not only be a major military handicap to the U.S., but would also have serious political effects on the U.S. position throughout Asia. American interests clearly would be served best by a continuation, in some form, of the present arrangements, with greatly increased Japanese participation in its own defense. Whether the present arrangements can be preserved in substance will depend in large measure on skillful U.S. diplomacy as well as on Japanese domestic politics (the two are by no means unrelated, particularly on the security question). American-Japanese economic ties and the full realization on the part of the Japanese of what an independent defense posture would really entail in the way of risks and resources will weigh heavily as positive factors in the Japanese decision. Yet, resurgent Japanese nationalism and a growing desire to translate economic strength into political influence will be arrayed against these factors and cannot be discounted by the U.S.

Relatively uninvolved up to now, the U.S.S.R. could find

itself increasingly concerned with security policy vis-à-vis Japan as a result of the 1970 decision. The Soviet Union's interest is likely to be ambiguous—in general, it would undoubtedly prefer a weakening of U.S. influence in Japan, but not necessarily at the risk of strengthening the Chinese hand or of creating a partial vacuum in Northeast Asia. Faced with such a choice, the U.S.S.R. might feel impelled to thrust itself into the situation to a far greater degree than in the past. For one thing, it is the only power besides the U.S. that can protect Japan from the Chinese nuclear threat, at least until the Japanese develop their own deterrent capability. For another, it has its own security interests to protect on its Pacific flank—interests which, in a period of Soviet-American détente, are served reasonably well by the continued U.S. presence in Japan. The U.S.S.R. therefore approaches the 1970 decision with more ambivalent and considerably less intense feelings than the U.S.

Finally, the Japanese decision will stir intense concern on the part of the other Asian non-Communist nations. In East and Southeast Asia, the credibility of U.S. power is likely to be measured in part by the Japanese decision. Equally important, it will be a test of whether the principle of mutual security against a monolithic and aggressive Communist China is preserved, or whether each Asian state should (or must) seek its own independent accommodation with China. A Japan striking out on its own—even to the point of having its own nuclear capability—may swell Asian pride momentarily, but Asians are realists enough to know that the whole of mutual security arrangements in Asia has always totaled more than the sum of its separate parts.

Communist China

Throughout this discussion of security problems and policies runs one common problem: China. The development of a credible Chinese nuclear capability results in a catalytic change in the security policies of both Asian and non-Asian states: China is likely to see its interests advanced by local war between or among other Asians; it appears to have an interest in furthering subversion and internal war in non-Communist Asian states. In brief, most of these developments are likely to enhance Chinese security, although miscalculation or conceivable longer-run developments (e.g., an independent, aggressive, nuclear-armed Japan) could have the opposite result.

Of course, it may be that China's perception of its security problems will change—indeed, the thrust of American diplomatic and security policy should be to induce such a change. Viewed pragmatically, Chinese interests might be advanced better by adopting a more conciliatory attitude toward the external world—e.g., Japan and other states might be induced to make economic aid available to support China's industrialization. This hypothesis usually is advanced on the basis of the similarity in China, in the future, of the process generally labeled "de-Stalinization" in the U.S.S.R. and Eastern Europe. It does deserve continuing study and evaluation, but we should keep in mind the fact that extensive change in the security outlook of the U.S.S.R. has been gradual and that it has taken place, in part, under the influence of successful containment policies and firmness on the part of the West.

The other Asian states, Communist and non-Communist, are likely to believe their security is reduced precisely by the same things that China insists are necessary for its security. Policies that might offer these states a reasonable degree of security in the 1970's are those that would result in containment as well as accommodation of China. This statement is based on an assumption that the cost of breaking containment can be made too high for China, and that, sooner or later, Chinese leaders will conclude that their nation's security can be enhanced by accommodation with Asian and non-Asian neighbors—in short, that the Chinese perception of security can be changed over time.

It is possible to argue that the interests of the U.S. and its allies might include encouragement or even positive support of subversion and internal war in such Asian Communist states as the People's Republic of China, the Democratic Republic of Viet-Nam, and the Democratic Republic of Korea. But the inherent and quite unpredictable or uncontrollable effects of large-scale destabilization should one of these governments collapse or be overthrown indicates caution. Certainly, in the decade of the 1970's, the interests of the U.S. and its allies could be served best by containment of and accommodation with China. As far as the policy of the U.S. itself is concerned, it will probably find it increasingly attractive to gain the cooperation of others in Asia and to avoid assuming the role of international anti-Communist gendarme.

The U.S.S.R. and its allies also have an interest in containment and accommodation. But, because of the long land frontier between the U.S.S.R. and the Mongolian People's Republic, on the one hand, and the U.S.S.R. and China, on the other, the U.S.S.R. might be tempted to contain China in North and Central Asia and in the Indian subcontinent, while tolerating Chinese offensive security policies in Southeast Asia.

Finally, throughout this discussion, there is an implication of an American-Soviet community of interests and cooperation. A word of caution is in order. No grand alliance is likely to emerge between the United States and the Soviet Union; nor are the two countries likely to develop a joint international gendarmerie (despite Chinese accusations to the contrary). In specific places and points in time, they could find their interests similar or even identical, and, when this happens, they might find it possible to work in parallel or in concert. When it does not, competition and even confrontation might result.

Policy makers and planners in both the U.S. and the U.S.S.R. should be alert to the increasing possibilities for cooperation between their countries—as well as to the likelihood of opposition from each other. At the same time, both the U.S. and the U.S.S.R. could demonstrate that the inherent conflict between the southern, eastern, colored, and poor peoples of Asia and the northern, western, white, and rich peoples of Europe and North America could be resolved peacefully rather than by force and violence—as the Chinese appear to believe.

6. *Internal Defense and the Less Developed Countries**

LIEUTENANT COLONEL PAUL F. GORMAN

> The great battlefield for the defense and expansion of freedom today is the whole southern half of the globe—Asia, Latin America, Africa and the Middle East—the lands of the rising peoples. Their revolution is the greatest in human history. . . .
>
> —John F. Kennedy (Special Message to Congress on May 25, 1961)

Looking across Pennsylvania Avenue from the White House, the President can see statues to Kosciusko, the Polish military engineer; to von Steuben, the German expert on military organization and training; and to Lafayette and Rochambeau, the French strategists and commanders. It is possible that these reminders of the debt we owe to foreign military assistance during our own revolution have comforted those who have assumed responsibility for extending U.S. military assistance across the developing world—and each President since Franklin Roosevelt has committed American soldiers and resources to conflicts in Latin America, Asia, or Africa.

---

* The views expressed in this essay are the author's own and do not necessarily represent those of the United States Government.

The Nature of Conflict

The future seems likely to be as stormy as, or stormier than, the past. The incidence of violence in the world does not appear to be declining. In February, 1958, there were in progress, world wide, twenty-three prolonged revolutionary wars, or insurgencies; in February, 1966, forty were being waged, including fourteen of the original twenty-three, and twenty-six other, similar wars. Over the intervening eight stormy years, there have been 164 internationally significant conflicts, involving eighty-two nations. Some 10 per cent of these conflicts were wars in the classic sense—overt clashes between conventional military forces of sovereign states. The other 90 per cent was divided almost equally between resorts to force in the political process within a state—primarily military coups d'état—and irregular or guerrilla wars. Virtually all of the 164 conflicts occurred in the developing nations of Latin America, Asia, and Africa, afflicting roughly four out of five nations in those regions. The incidence of violence in these lands shows an upward trend:

ANNUAL INCIDENCE OF VIOLENCE, WORLD WIDE*

	1958	1959	1960	1961	1962	1963	1964	1965
Conflicts per calendar year	34	35	42	43	47	59	56	58

In the fall of 1965, the World Bank published a study dividing 132 of the world's polities into four categories according to per capita gross national product. Relating the conflict data above to the World Bank figures, the following picture emerges:

* Based on data furnished by the Office of the Assistant Secretary of Defense for International Security Affairs, Department of Defense. Trends and figures in this and the following chart were cited by The Honorable Robert S. McNamara in a speech before the American Society of Newspaper Editors in Montreal, Canada, on May 18, 1966.

WORLD POPULATION, WEALTH, AND VIOLENCE*

Category	Per Cent of World's Population	Per Cent of World's Gross National Product	Number of Conflicts	Per Cent of Countries Afflicted
Very Poor Countries	29.6	4.4	70	87
Poor Countries	34.5	8.3 ⎫		69 ⎧
Middle Income Countries	11.7	10.0 ⎭	84	48
Rich Countries	24.2	77.3	10	37

Less than one quarter of the world's people now produce more than three quarters of its goods, the 800 million "rich" producing seventeen times as much as the 1,000 million "very poor." Moreover, the concentration of the world's income in a few countries—mainly those of the northern hemisphere—is intensifying. A century ago, the richest quarter of the world's people produced half of its goods; fifty years ago, they produced about two-thirds; today, as noted, they contribute about three-fourths. It is not poverty per se, however, that drives men to political violence. The fabric of revolution is hope, not despair. Men must be aware of deprivation but aspire to change before they become political capital. One of the grave difficulties of our times is simply that it is ever easier to perceive the widening gap between the standards of living in the northern and southern hemispheres. In the remote regions of the Andes, in the African market place, in dusty villages all across Asia, transistor radios and movies open vistas of new worlds.

This revolution of awareness and hope lies at the heart of

* Ibid., for conflict data. Wealth and population figures are from Escott Reid, The Future of the World Bank (Washington: International Bank for Reconstruction and Development, 1965), pp. 60–71.

the security problems facing the nations of the southern hemisphere. Their dilemma is not simply that their population growth nearly outstrips their economic progress; they face immediate political crises because their people are demanding more of government and expecting more of life in a material way. Heightened popular awareness of the continued economic success of the United States or of the economic "miracles" in Germany, France, Italy, and Japan only adds to the urgency of the crisis.

Development efforts, up to the late-1960's, have clearly been inadequate. Population growth rates have continued to exceed estimates, and wars, rebellions, and the extension of the Cold War into the Southern hemisphere have attenuated expected progress. Frustration contributes to instability, and to disequilibrium spiraling grimly toward violence. It is clear, therefore, that the developing countries must

> . . . accomplish deep-seated changes: in outlook, in social institutions, in economic organization. . . . The sheer bulk of the problems of underdevelopment—the number of mouths to be fed, the number of human beings to be maintained in decent shelter and gradually to be educated and made productive—continues to grow. If we do not begin to make faster progress in these matters, the prospect is for discontent, unrest and tensions that in the end must spill over national boundaries and ultimately infect the rich nations as well as the poor. . . . *

The development process characteristically involves urbanization and centralization of political life in the cities. Vivid contrasts are set up between life in the cities and in rural areas, and the urban areas attract people out of the countryside far beyond their capacity to shelter or employ them. Restive urban masses enter the political equation and rapidly become politicized. Uncoordinated and disproportionate growth occurs in politics, in the economy, and in society,

---

* George D. Woods (President, World Bank), Address to the Boards of Governors, International Finance Corporation and International Development Association, September 27, 1965, Washington, D.C.

creating groups of educated and expectant citizens who can find no satisfying employment; political parties headed by extravagant nationalist leaders who are chauvinistic and intolerant of internal opposition; secularization movements against orthodox religious ethics, customs, and organization, offering no replacing values; or a melding of any of the foregoing with ancient tribal, racial, or class antipathies.

The Role of the Military

In view of such explosive potential, the armed forces of these developing countries are of central importance. If the armies of these developing, threatened societies could be counted on to uphold governmental authority and to insure that the opportunity for peaceful change were held open, then the prospects for stability might seem brighter. But, as noted, nearly half of the violence visited upon the developing nations is attributable to actual or attempted coups. In the period 1958–66 there have been, on the average, eight of these a year. New nations are particularly vulnerable: Roughly half of the nations that came into being in 1958–66 experienced coups or mutinies. By early 1966, twenty-two of sixty-four non-Communist "poor" and "very poor" nations were ruled by soldiers.

Nonpolitical military establishments in the Anglo-American tradition are quite unknown in most of the developing world. For example, Asia's earliest encounters with the West were military, and its military establishments were intimately involved in the first steps toward Westernization. Japan's nationalism early acquired a militaristic hue, and, after the death of Sun Yat-sen and the emergence of Chiang Kai-shek, so did that of China. Mao's view that "political power grows out of the barrel of a gun"* sums up the Asian Communists' orientation. In South and Southeast Asia, only Malaysia,

---

* Mao Tse-tung, *Selected Works* (New York: International Publishers, 1954), II, 272.

Singapore, and India have escaped dominance by soldiers. In the Islamic world, Ayub Khan of Pakistan, the Shah of Iran, and President Nasser of Egypt emulate Riza Shah Pahlavi and Kemal Ataturk—each a soldierly apostle of modernism, each ruling consistent with a millennium of Moslem politico-military tradition.

In Latin America, the seizure of political power by the military is virtually commonplace. Though extreme, Bolivia's record is not atypical; its military coup in 1964 was the 180th revolution in 138 years of nationhood. Military men occupied the presidency of Latin republics 28.7 per cent of the time in the decade 1917–27; 38.5 per cent in 1927–37; 49 per cent in 1937–47; and 45.5 per cent in 1947–57. In the period since 1958, military men have occupied the office of president less than 30 per cent of the time; in this sense one can note recent progress toward constitutionalism.* Nonetheless, by any standard, Latin America is in revolutionary ferment; with weak civil governments everywhere under severe stress, it is doubtful that military intervention in politics is permanently waning.

Sub-Saharan Africa is no exception to the general rule of a politicized military in the developing world. African military traditions are altogether different from those of Oriental, Islamic, or Iberian cultures. Yet Quincy Wright noted that, among the primitive peoples, war as an instrument of national policy was most highly developed in Africa, and Africans stood highest in his measure of "warlikeness." Some Western observers of African military institutions have hoped that the military professionalism formed during the colonial tutelage would preclude the development of praetorianism after nationhood. They have been increasingly disappointed, for the apolitical precepts of Europe have not conspicuously figured in the armies of the Sudan, Congo, Algeria, Gabon, Dahomey,

* For lists of presidents, see S. H. Steinberg, ed., *The Statesman's Yearbook 1964–1965* (New York: St. Martins Press, 1965). See also Ronald M. Schneider, "The U.S. in Latin America," *Current History*, XLVIII, No. 281 (January, 1965), 1–8, 50.

Central African Republic, Upper Volta, and Nigeria. Also frustrated was the hope that since national armies were virtually non-existent in Africa until the 1960's, African armed forces might be eliminated or limited in size and sophistication of armaments. But possession of a comparatively modern, effective army, however small, remains a mark of status that few of the newly sovereign nations have been willing to forego.

The Congo's unpopular, ill-trained, and poorly led and equipped Force Publique reiterated the dangers of a disaffected, rag-tag army; in 1960, in the absence of any other security force, it was able to terrorize the nation's political life and to influence leaders and events. Significantly, many of the leaders of the new nations have responded to this type of danger by quite deliberately seeking to integrate the army leadership into their political elite.

However repugnant military intervention in politics may be to Americans, it is a dominant fact in the developing world. Moreover, a reformist coup d'état may be the least of several political evils to which the process of modernization might lead in a given country. Most coups of recent years have purported to be progressive or even revolutionary, rather than conservative. The Turkish Army considered itself "guardian of the revolution"; Nasser saw his army as the revolutionary "vanguard." The Burmese Army took over public administration and entered the grocery business to counter "economic insurgents" among "unpatriotic" merchants, bureaucratic ineptitude in the civil service, and faltering civilian leadership. General Juan Carlos Ongania of Argentina, a key figure in Argentine politics long before assuming power in June, 1966, summed up these sentiments in 1964 as follows:

> The armed forces are the right arm of the constitution. . . .
> Let us talk without euphemisms. . . . This is the only dialogue appropriate among soldiers.
> Obedience is due a government when its power is derived from the people, and for the people pursues the constitutional precepts set forth by the people. This obedience, in the last instance,

is due to the constitution and to the law, and it should never be the result of the mere existence of men or political parties who may be holding office because of fate or circumstances.

It should, therefore, be clear that the duty of rendering such obedience will have ceased to be an absolute requirement if there are abuses in the exercise of legal authority that violate the basic principles of a republican system of government, when this is done as a result of exotic ideologies, or when there is a violent breakdown in the balance of independence of the branches of government, or when constitutional prerogatives are used in such a way that they cancel out the rights and freedoms of citizens.*

Yet, few competent American analysts have found much praiseworthy in the reign of soldier-politicians. Morris Janowitz, for example, states categorically that "it is most difficult, if not impossible, for the military to manage the politics of a nation in the process of rapid economic development."† Others vehemently condemn the politically transgressing military as foes of progress toward democracy, holding that the military act primarily from institutional self-interest, that frequent military coups d'état are symptomatic of a sick body politic.

Nevertheless, it is possible to argue that military institutions of the emerging nations are compatible with a progressive attitude toward social and economic change. Of its nature, the military profession requires an international orientation—the soldier who would provide for the security of his country must continually measure the opposition abroad, compare it with his own, and seek ways to improve his capability. In the modern era, this seeking often involves travel and education abroad. Moreover, in the military profession, rewards are demonstrably high for modernity, espe-

---

* Lt. Gen. Juan Carlos Ongania (Army of Argentina), "The Government, the Armed Forces, and the National Community," *Final Report—Conference of the American Armies* (West Point, N.Y.: USMA, 1964), pp. 166–79.

† Morris Janowitz, *The Military in the Political Development of New Nations* (Chicago: University of Chicago Press, Phoenix Edition, 1964), p. 104.

cially in technology, and its practitioners tend to be receptive
to innovation, especially technical reform. These often combine with the soldier's nationalism into a drive toward
modernization in all sectors of society.

A nation's armed services are often its largest enterprise,
and military professionals are therefore uniquely experienced
in managing large amounts of manpower and sizable funds.
These experiences often lead the military to become a developmental and educational arm of the state. Examples
abound: Nearly all of South Korea's airline pilots, virtually all
its operators of heavy construction equipment, and 80–90 per
cent of its civilian motor vehicle operators and electronic
technicians learned their basic skills during their military
service; the Peruvian Army gives all its conscripts training in
literacy, hygiene, and national history, and provides advanced
vocational training to at least 1,600 conscripts annually; the
Service Civique of the Ivory Coast teaches conscripts improved hut construction techniques and stock-breeding practices, and that of the Malagasy Republic organizes its con-
script training as a prelude to homesteading.

In relatively primitive societies, the army is often the only
national entity functioning in the society; in its ranks, wearing
the nation's uniform, serving under the nation's flag, its citizens acquire meaningful ideas of national unity and dignity.
This is not to hold that military service is necessarily always so
beneficial. The stationing of rural conscripts in posts near
large urban centers may teach farm boys the delights of city
life, and thus add them upon discharge to the ranks of the
urban unemployed. Not all armies, by any means, follow
enlightened training programs. But armed forces can become,
and in many developing nations have become, an important
catalyst for social change.

Neither the political activity of armed forces in the emerging nations nor their socio-economic roles should obscure

their traditional mission of providing security to the state against foreign and domestic enemies. As the conflict data given above indicates, about half of the violence in emerging areas has taken the form of insurgency or guerrilla warfare. Such warfare—combat operations conducted by predominantly irregular forces that utilize tactics of surprise, brief and violent action, and studied elusiveness to compensate for lack of military strength—has been historically the resort of the weak, especially the technologically disadvantaged. Its modern history has been written along the outer edges of all the nineteenth century empires: The French had to contend with Abd-el-Kadr of Algeria, the British with the wily Boer and Afghan, the Americans with Aguinaldo.

The Communists, who are now among the principal practitioners of guerrilla warfare, have transformed it in two respects: They have converted an essentially defensive form of conflict into an instrument of strategic offense, and they have integrated combat thoroughly with their political, economic, and social doctrine. Their successes in Asia against the Japanese and the French stemmed from an elaborate military doctrine, from the thoroughness with which their political cadres communicated this doctrine throughout rank and file, from the gigantic scale on which they conceived and executed their feats of human organization, and, above all, from the dedication they inspired in and the discipline they exacted from their guerrilla organization.

There are, of course, many guerrillas who are neither inspired nor led by Communists—revolutionists seeking to force social change and modernization, ethnic separatists attempting to carve out their own polities from multinational states, tribal autonomists or simple bandits resisting the authority of the state. (But even these types of guerrillas have learned from, and are often used by, professional revolutionaries.) It is not, however, these miscellaneous struggles, but guerrilla warfare conceived and conducted by the Communists as a deliberate instrument of strategic offensive that is one of the foremost politico-military problems confronting the United States in the decade of the 1970's.

The stresses of modernization have created an environment admirably suited to guerrilla warfare all across the southern half of the globe. The Communists envisage frustrated and aspirant peoples as the terrain of their warfare, and the revolutionary literature of the Bolsheviks, the Maoists, the Viet-Minh, and the Fidelistos comprise a coherent body of insurrectionary doctrine that seems particularly relevant to such peoples. It is, moreover, a complete doctrine, which instructs on every aspect of revolt, from choosing appropriate political and social objectives to converting a shotgun into an antitank weapon.

Students from the developing nations have been steeped in guerrilla lore in the Soviet Union, the Communist nations of Asia, and Cuba. Significant numbers have returned to their homelands as professional revolutionaries, each an incendiary of special peril for an igneous society. The doctrine seems well-nigh irresistible, and its aura of triumph, above all, is the special glow that attracts new adherents; by emulating Castro, the young Latin concludes he can be not only "macho" but victorious; by following Mao and Ho Chi Minh, the young political movement or the young nation can successfully defy the greatest powers in the world.

Assistance from the West

More often than not, developing nations originally sought military assistance from the northern hemisphere powers for reasons unrelated to guerrillas or to Communist subversion. Many new nations simply retained military affiliation with a metropole. Each usually had more conventional security problems—one or more traditionally hostile neighbors, or a history of recourse to arms in regional disputes. But as Chinese and Cuban adventurers have pressed their designs on the developing nations, those nations have become increasingly concerned with internal defense against subversive movements and guerrilla warfare, and have called for military assistance against these threats as well.

Interesting differences have developed in the style of military assistance offered to the developing nations. The British have, on the whole, been the most consistently successful, and their approach is characteristically a cool, "the natives are restless tonight" pragmatism. They have preferred to regard insurgents as outlaws and to treat anti-guerrilla campaigns as manhunts as much as military operations. The French have been relatively more doctrinaire and pretentious. They attributed global significance to their experience in Indochina and Algeria: Like Charles Martel at Tours they stood, shield of the West. They devised an elaborate doctrine, heavily influenced by Mao and Giap, for *guerre révolutionnaire*, or, as they frequently referred to it, *guerre subversive. La guerre revolutionnaire*, distinct from *la guerre classique* and *la guerre nucleaire*, was, in essence, a combination of counterguerrilla and psychological warfare. In its principal elaboration, it is a doctrine for total war waged without resort to weapons of mass destruction—warfare in which mercilessly calculated violence, subversion, terror, torture, and intense politicizing, especially of rural areas, are systematically employed by both sides. The French military's frustrations—which they interpreted not as a failure of the doctrine, but of French politicians—seared the soul of their army, figured in its revolts in 1958 and 1961, and will influence its point of view in treating guerrilla wars for years to come.*

The bench mark for serious U.S. involvement in assistance to defeat subversive aggression and insurgency was the year 1958. That was a year of momentous endings: Retirement for

---

* For the impact of *la guerre revolutionnaire* on the French Army, see, *inter alia*, Peter Paret, *French Revolutionary Warfare from Indochina to Algeria* (New York: Frederick A. Praeger, 1964); Raoul Girardet, "Civil and Military Power in the Fourth Republic," in Samuel Huntington, ed., *Changing Patterns of Military Politics* (New York: Free Press of Glencoe, 1962); and Jean Larteguy, *The Centurions* (New York: Avon Book Corp., 1962), and *The Praetorians* (New York: E. P. Dutton & Co., 1963).

the Navy's battleships, for the Air Force B-36—last of the propellor driven strategic bombers—and for the Army anti-aircraft guns. It was also a year of propitious beginnings: An Army rocket carried aloft America's first satellite, Navy nuclear submarines sailed beneath the polar icecap, the Air Force initiated the second generation of ICBM's, and the Joint Staff came into being in a major Defense Department reorganization. Probably none of these departures was so significant as the strategic precept announced in the summer of 1958 by Secretary of State John Foster Dulles: Through propaganda, terror, agents, money, and arms for dissident minorities, one nation might destroy the independence of another; the U.S. would view such acts as inimical to its security, for, "if indirect aggression were to be admitted as a legitimate means of promoting international policy, small nations would be doomed, and the world would become one of constant chaos, if not war."*

Since then, in more than twenty nations of Latin America, Africa, and Asia, the United States has supplemented its post-World War II network of military alliances with explicit commitments—formalized by treaty or by unilateral declaration—to help defend against subversion. In a number of instances, these undertakings are more concrete than the assurances to the Republic of Viet-Nam that we have honored at great price.

Until the election of John F. Kennedy, the developing world remained largely peripheral for the U.S. military. Kennedy's interest and concern were quickly transmitted to the military. In early 1961, he announced that he was "directing the Secretary of Defense to expand rapidly and substantially, in cooperation with our Allies, the orientation of existing forces for the conduct of nonnuclear war, paramilitary operations and sub-limited or unconventional wars." In June,

---

* John Foster Dulles, Speech given before the National Convention of Veterans of Foreign Wars, on August 18, 1958; as reported in *The New York Times*, August 19, 1958, p. 12.

1962, he told graduating West Point cadets that to counter "wars of liberation" we needed "a whole new kind of strategy, a wholly different kind of force, and therefore a new and wholly different kind of military training." About a month later, speaking at the White House to graduates of a national interdepartmental seminar on counterinsurgency, he enjoined them to recognize that: "This is not merely a military effort . . . it requires . . . a broad knowledge of the whole development effort of a country, the whole technique of the National Government to identify themselves with the aspirations of the people. . . ."*

President Johnson continued President Kennedy's policies, and reported progress in a speech in June, 1964:

> Our adversaries, convinced that direct attack would be aimless, today resort to terror, subversion and guerrilla warfare. To meet this threat we began a large effort to train special forces to fight internal subversion. *Since January 1961 we have increased these specialized forces eight times.* We have trained more than 100,-000 officers in these techniques. We have given special emphasis to this form of warfare in the training of all military units. . . .
>
> But just as subversion has many faces, our responses must take many forms. We have worked to increase and integrate all the resources, political and social as well as military and economic, needed to meet a threat which tears at the entire fabric of a society.
>
> But success in fighting subversion ultimately rests on the skill of the soldiers of the threatened country. We now have 344 teams at work in 49 countries to train the local military in the most advanced techniques of internal defense. . . . We will continue to increase this strength until our adversaries are convinced that this course too will not lead to conquest.†

* President John F. Kennedy, *Public Papers of the Presidents of the United States, 1962* (Washington: U.S. Government Printing Office, 1963), pp. 535–36.

† President Lyndon B. Johnson, "U.S. Strength Continues Rapid Growth," Remarks at the Coast Guard Academy, New London, Conn., June 3, 1964; as quoted in the Supplement to the Air Force Policy Letter for Commanders, (Washington: Office of the Secretary of the Air Force, AFRP 190–92), No. 8, July, 1964, p. 2.

Statistics on U.S. efforts to train the soldiers of the developing nations are impressive. From the formal inception of the Military Assistance Program (MAP) in 1950 through 1960, only 85 U.S. training teams were deployed abroad for varying periods to instruct in counterguerrilla warfare and related subjects, and these were sent to only 14 countries. During 1965 alone, 364 teams were sent to 47 countries: The U.S. Army alone dispatched 179 teams—including 81 to Latin America, 79 to Africa and the Middle East, and 19 to the Far East; the U.S. Air Force sent out 123 teams; and the U.S. Navy, 62 teams. Also during 1965, the U.S. provided formal school courses to more than 15,000 foreign military professionals. These data do not reflect the activities of the nearly 10,000 U.S. military personnel stationed in developing countries with full-time assignments of providing advice and training to professional colleagues on the job; nor do they reflect material assistance, which amounted to about one billion dollars to the developing countries in the fiscal year 1965.* These undertakings—advisory and training missions, and material support—are a historically significant extension of the roles of the U.S. armed services.

It is difficult to measure with any precision the results achieved to date with our military assistance programs in influencing the roles of foreign armed forces in their own societies. Opponents of military assistance programs frequently suggest that U.S. military aid causes or encourages political intervention by assisted armed forces. The record does not support such concern, and those who work most closely with the military aid problem—our ambassadors

* For training team data, see Maj. Gen. W. R. Peers, USA, *Presentation to Delegates, Fourth Annual Senate Youth Program,* January 26, 1966 (Washington: Organization of the Joint Chiefs of Staff, 1966), p. 11; for military personnel, see U.S. Department of Defense, *Military Assistance Facts* (Washington: Dept. of Defense, 1965), p. 31. The data on formal school courses and material assistance were compiled from information available in the U.S. Congress, House of Representatives, Committee on Appropriations, *Foreign Assistance and Related Agencies Appropriations for 1966,* Hearings (Washington: Government Printing Office, 1965), p. 78.

abroad and U.S. officers administering the programs—are generally convinced that U.S. training and advice have aided importantly in moderating the political ideas of foreign officers and in influencing their behavior in constructive ways. Moreover, American assistance is extended only with the firm support of American civilian officials overseas, and with the full approval of incumbent governments, who evidently do not perceive it as a political threat. Indeed, since 1960, there have been at least six publicized occasions on which MAP-supported forces have protected their governments from attack by factions within its armed services.

Coups can, of course, be perpetrated by relatively small and militarily weak groups, since success is less a function of amounts of arms or equipment than of political perception and timing. Most modern coup attempts reflect not the size of the coup forces—these will usually exist in sufficient strength for a coup in any event—nor the amount of foreign aid, but the political stability and probity of the government. Moreover, most of these contemporary coups seem to have been popularly acclaimed; few of them can be attributed to the depravity or ambition of a military officer or clique.

American military aid policy can be credited at least partially with the broader interest taken by foreign armies in forwarding social and economic progress. "Civic action"—as the U.S. terms such undertakings—has not loomed large in the American military assistance budgets: Something like 1 per cent per annum has been usual. Civic action has, however, been an objective the U.S. has sought with whatever influence it could wield as a result of other assistance. The results have, by and large, been encouraging.

President Johnson's foreign aid message of February, 1966, typically called for military assistance with:

> Greater emphasis on civic action programs. We shall give new stress to civic action programs through which local troops build schools and roads, and provide literacy training and health services. Through these programs, military personnel are able

to play a more constructive role in their society, and to establish
better relations with the civilian population. . . .*

These nation-building efforts of the armed forces—helpful as
they may be—cannot, of course, provide a nation's main
developmental thrust. If the social and economic ills that so
often underlie movement toward either Communist insurgency or praetorianism are to be wiped out, a much broader
and more intensive development campaign is needed than the
armed forces can mount. In that context, other instruments
of American foreign policy—such as economic assistance,
surplus foodstuffs, and private capital flows—come into play.

Areas for Improvement

Looking to the future, it is clear that, despite laudable objectives and considerable progress in their achievement, U.S.
military assistance to the armed forces of developing nations
can be markedly improved, especially in the areas of personnel
management, doctrine, materiel, and organization.

Personnel. Except for the advisory group in Viet-Nam, military duty in the developing nations has not been regarded as
either important or rewarding by the "main line" U.S. officer.
The kind of person needed is well understood. At the 1965
meeting of the Association of the United States Army, the
presentation of the Deputy Chief of Staff for Military Operations stipulated that:

> Personnel who are assigned to such operations and activities
> must be military professionals, who know and respect technical
> competence and professional status . . . understand, appreciate
> and respect his hosts . . . their values, attitudes, and convic-
> tions, and what place they and their army hold in their own
> political process, economy, and social dynamics. Such an under-
> standing may in many instances necessitate a command of the

---

* President Lyndon B. Johnson, "Message to the Congress of the United
States (Foreign Aid Message)," February 1, 1966, in *ibid.*, p. 358.

language, and thorough study of the history, culture, and politics of the particular country. . . .*

Yet such duty has not enjoyed a suitably high priority. Symptomatic of this fact has been the scarcity of linguistically competent officers for assignment to key overseas positions. Ethiopia, for example, is a nation in which the U.S. has substantial security interests, to which limited military assistance has been flowing for more than a decade, and in which active military operations against insurgents were in progress during 1965, but at that time all branches of the U.S. armed services together had less than ten officers capable of speaking any Amharic.† Personnel management has placed numerous considerations of career development ahead of competence to advise the armed forces of particular countries. The inertia of three wars and two generations of oceanic and Europe-centered military policy, plus Congressional and public misunderstanding of the U.S. role in Latin America, Africa, and Asia—all these have acted to impede reform.

Doctrine. The skimpiness of military doctrine relevant to the roles and missions of armed forces in the developing nations has also been a prime contributor to the paucity of relevant military professionalism in our assistance programs. The counterinsurgency doctrine of the United States rests on dubiously slender appreciation of guerrilla operations in World War II and Korea, and postwar counterguerrilla experiences, especially those in Greece, Malaya, Indochina, Algeria, and the Philippines. The U.S. military profession has contributed comparatively little to its elaboration or further development. What professional energy has been expended has largely been a futile sifting of the same facts for universal

---

* Brig. Gen. R. C. Taber, USA, "The Army's Role in Stability Operations," Presentation to the Association of the U.S. Army, October 23, 1965 (typed manuscript).

† Department of Defense, *Study of Foreign Language Training Provided for Department of Defense Personnel and their Dependents—Worldwide* (Washington: Defense Language Institute, 1964), Annex A.

principles that might spark a better military doctrine—"force ratios," theories on "border closing," "population control" and the like—because this mode of analyzing conventional war was pursued successfully by Jomini, Clausewitz, and Mahan. Conventional war is homogeneous and symmetrical, in that the combatant forces resemble each other in composition and function, and each pursues the destruction of the other. Useful general guidelines can and have been written for the interaction of conventional forces. The violence prevalent in the developing areas, however, is generally neither homogeneous nor symmetrical, for one protagonist is usually a government, the other an antigovernment, not at all comparable in size, organization, or function. Whether the dissidents base their power within the army or elsewhere in the community, their objective is the polity. The form and pace of the conflict, therefore, vary according to the character of the incumbent regime and the afflicted society.

Too often, Americans have tended to assume that U.S. doctrine, organization, and training methods were sufficient models for all armies, and that our own preparedness for conventional or nuclear war conferred on us ample capability for coping with "lesser" forms of conflict—and for advising others how to do so. Experiences in South Viet-Nam in the mid-1960's have driven home hard lessons on the vacuity of this view, but they have stimulated a new body of doctrine and techniques that is also inapplicable to most improverished nations. Our massive application of modern communications, firepower, and aerial vehicles to counter guerrillas may result in military successes, but these are technically complicated and expensive solutions beyond the financial and technological resources of most developing nations.

Appropriateness aside, the United States has yet to develop military doctrine for this genre of warfare as extensive as that for nuclear and conventional war. This lacuna is evident, for example, in the curricula of Army schools:

EMPHASIS ON FORMS OF WARFARE*

By Percentage of Curricular Hours in Selected
U.S. Army Professional Schools
Fiscal Year 1965

Career Courses[a]	Nuclear	Conventional	Insurgency
Infantry	35	30	35
Armor[b]	11	79	3
Artillery[b]	21	70	3
Engineer[b]	8	21	15
Intelligence	8	87	5
Command and General Staff College[b] [c]	34	22	5

[a] Professional (branch) education for Captains and Majors, usually of some 35 weeks duration.

[b] Course includes other technical subjects not categorized under "forms of war."

[c] Professional education for selected Captains through Lieutenant Colonels, about 36 weeks duration.

These schools are not only the schools that train U.S. advisers to foreign armies, but they are also the schools foreign officers attend. For many a foreign army, for instance, a diploma from the U.S. Army Command and General Staff College represents the apex of professional education. But how relevant is that college's curriculum to the professionalism required by an Ethiopian officer, a Liberian, a Bolivian, or a Thai? Recognizing our own doctrinal poverty, are we not perhaps as likely to learn from foreign officers how to combat insurgency as we are to teach them? Indeed, is insurgency amenable to the same sort of doctrinal generalizations as are other forms of war, or do its political, economic, cultural, and environmental dimensions warrant different development? These are all questions to which the American military profession has, thus far, found few really satisfactory answers.

* U.S. Department of the Army, *Report of Department of the Army Board to Review Army Officer Schools,* Draft (December, 1965) Annex D, Appendix 14, p. 7.

Materiel. That American air and naval equipment is generally sophisticated beyond the needs and abilities of most developing nations is probably evident, but the proposition holds even for infantry gear. The design criteria for equipment for American forces do not necessarily yield items useful to other armed forces. Structural complexity, difficulty in training personnel to operate and maintain the equipment, and the necessity for extensive spare parts availability increasingly limit the transfer of standard U.S. equipment to developing nations. Helicopters are an example of this kind of problem.

Frequently American equipment is simply over-designed for the needs of other countries. Standard U.S. infantry battalion radios, for example, while comparatively simple and rugged, are designed to minimize interference with other sets in an electronically dense environment and to maximize security from enemy intercept and jamming. In the Asian or Latin American environment, these features are often useless, especially since they render the radios unequal to the distances over which many foreign infantry battalions must normally operate. In addition, foreign armies often need materiel the U.S. services simply do not stock; an example is the armored car, long since dropped as a U.S. standard item, but properly still in much demand throughout Africa and Asia.

There are undoubtedly many items or refinements of existing items suitable for use in less-developed countries, which might be produced by American research and development, but for which no U.S. military requirement has been stated and for which there is hence no effective demand. Finding a modality for bringing the inventiveness of American technology to bear more systematically on the military problems facing these nations through coherent research, development, and production programs could significantly enhance the efficiency of our assistance programs.

Organization. Military assistance, especially in the developing nations, is a highly political operation, which demands the closest attention of the Department of State. It is, however, administered by the Department of Defense. It is treated legislatively and budgetarily separate from other defense programs, despite the fact that it is deemed a key contribution to U.S. security: Secretary McNamara has regularly testified that he would prefer to see his own budget reduced before MAP was cut. Within the defense establishment, responsibility is exercised by the Office of the Secretary of Defense, the Joint Chiefs, and the Unified Commands—not the military services. But personnel management, military doctrine, and materiel development are all matters otherwise handled largely within the military departments, by the separate services.

However well suited this complex of arrangements may have been as long as MAP consisted essentially of a mechanism to transmit materiel to nations with security problems and capabilities similar to those of the U.S.—as was the case in the 1950's and early 1960's—its continuance as a means of assisting the developing nations needs serious re-examination. Not only have such arrangements dissociated the military assistance program from natural support among government agencies and within the Department of Defense, but they have also precluded strategic articulation between MAP and other long-range U.S. strategic planning. The MAP stepchild must be reared under far different and more changeable rules than any other defense program.

Of all the U.S. armed services, the Army has the greatest stake in finding a satisfactory solution to the problems sketched above. Armies dominate the security establishments of the developing nations, and usually play a highly significant political, social, and economic role in their society. Among the U.S. armed services, the Army conducts nearly 90 per cent of the schooling for foreign military students, provides approximately 75 per cent of all the personnel and equipment supporting civic action world wide, annually deploys overseas the preponderance of U.S. training teams, and furnishes three out of four officers serving in embassies, MAAGs, and Missions in Latin America, Africa, and Asia.* Moreover, the Army's experience in Viet-Nam has lent new urgency to its search for ways to help other armies help themselves.

The situation in Viet-Nam as of the late 1960's has cast dark shadows of doubt on all American military involvement in the less developed nations. A fundamental choice lies ahead. The nation can heed those who recount the genuine imperfections of past assistance as proof of American impotence in aiding militarily a nation attacked from within; those who invoke the immensity of the crises pending in the developing world as a reason for cutting off American military aid lest it lead to further costly ensnarement; those who cite U.S. missile and sea power as a sufficient contribution to world security and argue for disengagement from the lands and peoples of Asia and Africa. We can heed all these and draw back from our far-flung outposts to await the future with foreboding, or we can hold to the course pursued by every President since the 1940's—using the power and wealth of the United States to assist the evolution of a world community of culturally diverse, independent, peaceful, and cooperating nations. We can do so assured that, while not limitless, the wealth of the U.S. is considerable and growing, and that if the fraction of our national product invested in all

* These figures were computed from data obtained from the following:
DA General Staff, "Foreign Military Assistance," *Congressional Fact Paper,* CFP-ODCSOPS-13, November 15, 1965; *Foreign Assistance . . . ,* pp. 358, 894; Col. Edwin F. Black, USA, "Dragons Teeth of Freedom," *Military Review,* XLIV, No. 8 (August, 1964), 25; Paul C. Davis and William T. R. Fox, "U.S. Military Representation Abroad," in Vincent M. Barnett, Jr., ed., *The Representation of the United States Abroad* (New York: Frederick A. Praeger, 1965), p. 181; U.S. Department of the Army, General Staff, "Personnel Assigned to MAAGs, Missions, and Embassies," Disposition Form, DCSOPS to DCSPER, and Comments 2, 3 and 4 thereto (December 9, 1964); U.S. Department of the Army, *Report of the Department of the Army Board to Review Army Officer Schools,* Annex D, Appendix 14, p. 16; *Military Assistance Facts,* p. 30; Theodore R. Vallance and Charles D. Windle, "Cultural Engineering," *Military Review,* XLII, No. 12 (December, 1962), 60–64.

types of foreign assistance were restored to what it was in the late 1950's, there would be an enormous increase in the funds available to pursue this course. We can do so assured that the scientific, technological, and industrial strength of this country would not only help buttress the free world's walls against Communist aggression but also help build the solid foundations of economic and social growth needed to stabilize the developing nations.

We should not, indeed cannot, suppress or help others suppress the instability that is a natural concomitant of development; nor, when that instability occasionally generates internal violence, should we intervene. Samuel Huntington has rightly argued:

> Even in the United States, the process of modernization required the largest war of the century between 1814 and 1914. The likelihood that the nations of southern Asia, the Middle East, Africa, and Latin America will modernize their social and economic life without violent political dislocations seems relatively remote. Economic and social change requires political change. Without the constitutional tradition of peaceful change some form of violence is virtually inevitable.*

But we cannot expect the Communists to forego the temptation to try to turn developmental instability to their own ends. The "Rockefeller Report" of 1958 identified "concealed wars" as one of the more difficult problems facing the nation.

> These conflicts raise issues with which, in terms of our preconceptions and the structure of our forces, we are least prepared to deal. The gradual subversion of a government by concealed foreign penetration is difficult to deal with from the outside, even though the fate of millions may depend upon it. . . . Our security and that of the rest of the non-Communist world will hinge importantly on our willingness to support friendly governments in situations which fit neither the soldier's

---

* Samuel P. Huntington, *Changing Patterns of Military Politics*, p. 39.

classic concept of war nor the diplomat's traditional concept of aggression.*

In sum, the task confronting us in the less developed world is an exceedingly complex and formidable one—a task we have not yet adequately geared ourselves to handle in terms of preparing people, devising programs, generating resources, developing doctrine, or building organizations. Yet our success or failure in helping our friends in the less developed nations to succeed is likely to determine, in the long run, the success or failure of our own way of life.

* *International Security, The Military Aspect*, Rockefeller Brothers Fund (Garden City: Doubleday and Company, 1958), p. 24.

7. Arms Control and National Security*

LIEUTENANT COLONEL ROBERT G. GARD, JR.

In his address before the General Assembly of the United Nations on September 25, 1961, President Kennedy observed that "Every man, woman and child lives under a nuclear sword of Damocles. . . . The mere existence of modern weapons—ten million times more powerful than any that the world has ever seen, and only minutes away from any target on earth—is a source of horror and discord and distrust."† Since no nation in the thermonuclear age is beyond the reach of terrible devastation, absolute security is not obtainable, even for the most powerful. In pursuing its security interests, each nation must, therefore, weigh the degree of risk it is willing to assume in the light of competing values and demands on its resources. In addition, it must confront the prospect that armed conflict today, and to a greater extent in the years ahead, may lead to the destruction of the society its armed forces are designed to protect. These and other considerations have led the United States to join in an increased

* The views expressed in this essay are the author's own and do not necessarily represent those of the United States Government.
† Public Papers of the Presidents of the United States, John F. Kennedy, January 20 to December 31, 1961 (Washington: U.S. Government Printing Office, 1962), p. 620.

worldwide interest in arms control as a means of regulating force and promoting a safer international environment.

The Arms Control and Disarmament Act of 1961 defines arms control and disarmament collectively as "the identification, verification, inspection, limitation, control, reduction, or elimination of armed forces and armaments of all kinds under international agreement. . . ."* This definition seems unduly restrictive, since arms control is regarded generally to be more inclusive. For instance, neither the 1963 "hot line" agreement to maintain direct communications between Washington and Moscow nor the announcements by the U.S. and U.S.S.R. in 1963 and 1964 of defense budget cuts and reductions in the production of enriched uranium meet the criteria of the official definition. Nevertheless, all are usually regarded as arms control measures.

It appears preferable to define arms control in a manner more suggestive of the valuable functions it can perform; that is, as measures taken "in the interest of reducing the likelihood of war, its scope and violence if it occurs, and the political and economic costs of being prepared for it."† This definition encompasses appropriate unilateral adjustments in military postures and doctrines, often made to induce reciprocal, although not necessarily identical, actions by potential enemies. "Arms control" is the generic term; "disarmament"—the actual reduction or elimination of armament—is therefore one category of arms control.

In one sense, this less restrictive definition could be construed as so comprehensive as to include the totality of national security policy. Yet its utility is that it focuses on the intimate connection between arms control and national security and provides an appropriate perspective for the evaluation of arms control proposals. It may be contrasted with the

---

* Section 3(a), Public Law 87–297.

† Thomas C. Schelling and Morton H. Halperin, *Strategy and Arms Control* (New York: The Twentieth Century Fund, 1961), p. 2. The Schelling-Halperin definition limits arms control measures to those involving "military cooperation between potential enemies."

frequently-held view that military armament and disarmament are separate paths to the goal of international security—that "arms control is an alternative to our security effort, rather than a complement of it."* What is required, some argue, is a "move from security through armaments to security through arms control."†

The basic theme of this essay is that arms control is inseparable from national security policy, especially its military aspects, and should be viewed as an integral part of defense strategy. As former Deputy Secretary of Defense Gilpatric put it while discussing the relationship of arms control to deterrence strategy: "We don't have two policies. . . .We have one policy, which is to safeguard our national security."‡ Arms control measures have a direct impact not only on the means of waging war but also on the manner in which it is conducted. Military strategy can no longer be regarded as the conduct of warfare toward the sole objective of military victory, but must be concerned with limiting the scope of conflict after it has begun and terminating it successfully. Arms control measures can, but do not necessarily, enhance national security. Their desirability should be judged primarily in the light of their contribution to this objective.

General Disarmament

Many advocates of the special form of arms control known as general disarmament contend that the elimination of armaments, other than those needed for internal security, will preclude military conflict and therefore provide an escape from the potential destructiveness of war. They often overlook the realities governing the conduct of states in inter-

* Henry A. Kissinger criticizes this approach in *The Necessity for Choice: Prospects of American Foreign Policy* (Garden City: Doubleday & Company, Inc., 1961), p. 292.

† Louis Henkin (ed.), *Arms Control: Issues for the Public*, The American Assembly, Columbia University (Englewood Cliffs: Prentice-Hall, Inc., 1961), p. 17.

‡ U.S. Arms Control and Disarmament Agency, *Arms Control and Disarmament* (ACDA Publication 11, January, 1963), pp. 12–13, 16.

national affairs. Interstate relationships are fundamentally political, not legal; rivalries and conflicts of interest between and among states are inevitable. The institutions and accepted procedures for the settlement of disputes within the more advanced individual nation states do not obtain in the international environment. States with compatible basic goals usually resolve disputes through established and routine diplomatic processes. However, in the absence of a sovereign international body with an effective monopoly of force, conflict among states with incompatible goals is regulated in the final analysis by the national power of the states involved, with the potential application of military force as the ultimate arbiter. Reduction in the size of national armaments cannot eliminate this role of force in interstate relationships.* With some nations willing to use force to attain their objectives, others have no viable alternative to seeking power and influence in order to protect themselves against aggression and to safeguard their national interests. Weakness invites aggression; stability is maintained by the ability of one state or group of states to influence more bellicose nations to refrain from the use of military force. Military power is thus necessary to counterbalance the power of potential aggressors.

Some proponents of general disarmament understand the inescapable role of force in world affairs and call for an international enforcement agency more powerful than any combination of potentially aggressive states. They do not, however, recognize that fear of a highly destructive war is an insufficient basis for the degree of consensus necessary for a sovereign world organization. Others admit the need for power balances, but contend that these can be maintained at relatively low levels of national armament. They argue that comprehensive disarmament can be designed to provide acceptably balanced international security while avoiding the need for

* For an excellent analysis of the role of power in the international environment, see A. A. Jordan, Jr., "Elements of National Power," *Army,* April, 1966, pp. 69–76.

assessing the differential impact of partial arms control measures on the security of opposing states.* This approach does eschew difficult issues, but it seeks a solution to a far more complex problem. The unsuccessful negotiations on general disarmament, both during the interwar and postwar periods, demonstrate the difficult practical problems in achieving comprehensive agreements.

Khrushchev presented the Soviet proposal for "general complete disarmament" in the General Assembly of the United Nations on September 18, 1959. That proposal was a Cold War measure designed to capitalize on the frustrations and sense of helplessness of the less powerful nations, and to make the U.S.S.R. appear as the champion of world peace.† The plan and the statements in support of it avoid the complexities of necessary safeguards and the requirement for some means to settle international conflicts. Western attempts to expose this initiative as simplistic and unrealistic were ineffective against the propaganda advantage achieved by the U.S.S.R. After too long a delay, the United States countered in September, 1961, with an outline for "General and Complete Disarmament in a Peaceful World," which calls for balanced force reductions, emphasizes the need for safeguards, and makes specific the necessity for an international enforcement agency with adequate authority to restrain potential violators; there is, however, little likelihood of its being accepted.

The 1961 U.S.–U.S.S.R. "Statement of Agreed Principles" provides a sensible, if imprecise, approach to the disarmament issue. Measures are to be carried out "under strict international control," in agreed sequence, and by balanced stages, so that no nation can obtain a military advantage. Each stage

---

* See, for example, Jerome B. Wiesner, "Comprehensive Arms Limitation Systems," in Donald G. Brennan (ed.), *Arms Control, Disarmament and National Security* (New York: George Braziller, 1961), pp. 198–233.

† Soviet motivations in arms control are complex, according to Lincoln P. Bloomfield, Walter C. Clemens, Jr., and Franklyn Griffiths, *Khrushchev and the Arms Race: Soviet Interests in Arms Control and Disarmament, 1954–1964* (Cambridge: MIT Press, 1966).

is to be verified before proceeding to the next. Progress in disarmament would be accompanied by measures to strengthen institutions for the maintenance of peace and the settlement of international disputes by peaceful means. That these general provisions have been interpreted differently by the two nations is not surprising; there remain several basic points of disagreement, including the adamant unwillingness of the Soviets to allow meaningful verification on their territory. It is, however, the fundamental nature of international politics, as reflected in the arguments of both sides, rather than differences in the negotiating positions, that makes general disarmament highly unlikely in the foreseeable future. As Secretary of State Rusk put it, "deep-cutting disarmament really must be accompanied by a political settlement, a resolution of the issues about which people are tempted to fight."*

It is, nevertheless, advantageous for the U.S. to have a sensible plan for and to conduct negotiations on general disarmament, even though the attainment of that goal is obviously impractical without a basic change in the political structure of world society. It would be a mistake to permit the U.S.S.R. to pose as the sole advocate of general disarmament, thereby conceding to the Soviets important advantages in the international propaganda struggle.† Also, patient expositions of a responsible U.S. position serve to educate other nations and domestic proponents of disarmament in the complexities of arms control and the fundamental requirements for security in a world of sovereign states.

A more important reason for pursuing disarmament negotiations is that they permit an exchange of views on problems of security and on the military and political aspects of strategic policies. They provide an opportunity to highlight

* U.S. Congress, Joint Committee on Atomic Energy, *Hearings, on S. Res. 179, Nonproliferation of Nuclear Weapons,* 89th Cong., 2d Sess., 1966, p. 15.

† The view that arms control negotiations have been used almost exclusively as a psychological weapon in the cold war is the theme of John W. Spanier and Joseph L. Nogee, *The Politics of Disarmament: A Study in Soviet-American Gamesmanship* (New York: Frederick A. Praeger, 1962).

the dangerous features of the military confrontation, which in turn can lead to more practical arms control measures and a more stable international environment. In this regard, the U.S. should be especially careful in framing disarmament proposals, primarily to insure a useful dialogue, but also to avoid being placed in the potential dilemma of having either to implement a measure inconsistent with national security or to withdraw an offer with the consequent onus of apparent insincerity.

At the same time, the U.S. should attempt to reduce political tensions and increase peaceful international cooperation, among other reasons to provide a more favorable atmosphere for progress in arms control. Although the complex international environment of sovereign states places limits on the possibilities of establishing a genuine international community, it simultaneously offers opportunities for steps to promote it. As the United States works toward the goal of a world community guided by law, in which international differences are settled by peaceful means, its actions could lead ultimately to agreement on an effective international sovereign agency with means of enforcement, which, in turn, may make general disarmament feasible.

Selective Measures

One must not dismiss the potential utility of arms control simply because extensive disarmament must await the solutions to difficult political problems. While it may have been persuasive before the advent of nuclear weapons to argue that armaments were a product, not a cause, of political disagreement, it now is clear that the confrontation of highly destructive armaments is itself a cause of tension and insecurity. To contend that arms control agreements are infeasible if one party seeks world domination is to overlook even the basic mutuality of interest between potential enemies in avoiding a war that neither side wants and in containing its violence if war should occur nevertheless. Undoubtedly, there always has been such a common interest, but it has assumed far greater importance in the thermonuclear age. In short, although arms control is inseparable from political issues, its attainment is not dependent on the elimination of struggle and conflict. Indeed, a major incentive for arms control is precisely the prospect that political disagreement will lead to unintended military consequences. Reciprocally, successful arms control measures may make some contribution to improving the general political climate.

Strategic Deterrence

The most dangerous threat to U.S. security for the foreseeable future is attack by Soviet thermonuclear weapons on the continental United States. Secretary of Defense McNamara has warned that a general nuclear war would produce hundreds of millions of fatalities in the U.S.S.R., Western Europe, and the U.S. He has explained that even assuming the U.S. struck first, vast devastation by a Soviet retaliatory blow could not be precluded. Nor can this situation be altered fundamentally by significant additions to the military budget; even a three-fold increase in offensive and defensive strategic programs could not prevent tens of millions of American casualties. Moreover, the U.S.S.R. could offset the effects of such expenditures at a far lower cost.*

Herein lies the unfamiliar dimension of the problem of national security in the nuclear era. No conceivable increase in national power through unilateral armament or by obtaining allies can eliminate the threat to a nation's very survival.

---

* "Statement by Secretary of Defense Robert S. McNamara before the House Armed Services Committee on the Fiscal Year 1965–1969 Defense Program and 1965 Defense Budget, 27 January 1964," pp. 31–32. Improvement in Soviet forces since that time makes attainment of a U.S. first strike capability even more impractical. The corresponding statements of February 18, 1965, and March 8, 1966, repeat this general point, although not in the same detail.

Nevertheless, at an absolute minimum, it is essential for the U.S. to continue to maintain strategic forces adequate to sustain a surprise attack by the combined arsenals of the Soviet Union and Communist China and still deliver such a damaging retaliatory blow to both nations that they could not survive as political and social entities. Such a deterrent posture serves the cause of stability by eliminating the incentive for the U.S.S.R. or Communist China to attack the U.S., except under the most extreme provocation. Under circumstances of mutual vulnerability, nuclear powers have a mutual interest not only in preventing accidental war but also in avoiding dangerous confrontations that could lead ultimately to an exchange of thermonuclear weapons.

Early, unprotected models of the Intercontinental Ballistic Missile (ICBM) rendered strategic retaliatory forces, both bomber and missile, highly vulnerable. This created an unstable confrontation that placed a premium on each nation's striking first or launching missile forces quickly, perhaps on inaccurate information, before they could be destroyed by an enemy first-strike. Subsequent developments of relatively invulnerable submarine-launched missiles and hardened ICBM sites, along with better means of command and control, have created a more stable situation. Even in the event of a surprise first-strike, both the U.S. and the U.S.S.R. now are assured of the survival of powerful and effective retaliatory strategic forces, thereby reducing substantially the incentive for a preemptive attack.

Restraint by both sides on the development of strategic arsenals has also contributed to stability of the confrontation. For whatever reason, the Soviets did not create a strategic bomber force of a size to challenge U.S. superiority, nor did they produce ICBM's at a rate approaching their capability during the period of great American concern over a potential missile gap following the launching of Sputnik. The U.S. reduced earlier goals of its missile and aircraft forces and, shortly after the Cuban missile crisis, removed from the

United Kingdom, Italy, and Turkey the highly vulnerable Jupiter and Thor Intermediate Range Ballistic Missiles (IRBM's), which were likely to be destroyed unless launched in a first strike. Both the U.S. and the U.S.S.R. endorsed the United Nations resolution against placing weapons of mass destruction in orbit, and both have proposed an agreement not to place weapons on the moon or other celestial bodies. The advantages of prompt consultation in the event of emergency or accident were recognized by the installation of a direct teletype link between Washington and Moscow.

Despite the increased stability of the confrontation and some evidence of mutual restraint, deterrence could fail or a sequence of events might occur that could bring about a general war. In view of the size and destructive power of the strategic arsenals of both sides, a thermonuclear exchange would result in wide-spread devastation that many believe could destroy civilization. This creates a genuine world-wide interest in disarmament measures as the only hope for reliable security against the disastrous consequence of nuclear war. Yet, those who recommend the elimination or drastic reduction of strategic weapons frequently ignore the complexity of the problem of attaining stability with relatively small strategic arsenals.

Even if a formal agreement were reached, there would be no means of insuring the elimination of nuclear weapons. Indeed, "elimination" of nuclear weapons or even reductions to very low levels could make evasion highly attractive as a means to obtain significantly superior forces. If surprise assault promised an overwhelming advantage, the temptation to initiate nuclear war could be great. Clearly, in seeking means of reducing strategic forces, the potential gains must be weighed carefully against the risks involved. There are no simple solutions. For example, stability should not be equated with parity in numbers of ICBM's and bombers. Such factors as the hundreds of Soviet IRBM's targeted against Western Europe must be considered, along with the variety of weapons and delivery systems, the differences in yields, asymmetries in distribution of population and industrial capacity, and even the political situation and the intentions of adversary nations.

Although tacit limitation of additions to existing forces appears the most likely form of arms control in the near future, the maintenance of stability at lower levels of force should be explored, with the caution that too extensive reductions may place in jeopardy the very stability that arms control seeks to foster. On the other hand, intelligence capabilities should provide each side with sufficient knowledge of the other to allow maintenance of a balance essentially comparable to the present situation, in which there apparently is a tacit acceptance by the U.S.S.R. of a degree of U.S. superiority in strategic forces.

The complicating factor of revolutionary technological change cannot be ignored, particularly in considering such vital matters as strategic deterrence. At the same time that we seek stability, we have no choice but to continue research and development toward the creation of weapons that could end this stability. Ideally, it would be advantageous to the U.S. to regain the effective superiority over and invulnerability to Soviet strategic forces that obtained for a brief period after World War II. Technological change sufficiently radical to be decisive in this regard appears highly unlikely over the next decade; by its very nature, however, a technological breakthrough is unpredictable, and the possibilities of its occurring create uncertainty and genuine concern. At a minimum, the U.S. must attempt by its research efforts to prevent the U.S.S.R. from obtaining a decisive strategic superiority.

An anti-missile defense system is often cited as an example of a destabilizing technological development. Some argue that its deployment by either the U.S. or U.S.S.R. would threaten the effectiveness of the other's retaliatory capability and therefore would cause an ineffective but dangerous acceleration of the production of both offensive and defensive strategic forces by both sides. Others claim, however, that either side's deployment of the system would prove merely wasteful, since it is relatively simple to offset the effects of the large expenses required for the defensive system at a far lower cost by improving penetration aids in offensive weapons.* Yet an Anti-Ballistic Missile (ABM) system may be useful. Secretary of Defense McNamara has stated that although the Nike X is not capable of defending this nation against a sophisticated ICBM attack—one that includes a large number of nuclear warheads or warheads designed in such a way as to mislead the defense—it can defend against "the kind of attack China might direct against us in the decade . . . 1975 to 1985."† Thus, it appears that deployment of a limited anti-missile system may be useful in maintaining effective strategic superiority over an avowedly aggressive China, and also in protecting against a small-scale Soviet attack launched accidentally or for demonstration purposes. Also, it may be able to defend such key installations as ICBM sites. An intricate web of military, political, psychological, and economic factors must be considered in reaching decisions on such complex technical matters as the deployment of ABM's.

The potential for technological development not only challenges stability but also adds an element of risk to arms control agreements, particularly if such agreements generate a false sense of security. Formal treaties may invite overt as well as covert circumvention. It therefore seems prudent to include escape clauses similar to that contained in Article IV of the partial test-ban treaty, which permits a signatory power to withdraw whenever extraordinary events related to the subject matter of the agreement "have jeopardized the supreme interests of its country." Paradoxically, technological competition in research and development may itself provide a degree of

---

* *The Baltimore Sun*, February 12, 1967, p. 3; "Statement of Secretary of Defense Robert S. McNamara Before a Joint Session of the Senate Armed Services Committee and the Senate Subcommittee on Department of Defense Appropriations on the Fiscal Year 1968–1972 Defense Program and the 1968 Defense Budget, 23 January 1967," p. 55.

† U.S. Congress, Joint Committee on Atomic Energy, *op. cit.*, p. 99.

stability. The current space race supports Huntington's thesis that a qualitative arms race is less likely than quantitative competition to result in armed conflict.*

Regional Stability

While Soviet strategic forces constitute the most dangerous threat to the security of the U.S., a thermonuclear exchange appears the least likely form of conflict. More likely, even if less dangerous intrinsically, are wars in areas outside the territory of either superpower. These conflicts, however, have a high potential for involvement of the great powers, with the obvious attendant dangers. Generally, a balance of military forces offers a better prospect for regional stability than weakness in the face of a stronger power.

The European Case. A special case is the confrontation in Europe. It is essential that no power potentially hostile to the United States dominate the valuable human and material resources of Western Europe. The strength of NATO and the potential consequences of aggression apparently deterred the U.S.S.R. from attempting to expand further its sphere of control in Europe, thus creating relative military stability in the region. The continued division of Germany, the Berlin situation, and the stresses within NATO itself, however, make the situation potentially dangerous.

Despite modest British and French nuclear capabilities, the alliance is dependent on U.S. strategic forces to offset the massive Soviet nuclear power targeted against NATO Europe. But U.S. vulnerability to a Soviet retaliatory strike has called into question in some minds the credibility of U.S. willingness to employ strategic forces for any purpose except to deter or respond to attack against the United States. This is an important element in the crisis in confidence over NATO military strategy. For the Europeans, there is, however, no

---

* Samuel P. Huntington, "Arms Races: Prerequisites and Results," in Carl J. Friedrich and Seymour E. Harris (eds.), *Public Policy* (Cambridge, Mass.: Harvard University Press, 1958), pp. 41–86.

practical alternative to reliance on the U.S. commitment. A strong European IRBM force stationed in or near Western Europe is probably the most inherently logical means of insuring a reliable deterrent force for the allies, but the political preconditions for it do not exist. Individual national capabilities, each adequate for deterrence, are too expensive, potentially destabilizing, and, from the U.S. point of view, inconsistent with the objective of inhibiting the proliferation of nuclear weapons. Although U.S. actions in the Cuban missile crisis of 1962 demonstrated a willingness to threaten use of strategic forces for vital interests other than deterrence of attack against the continental U.S., Cuba's proximity to the United States made this example less than fully persuasive to Europeans. It appears prudent to make every effort to satisfy the legitimate requirement for allied participation in NATO nuclear planning and consultation on the use of U.S. strategic nuclear weapons in order to increase the credibility of our deterrent and to dampen the desires for expensive and relatively ineffective national or multinational nuclear forces.

The stationing of U.S. ground troops in Europe is also necessary to establish the credibility of the U.S. commitment to NATO. They serve to offset Soviet troops stationed in East Germany and insure against a rapid seizure of Western European territory by a relatively small attack. However, the substantial conventional option these forces are designed to provide has not been accepted or matched by the European Allies, who regard the deterrent aspect of NATO forces as overriding. The European nations prefer to retain the agreed strategy of the early use of nuclear weapons to defeat a relatively large-scale aggression and have configured their forces accordingly. In view of this, it seems that with careful political preparation, the U.S. could substantially reduce its ground forces stationed in Europe, perhaps by as much as one third to one half. Such a redeployment might well be accompanied by an attempt to obtain a regional arms balance involving the withdrawal of some of the twenty Soviet divisions from East Germany.

Other opportunities should be sought to reduce the intensity of the military confrontation; but, as the German Peace Note of March 25, 1966 observed, extensive progress in arms control and disarmament in Europe must be accompanied by a resolution of difficult political problems. It would therefore be a mistake to dismantle NATO in the foreseeable future or to reduce U.S. ground forces to a token commitment. Military weakness might tempt the very aggression by the U.S.S.R. and its allies that is apparently highly unlikely under the present circumstances. The NATO alliance and a sizable U.S. ground force presence in Germany not only contribute to stability but also serve an important political function in assuring all the nations of Europe that growing German military might is tied closely to the United States and NATO and will not be employed for aggressive purposes.

Less Developed Areas. Probably the most challenging and complex and, in the long run, the most critical, national security problem facing the United States in the coming decade is the economic, social, and political revolution in the developing nations. U.S. objectives include preventing Communist domination of these states, so that they do not become bases for operations against the nations of the free world, and assisting them in the evolution of institutions and values that facilitate the creation of free, viable societies. The basic causes of tensions in the developing areas usually lie outside the Cold War, but the competition for influence between and among the great powers can cause their involvement. Thus, it is generally in the U.S. interest to attempt to inhibit the outbreak of war in such areas, and, if it occurs, to terminate it as rapidly as possible without great-power confrontation. The objective should be to achieve regional stability at as low a level of

balanced military forces as is consistent with the requirements
for internal security of the individual states and protection
against aggressive neighbors. In the less developed areas of the
world, where conflict is most likely, the opportunities for arms
control initiatives appear to have received the least attention.*

In elaborating the U.S. position on this type of regional
arms control, Mr. William C. Foster, Director of the U.S.
Arms Control and Disarmament Agency, stated on April 19,
1966, that the initiative for arms limitations should come
from within the region concerned. He also indicated that any
agreement should include all important nations of the area
and should contain provisions to satisfy all interested parties
that the arrangement would be respected.† Since achieving
this kind of comprehensive agreement would be extremely
difficult, initiatives of lesser scope that could contribute to
regional stability deserve consideration and U.S. support.

In the past, the U.S. has provided military assistance and
negotiated arms sales with the principal objective of creating a
capability to resist overt Communist aggression. The recipient
nations have often accepted assistance in order to increase
their military capability against a regional neighbor, sometimes also a recipient of U.S. aid. Military assistance and sales
programs serve a variety of purposes, and decisions concerning
them must vary according to the particular situation; but
these programs should be assessed from an arms control
standpoint, with careful attention to the requirements for
regional power balances.‡ In situations of pronounced im-

* An excellent discussion of some of the issues is provided in Lincoln P.
Bloomfield and Amelia C. Leiss, "Arms Control and the Developing Countries," *World Politics*, October, 1965, pp. 1–19.

† Conference of the Eighteen-Nation Committee on Disarmament, "Final
Verbatim Record of the Two Hundred and Fifty-Seventh Meeting," ENDC/
PV.257, April 19, 1966, p. 18. *The New York Times*, April 20, 1966, p. 14.

‡ The charge is often made that arms control considerations do not receive
sufficient attention in the development of military assistance and arms sales
programs. See, for example, U.S. Congress, Senate Committee on Foreign
Relations Staff Study, *Arms Sales and Foreign Policy*, 90th Cong., 1st Sess.,
January 25, 1967.

balances, such as the smaller states bordering on the U.S.S.R. and Communist China, it is impractical to provide more than a delaying force against attack by the larger power. Although each case must be evaluated on its own merits, if the security of these states is important to the U.S., only limited military assistance coupled with a security guarantee seems generally preferable to supporting forces too large for other legitimate security needs. Indeed, it may be desirable to use incentives of economic and technical assistance to encourage certain countries to reduce their forces and concentrate on internal development.

The U.S. should try to prevent the introduction of new, relatively sophisticated armaments into underdeveloped areas. Agreed reductions from existing levels are more difficult, but they, too, should be sought as appropriate. Although it will not be easy to obtain, the U.S. should also seek agreement among its allies to limit arms transfers. The Soviet Union poses a separate problem. In order to weaken U.S. influence and enhance its own, the U.S.S.R., in some cases, has an interest in creating the very instability that arms control is designed to prevent. Yet its initiative for the Tashkent Conference, following the 1965 conflict between India and Pakistan, suggests that the U.S.S.R. may recognize an interest in stability in at least some underdeveloped areas, both to inhibit the growth of Chinese influence and to prevent conflict situations likely to result in Soviet involvement with the United States. Thus, arms control discussions with the Soviet Union on regional stability might be productive, since it may prefer in an increasing number of instances to compete for influence by peaceful means. It seems likely that the U.S.S.R. could prevent arms sales or grants by Eastern European nations such as Czechoslovakia.

Communist China has the greatest professed interest in creating instability and promoting military conflict in the emerging nations of the world; thus far, however, the Chinese have acted with comparative restraint, perhaps only because they do not have the capability to provide more than token amounts of sophisticated military equipment to other states. Although it apparently has shown no interest thus far, we should attempt to engage China in arms control discussions through both unofficial contacts and in formal negotiations, thereby exposing the Chinese leaders to U.S. views on the problems of international security and the dangers of military conflict. Whatever their formal reaction, they might well discover areas of common interest with the U.S., at least in making unintended conflict less likely.

The developing states must be provided other sources of security if they are to exercise restraint, beyond that imposed by economic necessity, in obtaining arms. Regional organizations for mediation and arbitration provide one alternative. As another approach, regional or international observer and peace-keeping forces could prevent conflict during periods of high tension or secure and police a cease fire after conflict has begun. For this purpose, it appears preferable to rely on forces supplied by the smaller powers and to limit great power involvement to necessary logistical support.

Insurgency—externally fomented and supported, as in South Viet-Nam—appears to be the most likely form of conflict for the foreseeable future. Perhaps the most appropriate "arms control" measure to prevent insurgencies is to assist developing countries in their efforts to attain economic and social progress. As Secretary of Defense McNamara stated on May 18, 1966, "In a modernizing society, security means development."* While we cannot expect the uninterrupted and smooth transformation of these states into stable and viable political entities uniformly sympathetic to our objectives, especially in the short run, we must risk temporary difficulties to avoid far more serious disruptions later. Yet, at the same time, we must also be prepared to take appropriate

* Department of Defense, News Release, "Address by Robert S. McNamara, Secretary of Defense, Before American Society of Newspaper Editors, Queen Elizabeth Hotel, Montreal, Canada, Wednesday, May 18, 1966," p. 8.

military action when required. In this regard, it is important to be chary of agreeing to limitations of conventional forces, for it is extremely doubtful that such agreements would take into account the forces of smaller powers, such as Viet-Cong guerrillas or even North Vietnamese regulars.

Nonproliferation of Nuclear Weapons

Sought with varying frequency and intensity, the major arms control policy objective of the U.S. since World War II has been to prevent the proliferation of nuclear weapons. Although such weapons create great international insecurity, because of their potential for instantaneous massive destruction, our position then and since on the desirability of possessing them has been ambivalent. While we wished to deny these weapons to others, we believed that our own security and that of our Western European allies was dependent on them.

In June, 1946, the United States offered in the United Nations Atomic Energy Commission the Baruch Plan to prevent the military application of atomic energy through the international ownership and operation of all atomic facilities. Whatever its other merits, the U.S. plan offered the Soviets little incentive to agree, even had they desired effective international control of atomic energy. The plan called for the establishment of an extensive system of international control of atomic materials and facilities that would have precluded Soviet development of the atomic bomb. The U.S., for its part, offered to cease manufacture and dispose of weapons only after "effective operation" of the control system and the acceptance of "condign punishments" for violations. In his presentation of the U.S. position, Baruch went so far as to stipulate that "before a country is ready to relinquish any winning weapons it . . . must have a guarantee of safety, not only against the offenders in the atomic area but against the illegal uses of other weapons—bacteriological, biological, gas—perhaps—why not? against war itself."*

The next significant U.S. initiative to inhibit the proliferation of nuclear weapons was the U.S. Atoms for Peace Plan presented to the United Nations by President Eisenhower, in December, 1953. Assuming that there would be a widespread demand for large atomic reactors, the U.S. proposed that nuclear fuel be made available to an International Atomic Energy Agency (IAEA), which would provide technical assistance to nations for peaceful uses of nuclear materials. The IAEA would inspect atomic installations to guard against diversion of materials for the production of weapons. The IAEA was established in 1957, and systems of safeguards were adopted in 1960 and 1965. Although there has been only limited use of the IAEA, its growth has been steady. U.S. policy continues to urge placement of atomic facilities under IAEA inspection for assurance that materials are not being diverted to weapons production.

The test ban agreement is also related closely to the non-proliferation proposal. Following the contamination of Japanese fishermen resulting from a U.S. thermonuclear test in 1954, the Soviet Union capitalized on world sentiment by calling for the conclusion of a test ban agreement. The U.S. insisted on coupling the test ban to other arms control measures until 1959. Test ban negotiations began in October, 1958, but foundered repeatedly on Soviet reluctance to allow inspections in the U.S.S.R. The Soviets guardedly agreed to a token number of inspections, which they knew the U.S. would regard as inadequate to verify a ban on underground testing. Finally, by exempting underground tests, and thereby avoiding the issue of on-site inspections, the "Treaty Banning Nuclear Weapons Tests in the Atmosphere, in Outer Space and Under Water" was concluded in the summer of 1963.

---

* U.S. Department of State, *United States Atomic Energy Proposals*, Department of State Publication 2560 (Washington: U.S. Government Printing Office, 1946), p. 7.

More than one hundred nations have signed the agreement, although France and Communist China, both with active atmospheric test programs, have not.

The test ban treaty does not address non-proliferation directly, nor does it include a prohibition against the transfer of weapons from a nuclear to a non-nuclear power. The non-proliferation of nuclear weapons was not formally considered as a separate issue until 1964. The Communist Chinese atomic explosion on October 16, 1964, focused attention on non-proliferation and, in fact, led to a flurry of activity resulting, on August 17, 1965, in the U.S. "Draft Treaty to Prevent the Spread of Nuclear Weapons." Two weeks later, the U.S.S.R. rejected this proposal, and, on September 24, presented its version in the United Nations. Despite the maneuvering for position, both sides share an interest in preventing the proliferation of nuclear weapons.

Nuclear technology is becoming less complex and more familiar throughout the world. Although estimates vary, there is no question that several other nations could obtain nuclear weapons in a matter of only a few years, and many could achieve this capability over the next decade or two. Sophisticated delivery systems necessary for superpower status are more difficult and expensive to develop, but aircraft and simple missiles would enable less powerful nations to employ these weapons against each other or perhaps even on the overseas installations of the more powerful nations.

An increase in the number of nuclear powers would itself make the world power balance more complex and dangerous, and it would also make more likely the use of these weapons, either intentionally or by accident. The attainment of nuclear arms by one of the nations involved in an ethnic or territorial dispute would increase tensions sharply. There would be a high incentive for such a nation to exploit its advantage through nuclear blackmail or a pre-emptive attack, either before its enemy in turn obtained an offsetting capability, or even after he did, since the initial weapons systems are likely to be relatively primitive and highly vulnerable. Most dangerous is the possibility of great power involvement in a local nuclear conflict, which could lead to a large-scale thermonuclear war. Perhaps less serious in the short run, but nevertheless important, is the fact that expenditures by the poorer developing nations for a nuclear capability would siphon funds away from the critical needs of economic development.

It does not follow that a non-proliferation treaty in itself will prevent the spread of nuclear weapons. But agreement by the major nuclear powers and others would place considerable pressure on the remaining nations to subscribe to its conditions. A formal treaty would represent a public commitment —with international legal, moral, and political restraints—to abstain from acquisition of nuclear weapons. Thus, a treaty should at least create an environment in which countries disposed to acquire these weapons would be less likely to seek them.

It appears useful to press for a non-proliferation treaty to obtain the advantages that would accrue. The U.S. position that non-proliferation means no increase in the number of entities exercising control over nuclear weapons is designed to allow for the unlikely eventuality of a European nuclear force. This position provides the U.S.S.R. an opportunity to capitalize on the almost universally strong feeling against German acquisition of nuclear weapons, by contending that participation by Germany in a European force could eventually lead to unilateral German possession. Arrangements satisfactory to our allies, especially Germany, for consultation on nuclear planning within the NATO Nuclear Defense Affairs Committee and the subsidiary Nuclear Planning Group should enable us to obtain their support for a non-proliferation treaty that retains the consultative option, but prohibits the transfer of weapons to any non-nuclear state or group of states. Although it seems improbable in the foreseeable future, should political evolution make a European nuclear force both possible and desirable, a reservation in the treaty allowing for withdrawal could be invoked.

The U.S. should coordinate its negotiating position with allies and other key nations, but even then it may prove easier to conclude a non-proliferation agreement with the U.S.S.R. outside the Eighteen-Nation Disarmament Committee than within it—and then have both sides encourage other nations to subscribe to the treaty. The U.S. and U.S.S.R. should, in any event, exert diplomatic influence to encourage non-nuclear powers to refrain from developing nuclear weapons. To obtain the agreement of some non-nuclear powers, it probably will prove necessary to provide guarantees not only against the use of nuclear weapons but also against other threats to their security. The President has reiterated on several occasions his statement following the first Chinese atomic detonation that "nations that do not seek national nuclear weapons can be sure that if they need our strong support against some threat of nuclear blackmail, then they will have it."* The means of providing even this assurance, however, present difficult problems. We should not hesitate to investigate prospects for joint action with the U.S.S.R. or to seek understandings that there will be no interference by the Soviets in cases of guarantees in which they are unable to participate. The United Nations could prove useful in legitimizing such assurances.

Another means of inhibiting nuclear weapons proliferation is through regional arrangements for nuclear-free zones. The U.S. has conditioned its endorsement of such measures on a number of stipulations, undoubtedly in part because of concern over the possible loss of transient rights for its own nuclear weapons. Despite such difficulties, on balance it would appear favorable to U.S. interests to encourage agreement on nuclear-free zones in those areas in which nuclear weapons have not yet been introduced and where there is

* *Public Papers of the Presidents of the United States, Lyndon B. Johnson,* July 1 to December 31, 1964 (Washington: U.S. Government Printing Office, 1965), p. 686.

little or no likelihood of invasion by massive Communist land armies.

Development of Policy

National security is an inordinately complex problem, which cannot be divided into clearly identifiable and separable parts. Among other considerations, the formulation of security policy involves the task of relating force to national objectives that are often conflicting, continuously compromised, and seldom realized. Theoretical constructs notwithstanding, military strategy is not evolved systematically from clear statements of political purpose but it is the product of balancing requirements and capabilities to achieve competing objectives. Nevertheless, national security policy, particularly its military aspect, should be formulated with the clear purposes of making war less likely and mitigating its effects should it occur. In this sense, arms control policy not only must be consistent with military strategy, but also can be considered as an enlargement of it.

As with other aspects of security policy, the problem of arms control is itself highly complex. Measures improving one component of security may degrade another, but the objective should be to reduce hazards by a factor greater than the induced risk. The problem is complicated by the inability to predict technological developments that may make an agreement ineffective or even dangerous. Considerations such as these led Mr. John J. McCloy to call the subject of arms control "profound" in that it affects "so many aspects of our national life, not only our defense policy and our foreign policy, our atomic energy policy, our intelligence policy, but even our economic and social structure."* Actions are the clearest evidence of policy. It is essential that the principal

* U.S. Congress, Senate Committee on Foreign Relations, *Hearings on S.2180, a Bill to Establish a United States Disarmament Agency for World Peace and Security,* 87th Cong., 1st Sess., 1961, p. 40.

departments and agencies of government incorporate arms control concepts in the formulation of national security strategy and programs.

On September 26, 1961, President Kennedy signed the bill establishing the United States Arms Control and Disarmament Agency (ACDA). Although sections of the Act appear contradictory, there is no question that in practice the Director of ACDA is responsible to the President for the preparation and interdepartmental coordination of arms control policy proposals. The Act designates ACDA as "a new agency of peace," suggesting a conflict between its mission and those of the Departments of State and Defense, despite the caveat that "Arms control and disarmament policy . . . must be consistent with national security policy as a whole."* Inherent in the existence of a separate ACDA, especially since it has responsibility for the negotiating function, is encouragement of its personnel to pursue arms control as an objective for its own sake. The First and Second Annual Reports of ACDA make explicit, and the succeeding reports imply, that successful negotiations are "the chief purpose" of the Agency and "the goal to which its energies are directed."†

An interdepartmental Committee of Principals reviews and coordinates major arms control proposals, thereby insuring that the diverse interests and statutory responsibilities vested in other executive agencies are brought to bear on arms control matters. The Committee is composed of the Secretaries of State and Defense, the Chairman of the Joint Chiefs of Staff, the Director of ACDA, the Chairman of the Atomic Energy Commission, the Director of the Central Intelligence Agency, the Special Assistants to the President for National Security Affairs and for Science and Technology, the Administrator of the National Aeronautics and Space Adminis-

* Section 2, Public Law 87-297.

† "First Annual Report of the U.S. Arms Control and Disarmament Agency," in U.S. ACDA, *Documents on Disarmament*, 1961, p. 751; "Second Annual Report of the U.S. Arms Control and Disarmament Agency, January 28, 1963," in U.S. ACDA, *Documents on Disarmament*, 1962, II, 1281.

tration, and the Director of the United States Information Agency. Thus, despite the existence of a separate ACDA, it is unlikely that major arms control initiatives or recommendations will reach the President without the consideration of their implications for national security. Perhaps more pertinent is the question of whether ACDA is consulted on, and makes an appropriate contribution to, the broad range of national security and foreign policies.*

Potentially the most serious disadvantage of a separate arms control agency is that, despite the functioning of the Committee of Principals, the executive departments primarily concerned with national security policy will tend to give minimum creative attention to arms control initiatives and will generally limit their consideration of arms control to reacting to proposals that originate in ACDA. ACDA has a special, but not exclusive, mandate to initiate arms control policy recommendations. Arms control conceived as an enlargement of the scope of military strategy is compatible with the responsibility of the Department of Defense, which should be as concerned with security through arms control as by any other means.

As stated in the Act, arms control is "an important aspect of foreign policy." The Secretary of State, as the primary Cabinet officer for national security policy, "should be able to advise the President on the full range of national security matters from the point of view of their relation to foreign problems and policies," and should bear chief responsibility "for overseeing and coordinating our manifold foreign policy activities on the President's behalf."† It appears from his testimony, however, that the Secretary of State not only has

* See, for example, "Peace Studies Await a Call," *The Washington Post,* March 26, 1967, p. B3. The allegation "that the Agency was often not permitted to carry out its functions," is attributed to "officials" of ACDA in *The Times* (London), January 31, 1967, p. 8.

† Henry M. Jackson (ed.), *The National Security Council: Jackson Subcommittee Papers on Policy-Making at the Presidential Level* (New York: Frederick A. Praeger, 1965), pp. 27, 69.

delegated the development of arms control initiatives to the Director of ACDA, but also has placed confidence in that Agency to insure that arms control policy recommendations are consistent with national security policy. When questioned on the handling of arms control proposals within the Department of State, the Secretary stated his conviction that the Director of ACDA insured that arms control policy was consistent with other security considerations and that the Foreign Service Officers detailed to the Agency provided the required coordination with the Department of State.*

During the hearings on the establishment of ACDA, Secretary of State Rusk took the position that, although the Agency should function under the direction of the Department of State, it should be independent to avoid any "accident of bureaucratic rivalry" that would make it appear that the State Department was trying "to put the Department of Defense out of business."† This statement suggests that both the State and Defense departments viewed arms control in a manner inconsistent with its purpose and importance. Bureaucratic rivalry must inevitably characterize policy formulation in complex interdepartmental national security matters not relegated to a subordinate status. Although the Committee of Principals provides a forum for interdepartmental coordination, it is essential that each of the principal departments responsible for national security recognize the contribution that arms control can make to national security and insure that arms control considerations receive adequate attention in the formulation of national security policies and programs.

It is clear that, in the years ahead, national security policy

* U.S. Congress, Senate Committee on Armed Services, *Arms Control and Disarmament: Hearings, Before the Preparedness Investigating Subcommittee,* 87th Cong., 2d Sess., 1962, pp. 95–97.

† U.S. Congress, House Committee on Foreign Affairs, *Hearings, on H.R. 7936 and H.R. 9118, to Establish a United States Arms Control Agency,* 87th Cong., 1st Sess., 1961, p. 57; U.S. Congress, Senate, *Hearings on S. 2180,* pp. 19, 26.

will remain a highly complex issue requiring the closest inter-
weaving of arms control initiatives with other aspects of
national strategy. This challenge

> requires of us the degree of maturity that makes it possible to be
> strong and firm in resisting political thrusts, prudent in the
> exercise of power, energetic in seeking safeguards to reduce the
> risk of war, and encouraging to processes of change which may
> moderate the underlying causes of conflict—without regarding
> these lines of action as contradictory, as either "hard" or "soft."*

*Marshall D. Shulman, *Beyond the Cold War* (New Haven: Yale University Press, 1966), p. 88.

8. *National Security Policy and International Organization*

RUTH B. RUSSELL

The United States ended World War II as the leader of the victorious military alliance and as the chief sponsor of the United Nations, the permanent organization established to maintain future international peace and security. The prewar concept of providing for national security through political isolation and defensive military strength had been abandoned during the course of the conflict. Americans in general accepted the idea that their nation would provide world leadership, but, at the same time, they had little desire to play a modern equivalent of the grand-imperial role of dominant states in past eras. Nor did they have any clear idea of what changing conditions of national and international politics might mean in terms of the responsibilities inherent in their new leadership role. Depending on their temperament, Americans in 1945 were inclined to conceive of the situation in oversimplified form along one of two contradictory lines.

One, primarily a military approach to world leadership and national security, reasoned that ownership of the most powerful industrial economy in the world and possession of the atomic bomb, with means for its delivery, would in themselves provide adequate national security and permit the

United States "to police the world" by the threat of using the bomb.* This view grew out of American strategic thinking, which, in the immediate postwar period, continued to concentrate on the traditional aim of safeguarding the homeland and of preparing to fight, if necessary, a defensive war. In the contemporary context, a defensive war was construed as action against Soviet aggression. Such a position, based on industrial-atomic primacy, had the domestic political virtue of requiring the least immediate sacrifice in men and money when contrasted with the costs of maintaining a more flexible military establishment geared to differing levels of possible conflicts in different parts of the world.

The other trend of American thought was primarily political: It relied on the existence of the United Nations, and on United States membership therein, to maintain international peace—and thereby national security also. Those who held this view seemed to assume that the world organization would somehow insulate the United States itself from the hurly-burly of world politics, even when the United States was not politically isolating itself as it had in the past. They failed to understand that the Charter's system of collective peace enforcement would require the United States to meet the Soviet Union as a political-military rival outside the United Nations if and when Washington's objectives were thwarted by a veto of Security Council action by Moscow.

These two approaches to maintaining peace and the national security were not always considered to be mutually exclusive. President Truman, for example—sharing the predominant military view that the atomic monopoly guaran-

---

* Gen. Maxwell D. Taylor (*The Uncertain Trumpet* [New York: Harper & Row, 1960], p. 4), describes how, in 1945, "Our own people [including himself at the time] were quick to believe that our armed forces had in the air-delivered atomic bomb the absolute weapon which would permit the United States . . . to police the world through the threat of its use. Thus, in 1945, a new strategic creed, eventually to be known as Massive Retaliation, came into being. . . ."

teed national security—optimistically believed in 1945 that the United Nations could replace "the old power politics," of which he disapproved in typically American fashion.* Both these assumptions, however, foundered on the developing Cold War.

The atomic monopoly, it turned out, did not in itself discourage the economic, political, or covert military actions of Moscow and local Communist groups in seeking to gain control of European and Near Eastern governments; nor, in the Far East, was it any help in influencing the internal struggle in China in favor of Chiang Kai-shek. But if the United States was unwilling† to threaten the Soviet Union with atomic bombs as an indirect means of supporting internally threatened non-Communist governments in Greece, Italy, France, or China, then it would have to face the need, sooner or later, to undertake lower-level military responsibilities in foreign areas not traditionally considered vital to the national security. If the United States was not prepared to allow the Soviet Union to take over the role of world domination anticipated by Communist ideology, it would have to undertake new direct obligations in the field of "power politics" in order to stop the spread of Communist influence. If the United States succeeded in doing both those things, however, the United Nations would hardly be able to develop its full potentialities, as foreshadowed in the Charter, which depended upon a high degree of cooperation among its members, in particular among the great powers. But the actual state of international conflict was what made the other—national—actions necessary in the first place and limited what

* Harry S. Truman, *Memoirs* (Garden City, N.Y.: Doubleday, 1955), I, 245–46. For the attitude of many U.S. officials during World War II on "power politics" and its replacement by a world organization, see Ruth B. Russell, *A History of the United Nations Charter* (Washington, D.C.: Brookings Institution, 1958), esp. pp. 181, 484, 490, 963.

† Or unable—in the early postwar period, atomic weapons were in short supply, as were conventional forces, once the hasty demobilization was completed.

could be done through the U.N. to maintain international peace.*

Logic alone might have dictated an American policy of foregoing all effort to develop the world organization until the Communist–non-Communist conflict had been resolved in favor of the United States. Governments, however, even less than individuals, do not arrive rationally at lucid and consistent major policy determinations, from which future foreign policy then flows. The United States seemed to want both a strong national security policy and a strong international organization at the same time, but it was unwilling to pay the military price of the first and unable to bring about the political cooperation necessary to the second.

American policy since 1946 can be seen, therefore, as an attempt to adjust inconsistent approaches to the conflicting demands inherent in the complex situation that resulted. That situation never presented itself in terms of a neat and clear choice between the two oversimplified alternatives summarized above. Circumstances kept changing with time, and United States actions were themselves one of the determining factors in how they changed. The novelty of many specific postwar problems facing the United States as a result of the now-commonplace revolutions in technology, in the political, social, and economic aspirations of peoples around the globe, and in population growth, was matched by the novelty for governments of operating in entirely new ways on the international scene. This last was of greater importance for the United States, given its history of isolationism, than for many other members of the United Nations; but the other "revolutions" also affected the character of diplomatic relations so strongly that all governments proved to be relative novices in their ability to operate effectively through the many new

---

* Thus, when the U.S. took the question of Korea to the General Assembly in 1947, having failed to agree with the Soviet Union on methods to elect a national government and to reunify the country divided between their two occupation zones, there was no way by which the Soviet Union could be made to accept the recommendations of the Assembly in the matter.

international agencies created to meet the new circumstances.

The record of United States policy in relation to international organization, in its attempt to maintain both national security and international peace, has been an irregular one as a result of all these complexities. Neither dependence on military strength alone nor on international organization alone has controlled Washington's policy, although, in our pluralistic system, even the extremes, both of preventive war and of pacific achievement of world government, have found their advocates. The actuality has been more complicated. The effort of most Administrations most of the time has been to maintain the stance described by President Johnson in April, 1964: "Our guard is up, but our hand is out," he declared.* The policy, like the posture, has been a difficult one to maintain. Not surprisingly, it has led to official ambivalence and inconsistency on more than one occasion.

A *"Police Action"*

The drafters of the United Nations Charter believed that one reason for the failure of the League of Nations was its inability to apply military sanctions against an aggressor. The provision of adequate enforcement means was therefore considered necessary to the success of the new security system. The pattern of Anglo-American strategic direction of World War II provided precedents for the embryonic enforcement system written into the Charter. The allied war leaders, assisted by the Combined Chiefs of Staff, had made the key political-military decisions. (Articles 46–47 provided, in effect, that the permanent members of the Security Council, assisted by the Military Staff Committee, would do the same.) The question of theater command had normally devolved on the government that controlled the major forces in the area. (Article 47 left "questions relating to the command of" armed forces to be used by the Council to be "worked out

* U.S. Department of State *Bulletin*, L, 1964, 607.

subsequently.") Wartime forces had come from all allied states according to their capabilities. (Article 43 provided that all member states would make special arrangements with the Security Council to provide forces and facilities for enforcement purposes on its call.) The major allies had provided the largest forces during the war. (As permanent Security Council members they would presumably do the same under Article 43 agreements, thus justifying their privileged position in the directing organ.) *

In concrete terms, however, it proved impossible for the Military Staff Committee to agree in 1946–47 on the contributions of forces the five permanent members should undertake to provide in Article 43 agreements. These, it was agreed, would form the military basis of the whole enforcement system. The United States wanted the international forces to be "large enough to bring to bear against any breach of the peace anywhere in the world balanced forces drawn from the most powerful and best equipped forces that could be provided by members."† Emphasis was to be on naval and air arms, with contributions according to the capacity of each country. The system, by American thinking, would thus give the United States a dominant role and, therefore, command of the forces. The Soviet Union, on the other hand, advocated small forces, contributed on an absolutely equal basis by the permanent members—an "absurd plane-for-plane, gun-for-gun, man-for-man proposal," as General Matthew Ridgway described it.‡ It was a concept consistent with the Soviet

* Wartime thinking was somewhat amusingly carried over into the special provision of Article 45, that any air-force contingents pledged under Article 43 agreements should be held "immediately available." According to General Ridgway, the U.S. Air Force originally proposed that "the entire contribution of the Big Five should be in air power and that the control of this first international air force should be vested in the United States commander." Matthew B. Ridgway, *Soldier: The Memoirs of Matthew B. Ridgway* (New York: Harper, 1956), p. 169.

† *UN Security Council Official Records* (SCOR), 2d year, No. 43 (June 21, 1947), p. 955.

‡ General Ridgway was the U.S. representative on the Military Staff Committee and also military adviser to Bernard Baruch on the Atomic Energy Committee. Ridgway, *op. cit.*, p. 170.

leaders' obsession that the Big Five should make identical contributions to the United Nations in almost every way, and with their suspicion of international cooperation in general. Small-sized forces, moreover, were also consistent with the fact that the veto privilege meant that they would not be used against one of the permanent members.

United States leaders saw the Soviet position on international military forces, especially when combined with the Soviet attempt in disarmament discussions to prohibit the use of atomic and other mass-destruction weapons, as an attempt by "the Russians . . . to strip us of all our present technological and scientific superiority and to elevate the USSR to the position of dominant military power."* The two governments' approaches were clearly irreconcilable, and, in the Cold War atmosphere, both governments were more concerned to blame failure on the other than to seek any basis of adjustment. The abortive negotiations at least demonstrated that the Charter's security system would not work without the cooperation of the two major military powers. In its place, the United States—spurred by the Berlin Blockade and the Communist takeover in Czechoslovakia in 1948—turned to collective defense under the North Atlantic Treaty as the means to contain what it saw as the one great threat to international peace, namely, international Communism under monolithic Soviet control. Although brought under the umbrella of Article 51 of the Charter, NATO was generally regarded as a substitute for (rather than as a supplement to) the United Nations system. In this period, the military containment approach was heavily predominant.

The anticipated military aggression came in June, 1950—in Korea, however, rather than in Europe—and Washington interpreted the North Korean invasion as a move by international Communism against the non-Communist world as a whole. In these terms, the area had to be defended despite the "defensive perimeter" military concept, which, Secretary

* *Ibid.*, pp. 171–72.

of State Dean Acheson had publicly stated in January, excluded Korea from direct United States military protection.* The local military situation and the nearness of American occupation forces in Japan facilitated an immediate military response. With no regional security organization available, the United Nations offered a focus for immediate political action. The Security Council, in the absence of the Soviet representative, was able to recommend that members aid the Republic of Korea under a United Nations Unified Command, and asked the United States to appoint a commander and to report to it "as appropriate" on the course of action taken.† The request for reports was the only provision for any United Nations "supervision" of the international operation. The military situation justified the United States' claim to predominance in its strategic direction, but the extent to which Washington refused any element of international direction made it clear that American military officials, at least, regarded the United Nations connection as nominal.‡ The operation was internationalized, however, to a politically important extent by contributions of troops from sixteen countries and ancillary support from about thirty.

The Security Council resolution set the objective of the

* U.S. Department of State *Bulletin*, XXII, 1950, 116.
† UN Doc. S/1511, June 27, 1950.
‡ Gen. Douglas MacArthur was appointed UN Commander. His chain of command was through the Chief of Staff (U.S. Army), to the JCS, to the Secretary of Defense, to the President. His reports to the United Nations were subject to revision in Washington before transmission to the Security Council. Early proposals for a "Committee on Coordination of Assistance to Korea" (of states contributing forces to the UN Command), for some kind of joint command, for an "international brigade" (of volunteers from countries unable to contribute an organized battalion), even for designating the Korean Hqtrs. of the U.S. Eighth Army (operating headquarters for all ground forces) as those of the "First United Nations Army," were all turned down. Only after the entry of the Chinese in the North was a committee of ambassadors established in Washington (of states contributing forces) for consultative purposes. On these aspects, see Trygve Lie, *In The Cause of Peace* (London and New York: Macmillan, 1954), pp. 336–39; and Leland M. Goodrich, *Korea: A Study of U.S. Policy in the United Nations* (New York: Columbia University Press, 1956), pp. 121 ff.

enforcement action in limited terms: "To repel the armed attack and to restore international peace and security in the area." The United States and other United Nations members understood this to mean, "solely for the purpose of restoring the Republic of Korea to its status prior to the invasion . . . and of re-establishing the peace broken by that invasion."* Although the conflict was unprecedented as the first war in history fought specifically in the name of organized collective security, such a limited objective was consonant with the military aspects of the Charter concept of maintaining international security—that is, of restoring the *status quo* and ending hostilities quickly, thus proving that aggression would not pay. But a limited objective in such a major conflict was also a novelty in United States military experience. Early acceptance of the limited goal was superseded when American anticipation of a decisive military victory and of surrender by the North Koreans appeared to make possible a final settlement of the problem of Korean unification. That expectation was rudely shattered by failure of the North Koreans to submit before the entry of Chinese "volunteers." This new factor brought to a climax a deep split in United States official circles, between advocates of the original, limited collective-security victory and proponents of victory over international Communism even at the possible cost of generalized war.†

In the end (pressed by allies and neutrals alike), the United States limited the war to the Korean Peninsula. The Truman Administraton and the Joint Chiefs of Staff felt that broadening the conflict to include mainland China would risk the loss of many allies, weaken the defense of Europe, and ". . . involve us in the wrong war, at the wrong place, at the

---

* Secretary of State Acheson, U.S. Department of State *Bulletin*, XXIII, 1950, 46.

† The latter view found its classic statement in General MacArthur's oft-quoted remark, ". . . there is no substitute for victory." (Speech before Congress, April 19, 1951.)

wrong time, and with the wrong enemy," as General Omar Bradley so aptly phrased the situation.* The Korean military conflict was eventually halted by a military armistice in 1953, on an improved defensive line near the 38th Parallel where it all began, but the political conflict remains unresolved.

Had the original objective of repulsing aggression in Korea remained unchanged, the military results might have been about the same, but they would have been achieved at far less cost. The experience would not have been as traumatic as it was for many American officials (especially the military) and for the American public generally, since the limited victory sought would have been achieved. The Uniting for Peace resolution, in 1950,† was at first hailed as a means of overcoming the Soviet veto and as leading the way to an effective system of international enforcement even against the will of a great power. But the military intervention did not succeed as anticipated, and, by 1953, the stalemate in Korea had led to widespread American disillusionment with United Nations "collective security" and all its works.

One result of these developments was to give great impetus to the United States' negotiation of a whole new series of regional and bilateral security arrangements to contain Communism. But Korea also proved to have marked the end of Communist attempts to expand by means of organized military attacks in areas where United States interest was great enough to raise the possibility of direct response. Instead, the

---

* *Military Situation in the Far East*, Pt. 2, p. 732: Hearings before the Committee on Armed Services and the Committee on Foreign Relations, U.S. Senate, 82d Congress, 1st Session.

† UN Doc. A/1481, Nov. 3, 1950. The resolution, besides providing for a speedier convening of the General Assembly in the event of Security Council failure to act because of a veto, also sought to establish the machinery for Assembly supervision of military sanctions within the limits of its recommendatory authority. It recommended that members earmark units of their armed forces for future U.N. use; authorized the appointment of a panel of military experts to advise the governments about setting up such earmarked units; established a Collective Measures Committee to study further methods to improve U.N. ability to meet future acts of aggression; and set up a Peace Observation Commission for use before the actual outbreak of aggression.

Soviet Union and its allies encouraged revolution and disorder in areas emerging from colonial or semicolonial status. The new activity in underdeveloped areas was harder for the United States to deal with, but less immediately threatening to its vital interests. The United Nations had an entirely different role to play in helping to maintain peace and security in the face of this kind of threat.

Peace-Keeping Operations

In 1956, the welter of inter-Arab rivalries, Arab-Israeli conflicts, and Arab-Anglo-French disputes finally erupted in the Israeli invasion of Egypt, which was followed closely by British and French intervention on the plea of protecting the Suez Canal. This action by major allies of the United States was taken without its consent, or even knowledge, and was promptly condemned by Washington. In this situation, Soviet Premier Khrushchev proposed to President Eisenhower that their two governments, as permanent Security Council members, should jointly initiate assistance to Egypt on the expiration of a twelve-hour ultimatum to the three invaders to halt the military action.* The Soviet proposal neatly adapted to the new occasion the form of initial U.N. action in Korea.

Notwithstanding his initial reaction to the invasions, President Eisenhower did not want to join in the proposed U.N. resolution, which would bring Soviet forces into the Middle East under United Nations auspices; to leave Moscow in the position of Egypt's best "friend in need"; or to counterbalance Soviet aid to Egypt by supporting the intervention, of which he disapproved in principle and because of the inherent risk of escalation. The Eisenhower Administration eagerly grasped an alternative it found in a Canadian proposal for an impartial, noncombatant, international military force. This body would not seek to enforce the peace against the invading

* For the Eisenhower-Khrushchev correspondence, see Paul Zinner (ed.), *Documents on American Foreign Relations, 1956* (New York: Harper, 1957), pp. 355–58.

armies, but, with Egypt's consent, would simply secure the peace, primarily by its continuing presence after the agreed withdrawal of the foreign forces and until settlement of the underlying political conflicts was reached. Through United States pressure, Commonwealth persuasion, and Soviet threats, Great Britain, France, and Israel were induced to accept a cease fire and to agree to withdraw in favor of the proposed United Nations Emergency Force (UNEF). Almost as important, their acquiescence was obtained prior to the Security Council meeting at which the Soviet Union intended to seek approval for action against aggression. The United States thus escaped from the dilemma posed for it by the Soviet proposal, and the United Nations found itself deploying an international "peace-keeping" force of a character not anticipated in the Charter and wholly different in function from the international sanctions forces in Korea.

UNEF was, in its commander's view, a true (not a para-) military force, but with a purely pacific mission.* It was composed of some 6,000 troops supplied by eight states in organized national contingents. The permanent members of the Security Council were excluded from direct participation, although the logistical support provided by the United States was absolutely essential. UNEF could use its arms only in self-defense—interpreted in United Nations terms to mean that it never initiated the use of force, never applied more than the necessary minimum of force, and used even that minimum only when all efforts at peaceful persuasion had failed.

---

* Lt. Gen. E. L. M. Burns, *Between Arab and Israeli* (New York: Ivan Obolensky, 1963), p. 313 n. General Burns objected to diplomatic use of the term "paramilitary" to describe UNEF. Its inappropriate use, he thought, "perhaps arises from a misapprehension that a military force in all situations invariably and necessarily uses all the arms and means at its disposal to achieve its object. This, of course, is not so, and an army can give 'aid to the civil power' under great restrictions as to its use of arms. In my view, UNEF is certainly a military force, but with a strictly limited and defined task and mode of action prescribed for it." For a detailed account of UNEF, see also Gabriella Rosner, *The United Nations Emergency Force* (New York: Columbia University Press, 1963).

Secretary-General Dag Hammarskjöld later pointed out that such an impartial peace-keeping force:

> . . . must constitutionally be a non-fighting force, operating on the territories of the countries concerned only with their consent and utilized only after a decision of the Security Council or General Assembly regarding a specific case, for those clearly international purposes relating to the pacific settlement of disputes which are authorized by the Charter.*

Although far larger than any earlier U.N. peace-keeping field mission—such as the Observer Group in Kashmir or the Truce Supervision Organization in Palestine (UNTSO)—UNEF's function was politically similar. Its first commander and his staff were even drawn from UNTSO. In spite of the similarities, the sheer novelty of an international military force commanded by Secretariat officials under General Assembly direction was so great that its limited authority and strictly pacific function were widely overlooked.

Advocates of the United Nations responded with excessive enthusiasm to this "new" device. They saw it as a break-out from the impasse the United Nations had reached, because it gave the U.N. a role in maintaining international peace and security on the periphery of the Cold War, even if it could not play such a role in relation to direct super-power conflict. If the United States and the Soviet Union could not cooperate to enforce the peace, they could, apparently, cooperate to keep out of situations not of vital national interest to either, thus reducing the tendency of "brushfire" conflagrations to escalate to more dangerous super-power confrontations.

UNEF (and an observer group of some 600 men in Lebanon in 1958) were so successful that when the newly independent Congo was thrown into chaos by the mutiny of the Congolese

* U.N. Doc. A/3844/Add. 1, *Introduction to the Annual Report of the Secretary-General on the Work of the Organization: 16 June 1957–15 June 1958,* p. 2.

Army and the return of Belgian troops, the Security Council had little trouble deciding on another military force as part of the broader United Nations Operation in the Congo (ONUC).*

Unfortunately, ONUC soon became a contentious political issue. In brief, it can be said that because of the different mission of ONUC (to assist in the maintenance of internal order in a situation where no stable government, or even a generally recognized one, existed) as contrasted to that of UNEF (to separate firmly established governments that had agreed to remain apart), ONUC was unable to operate according to the principles laid down in the Suez situation by Secretary-General Hammarskjöld. In addition, ONUC suffered because various U.N. members, at different times, either actively opposed the operation or sought to turn the impartial U.N. force to the ends of one or another of the internal Congolese factions. The Congo situation reflected not only the broader controversies of the great powers and their endeavors to diminish the influence of one another in the country, but also the ambitions and rivalries of various African states. In spite of these difficulties, ONUC was maintained until June, 1964, and in general completed its military mission.

The violent controversy that developed within the United Nations over the politics of the Congo operation was marked by the refusal of a number of members (especially the Soviet Union and France) to pay their assessed share of ONUC costs. This created a financial crisis within the United Nations, which in turn led to a related constitutional crisis over the authority of the General Assembly to initiate peace-

---

* For a more detailed consideration of the Congo Force, see Ernest W. Lefever, *Crisis in the Congo* (Washington, D.C.: Brookings Institution, 1965). For a comparison of UNEF and ONUC, especially in connection with the application of Hammarskjöld's principles, see Ruth B. Russell, *United Nations Experience with Military Forces: Political and Legal Aspects* (Washington, D.C.: Brookings Institution, 1964), pp. 50–67, 79–123.

keeping missions and to assess the member states for peace-keeping costs.*

Meanwhile, events called for new peace-keeping operations: a small security force in West Irian (1962–63), a minor observation mission in Yemen (1963–64), another substantial force in Cyprus (UNFICYP, 1964), and an expanded India-Pakistan observation mission (UNIPOM, 1965) to supplement the original, which had been on the Kashmir cease-fire line since 1949. To all of these, as well as to the continuing UNEF and Palestine Truce Supervision Organization, the same general characteristics of pacific-settlement operations applied, their varying sizes, mandates, and details of organization and operation notwithstanding.

Ways were devised to finance these missions outside the regular United Nations budget. In Yemen and West Irian, the parties in controversy shared the costs. In Cyprus, the force participants and other voluntary contributors, including the United States, have borne the burden. These contributors represented only a handful of states, and they have not covered the costs fully, so that the Secretary-General has had to plead for greater contributions on each renewal of UNFICYP.†

Problems of Peace-Keeping

The weaknesses that have afflicted the various peace-keeping operations described above are both technical and political in nature. The technical failings are easier to define because of their more concrete nature, and thus have received most of

* Special committees on peace-keeping operations (Committee of 33) and on finances (Committee of 14) were established to study these problems and report to the 21st Assembly. As of mid-1966, they had found no way to resolve either problem. For further consideration of the development of both problems, see Ruth B. Russell, "United Nations Financing and 'The Law of the Charter,' " *Columbia Journal of Transnational Law* (March, 1966).

† See the Secretary-General's letter to all member states, June 21, 1966, reporting a deficit at that date of over $3,000,000. U.N. Doc. S/7376, June 23, 1966.

the attention. Moreover, there is considerable expertise on the practical aspects of peace-keeping, although it needs to be organized and made readily available to interested governments. All peace-keeping missions have been *ad hoc* affairs, with the inevitable confusion attendant on deploying military force under emergency conditions and without prepared plans. Most proposals to strengthen international peace-keeping machinery, therefore, concern overcoming these *ad hoc* hazards. They commonly suggest that member governments should hold available suitably trained and equipped personnel and should authorize an adequate planning staff at United Nations Headquarters. The requirements are not difficult to formulate; any competent military staff officer could program them adequately on the basis of available experience. There is no mystery, in short, about what needs to be done to organize and maintain an effective system of peace-keeping "forces" on a ready call-up basis.

The great difficulty concerns securing the necessary political cooperation in disputes that arise among the most important members of the U.N., which would have to organize the system. For it is a melancholy fact that only when fear of action outside the organization has become greater than fear of action through it has it been possible to mobilize enough political support to authorize the major peace-keeping operations. And when that initial accord proves tenuous, as it did in the Congo, the effectiveness of the mission is diminished if not destroyed. In such circumstances, it may be better, as Lincoln Bloomfield pointed out, to continue the *ad hoc* system with only such preparatory steps as can be made on the current do-it-yourself basis, chiefly by such stanch middle powers as Canada, the Scandinavian countries, and others that have been the backbone of peace-keeping.* In this way, new ventures can be undertaken when sufficient accord exists without clashing over the still unresolved constitutional and

* Lincoln P. Bloomfield, "Peacekeeping and Peacemaking, "Foreign Affairs (July, 1966), pp. 675–76, 679–80.

financial principles on which the United States remains at odds with the Soviet Union and France.

Analyses of experience on the operating side—in the Congo, for example—have found that the vagueness of ONUC's mandate and the inadequacy of its authorized means in relation to its objectives were major causes of its difficulties. It is easy, then, to suggest that clear mandates and adequate means are necessary for improved peace-keeping. This conclusion, however, ignores the tense political situation in which such missions are established. They have often been almost literally a last resort, little more than a procedural measure on which the parties in conflict could be brought to agree when nothing better was available or acceptable.

In Cyprus, for example, neither Commonwealth, NATO, nor Anglo-American diplomacy stemmed the mounting tensions. By March, 1964, only enough accord could be mobilized to obtain agreement on UNFICYP for a three-month period, with a weak mandate in relation to the Cyprus Government. Furthermore, partly because of the growing financial difficulties within the United Nations, there was general indifference to the call for men and money—unlike the initial responses to both UNEF and ONUC. Secretary-General U Thant had difficulty in putting together an acceptable force and in obtaining pledges of funds to finance UNFICYP. Vagueness of mandate and inadequacy of means may thus be the price for any operation at all when acute political conflict makes it impossible to muster the votes in either the Security Council or the General Assembly for a precise definition of agreed objectives.

It does not necessarily follow, moreover, that precision itself is the key to a successful mission. The mandate for the Yemen observer mission (UNYOM) was quite clear: To observe the agreed disengagement of the U.A.R. and Saudi Arabia from their respective involvements in the Yemeni Civil War. Although the highly visible Egyptian troops were not withdrawn, the 200 men in UNYOM were in no position to force them out, and they would not have been even if they had had a stronger mandate. The mission could only report that the withdrawal was not being undertaken. This situation led eventually to the withdrawal of the observers rather than of the Egyptian troops. UNYOM's fate was not a function of the clarity of its mandate.

Continuation of a mission is no guarantee that the peace will be kept indefinitely, as Kashmir and Palestine have shown. The costs of such continuing operations, even without renewed violence, have intensified the search for ways to remedy the failure of peace-keeping operations to lead to final settlement in some cases. In Cyprus, for example, much greater than normal stress was put on the appointment of a separate political mediator in tandem with the peace-keeping officials. His efforts have yet to gain the acceptance of the disputing parties, serving chiefly to illustrate once again that the political problem is fundamental rather than the technical issues of machinery and procedures.

Settlement of Conflicts

The relationship between peace-keeping and settlement is often misunderstood. When violence is seriously threatened or has actually broken out, the Security Council or the General Assembly, acting as settlement agencies, may be unable to bring about settlement between the parties in conflict. If the Council can agree that the situation constitutes a threat to the peace and if it can mobilize the means required, it has the authority to order enforcement action—that is, diplomatic, economic, or military sanctions—as a means of forcing the maintenance of peace. If it cannot or does not wish to go that far, either Council or Assembly may be able to get the parties to agree at least to cease (or not to start) open hostilities, while an impartial U.N. presence of some sort is utilized to assist them in maintaining the agreed state of suspended violence. That field presence (whether the personnel are political or military) in itself neither stops the violence nor brings about further progress toward settlement. It is, in the last analysis, the governments concerned with maintaining the peace—whether they are acting collectively through the U.N., or separately in support of the organization's collective efforts—that must use the time bought by the acceptance of a peace-keeping mission to persuade the parties in conflict to accept a settlement also.

However, such apparently permanent peace-keeping missions as those in Kashmir, Palestine, and the Gaza Strip, and perhaps that in Cyprus, have led many to conclude that such operations themselves "freeze" a conflict situation rather than promote settlement. The charge overlooks the fact that settlement was impossible in the circumstances that originated the peace-keeping intervention. It is more accurate to say, as the Secretary-General has, that there is a tendency for some missions to become "an accepted and semipermanent part of the way of life in [their] areas," thus reducing "the sense of urgency" that might stimulate the parties to seek settlement more seriously.* The charge also overlooks the record of successful peace-keeping missions, in the sense that the political dispute that brought them into being was settled. Such missions have ranged from one-man mediators to the 1,000-man West Irian Security Force. The blame, therefore, belongs in the first place on the governments that fail to carry out their basic obligation under Article 2(3): to settle their disputes "in such a manner that international peace and security and justice are not endangered."

There is no simple answer to improving the settlement record. Where disputes are passionate and deepseated—such as in the ideological aspects of the Cold War, or in the vital conflicts between Arab and Israeli, or between Indian and Pakistani—they tend to be intractable to reasonable persua-

* U.N. Doc. A/6000/Add. 1, *Introduction to the Annual Report of the Secretary-General on the Work of the Organization: 16 June 1964–15 June 1965*, p. 7.

sion. Diplomatic "arm twisting" by stronger powers able to influence less powerful states can sometimes bring about settlement of disputes between the latter. But as long as the level of conflict between the super-powers remains high, it both threatens the peace directly and tends to cancel out their respective abilities to restrain lower-level violence among smaller states or to use their diplomatic influence on behalf of settlement. Even when the Soviet Union and the United States had a common interest in damping down the Indian-Pakistan conflict in 1965, the specter of Communist China in the background—supporting Pakistan and taunting the Soviet Union for betraying the Communist cause—diminished the influence that flowed from the common Soviet-American goal.

Regional security arrangements such as NATO, SEATO, and CENTO, on the other hand, are no more effective in resolving disputes among their members than is the United Nations. For example, the differences among NATO members about Suez, the Congo, and Cyprus were not taken care of through that organization and led, as a result, to major U.N. peace-keeping operations in those areas. The argument sometimes advanced—that it is the purpose of NATO to deter the Soviet threat in Europe, not to resolve such intramural disputes—is accurate enough, but it overlooks the fact that such extra-Communist conflicts involving NATO powers frequently draw the threat, if not the reality, of Soviet intervention. In a world of proliferating atomic weapons, such threats may start the escalation process toward that more direct confrontation the regional security arrangement seeks to prevent. In such situations, peace-keeping operations have played their part in bringing the violence under control, even if the time they gained has not been successfully used to achieve settlement. From the point of view of the United States, as well as of the United Nations, therefore, it is important to maintain the organization's ability to mount such undertakings, despite their weaknesses.

U.N. Efforts and the Great Powers

It should be clear from the above that the circumstances of the current conflict in Viet-Nam rule out effective use of the United Nations in connection with United States' efforts to force Hanoi to the conference table. Yet many Americans, failing to see this, have argued for taking the issue to the U.N. In January, 1966, when it resumed bombing of North Viet-Nam after a 37-day pause, the Johnson Administration evidently sought to satisfy such critics by concurrently asking the Security Council to support a call to Hanoi to agree to "immediate discussions without preconditions" in order to arrange a conference on settlement negotiations.* By then, however, most U.N. members viewed the situation in Viet-Nam as, in reality, a conflict between the United States, Communist China, and the Soviet Union. With Peking excluded from the organization and with Moscow apparently determined neither to support nor to have to veto a call for settlement negotiations, the Council refused to discuss the matter substantively.†

The only way in which the U.N. might be brought into the picture in a peace-keeping capacity, therefore, is for the parties in conflict to agree on a cease fire, which international observers could verify, or on a truce line that they could patrol. (Even in that situation, strengthening of the International Control Commission would seem more likely than a new U.N. mission.)

The United States finds the U.N. reluctant to deal with the

---

* Text of proposed U.S. draft resolution, U.N. Doc. S/7106, January 31, 1966. See Ambassador Goldberg's somewhat different explanation of the Government's move, in *United Nations Financial Situation*, pp. 84–87, 99–101. Hearings before the Subcommittee on International Organizations and Movements, of the House of Representatives Committee on Foreign Affairs, House Report No. 1564 (89th Congress, 2d Session).

† It almost refused to put the item on the agenda, and confined itself thereafter to informal "consultations" by the Council president on the best way to deal with the subject further. It found none, and the Council held no debate on the substance of the U.S. submission.

Viet-Nam issue on Washington's terms, but it is itself reluctant to go along with the desire of the majority of U.N. members to apply stronger sanctions against the white governments in southern Africa. With the advent after 1960 of many new African members in the organization, their main concern to bring all Africa to independence and racial equality was increasingly reflected in General Assembly (and later in Security Council) resolutions to speed self-determination for the Portuguese colonies and South West Africa and to bring an end to apartheid in South Africa. Since neither Portugal nor South Africa had changed their policies in response to the U.N. resolutions, the frustrations of the African members were already great by November, 1965, when the British self-governing colony of Southern Rhodesia unilaterally declared its independence after futile negotiations with London for a formal grant of independence. The crucial difficulty had been Rhodesian refusal to liberalize its white-supremacy political system in favor of the African majority.

Great Britain declared the breakaway Rhodesian government to be in rebellion and instituted economic and financial sanctions against it, optimistically predicting that such action would shortly cause the government's downfall. In the Security Council, however, London opposed African desires for the immediate application of military sanctions, and the Council contented itself with endorsing British efforts at that time.* In April, 1966, with the rebel regime still in power and with a serious leakage in the petroleum embargo threatened by shipments through Mozambique, the Security Council declared that the situation constituted a threat to the peace and called on Great Britain to become, in effect, the "chosen instrument" of the organization to enforce the petroleum ban, by military measures if necessary.†

Aware of the failure of its partial sanctions, the British resumed talks with Rhodesia later in April in search of a

* S/Res. 217 (1965), adopted November 20, 1965.
† S/Res. 221 (1966), adopted April 9, 1966.

peaceful resolution of the dispute. African governments saw this as a betrayal of their interests and insisted on calling for strong military sanctions in another Council meeting. Their draft resolution was defeated, but a British veto would probably have been used had it been necessary to prevent adoption of the resolution.* Neither London nor Washington was ready to use its armed forces to overturn the Rhodesian regime, either directly or through enforcement of a total blockade. The African states did not have the power to do the job themselves. The Soviet Union provided strong political encouragement for the more radical African demands but, whatever its covert assistance, did not offer any large-scale military help.

British and American reluctance to enforce political change applies even more strongly in connection with Portugal and South Africa. Although Washington and London cooperate in the arms embargoes recommended by the United Nations against both states, they do not observe similarly recommended economic boycotts. Earlier doubts about the effectiveness of possible economic sanctions against either country have only been reinforced by the Rhodesian experience.

In the United States, neither Congress nor the public are generally cognizant of the wider issue for American foreign policy, which may be expressed as determining when resistance to change (which is necessary to meet standards favored by overwhelming majorities in the United Nations) constitutes in itself a sufficient threat to the peace to justify enforcement action through the Security Council. Ambassador Goldberg has explained the United States' backing of British policy in Rhodesia in terms of supporting self-determination (as Washington is doing in Viet-Nam) and of curbing potential racial violence in Africa.† The reaction of columnist John

---

* U.N. Doc. S/7285, May 10, 1966. The resolution was defeated by the abstentions of a majority (including Great Britain, the United States, and France), rather than by actual negative votes.

† See, for example, his statement in the Security Council, May 19, 1966, text in U.S. Department of State *Bulletin*, LIV, 1966, 986–91.

Chamberlain, however, is probably more representative of American opinion on the U.N. action:

> It took absolutely no courage [he wrote] . . . for a majority in the U.N. Security Council to endorse British interference with those Greek and Liberian tankers which [were] bent on off-loading oil in Portuguese Mozambique. . . . But when it comes to imposing sanctions on real bullies who have actually broken the peace of the world, the majority that dominates the . . . Council is as yellow as the saffron in a Vietnamese Buddhist monk's robe.*

President Johnson has been unable to persuade some people in the United States that this country should fight to enforce the right of the South Vietnamese to self-government against the threat of Communist rule. He would have an even harder task convincing a large segment of the American public that the country should go to war to enforce the right of black Africans to self-government against the actuality of minority white rule. On the other hand, to insist that threats to the peace are only to be defined in terms of military aggression and foreign-supported guerrilla actions is to ignore certain aspects of the Charter† and of recent United Nations history, as well as to make mockery of many American professions of principle.

As the issue of recognizing resistance to change as a possible threat to the peace becomes more acute, U.N. consensus on the objectives of both enforcement and settlement actions will become more difficult to achieve. Yet such consensus, as experience shows, is essential to effective collective action to maintain the peace. The dilemma will only be exacerbated if

---

* *Washington Post*, April 23, 1966, p. 7. "Opinion," in this context, refers only to the undoubtedly small minority of Americans who are even aware of the Security Council's actions or of U.S. policy in connection with them.

† The domestic-jurisdiction reservation is specifically made inapplicable in cases of enforcement [Article 2(7)]. It was understood at San Francisco that enforcement covered domestic matters that might become sources of international disorder. Ironically, the racial policies of the Nazis were one of the examples in mind, in 1945, as a domestic source of international conflict. See Russell, *A History of the United Nations Charter*, pp. 900–10.

and when the bellicose People's Republic of China is seated in the world organization. If the other members, especially the great powers, are firm in their support of the U.N., however, an obstreperous China need not ruin the organization any more than an obstreperous Soviet Union did in its first years. And if they are not thus firm, it will not be China alone that destroys the institution.

Disarmament

Concepts of the requirements for national security and international peace have been adapted in significant ways to the changing circumstances of the revolutionary post–World War II period. The two oversimplified approaches prevalent in 1945 have given way to far more complex analyses of the problems and of appropriate policy approaches to them. The original conflicting approaches, nonetheless, still exist and are still being simultaneously sought, so far as official policy statements go. Curiously enough, they can perhaps be seen best in the differing interpretations given to the United States plan for general and complete disarmament (GCD).

The political approach espoused by the United Nations in 1945 has developed into a long-term (Stage III) plan: The peace is to be kept in a disarmed world (where national arms beyond those needed for internal security are banned) by an elaborate peace-keeping structure topped by a UN Peace Force, stronger than any national forces that can be mobilized against it. Officially, this is described as "strengthening" the United Nations machinery, although logically (as is usually admitted unofficially) it would mean the development of a world government.

The 1945 military-atomic approach has been elaborated into one that considers the complexities of the nuclear deterrent system and the strategy of conflict, which concerns itself with collateral arms-control measures as one means of stabilizing the dangers of the deterrent system. Officially, Stage III of the GCD plan is described as something possible only in the distant future, although, unofficially, adherents of nuclear deterrence generally admit they see nothing but propaganda value in the formal proposal.

Thus, both approaches reflect a surprising confidence in the ability to achieve international peace by control of the weapons of potential holocaust—one by controlled armament, the other by controlled disarmament (although Thomas Schelling has rightly pointed out that it is hardly accurate to describe the Stage III situation as a "disarmed" world).* While both presume the prevention of general nuclear war, neither would result in the kind of pluralistic world of national states existing in a system of reasonably peaceful international relationships that the Charter anticipates. That is still the system desired, according to United States policy statements, although the strategy of conflict cannot achieve, since it subserves to its own objective of deterrence, the political, economic, psychological, and military resources of the nation. Nor can world government achieve it, since that would require surrender of the national states as the controlling units of power.

There is in logic a third approach, which has never been developed theoretically as have the other two, but which, in its inconsistent way, the very ambivalence of United States policies has most nearly approached. That is, to maintain the strength of the nuclear deterrent against Communist expansionism, while utilizing (to a far greater degree than has been done) the U.N. and other international agencies to alleviate the underlying causes of conflict that, in today's world, threaten to escalate out of control, however small their beginnings. This approach might be said to apply the original concepts behind the Charter to the circumstances of the present. In practice, however, the constructive aspects of that two-fold approach have never been seriously sought on a scale

---

* Thomas Schelling, *Arms and Influence* (New Haven, Conn.: Yale University Press, 1966), p. 251.

even remotely comparable to the effort put behind the actual military approach. "Our guard is up," but our "outstretched hand" has never been equipped with adequate political and economic tools, such as the U.N. system might be capable of providing.

9. The Central Role of the President in the Conduct of Security Affairs

GENERAL OF THE ARMY DWIGHT D. EISENHOWER

In assuring the nation's security, the role of the President is central; it is his highest concern and his primary duty. No other responsibility demands more of his attention and effort, even though many others are of great significance to the nation. The various factors that make up this one preoccupation are so broad in scope and so involved in their complexity that his effort must primarily take the form of directing and guiding the governmental agencies specifically concerned in these affairs and of seeing that they provide him the knowledge, analyses, and advice he needs in making the personal decisions and issuing the necessary basic directives. To do this well, he needs assistance—staffs of intelligent, proficient, and dedicated individuals.

While it is manifestly impossible, because of differences in personality, background, training, and experience, to plan uniformity in the ways which Presidents use their assistants—especially in matters affecting national security—there may be some value in considering one President's experience for the light it can throw on the basic requirements of any.

Consequently, the following must be regarded as more personal than general.

The measures developed to enable the President to fulfill his role should meet the stiffest test. That is, they should safeguard the nation's security at crisis points, or at times of profound change in the international scene. In my Presidency, these included such instances as bringing an end to the war in Korea; adjusting our armed forces at that time to a proper posture of long-term security without pell-mell demobilization; introducing, subsequently, into our defense machinery thermonuclear weapons and guided missiles—not to mention earth satellites; assuring the safety, in the face of constant Red Chinese threats, of Formosa and the off-shore islands; aiding in the growth of friendly underdeveloped countries during the same years; and taking countermeasures against the emergence of difficulties in Southeast Asia and Cuba from 1959 onward. Such problems as these were of the first rank in considering the security of the United States and in the hope of achieving a world order based on peace and mutual respect among nations.

Though a President might be a student of Clausewitz, Jomini, von Moltke, and other military writers, and though his understanding of war's basic nature might be clear, yet situations of actual or probable conflict change so rapidly and the weaponry of modern military establishments increase their destructiveness at such a bewildering speed that he will always need the vital studies, advice, and counsel that only a capable and well-developed staff organization can give him.

The Joint Chiefs of Staff

These observations about the importance of assistance in security matters lead me to a special word concerning the President's use of his Joint Chiefs. Here again, I return to personal experience. By and large, the Joint Chiefs of Staff are not only the President's advisers on military matters, but they are part of the chain of command through which he controls "military operations," especially over the "Unified Commands." The Joint Chiefs of Staff stand at the apex of purely military responsibility. I have known, rather intimately, the successive members of the Joint Chiefs from 1942 to 1965. They have been among the best and finest officers I have met in the United States or any other country. They invariably provide a central core of responsible advice on basic strategy and strength; and theirs is unquestionably the most competent, dedicated, and disinterested counsel on military matters available to the President. Accordingly, their advice should never be lightly disregarded, even though it will frequently not be unanimous on details of forces and their application.

The relationship between the President and the Joint Chiefs of Staff must be close and direct, even though, in the normal case, the President will not be experienced in military matters. No intermediate authority or individual should ever have the right to dilute, to change, or to edit the opinions of the Joint Chiefs of Staff, when these are desired by the President.

In approaching the entire national security problem, the President must necessarily coordinate requirements for purely military strength or action with the over-all strength of the country, which he must preserve unimpaired. In this concern, he goes beyond the Joint Chiefs. He not only depends on the Secretary of Defense, but also on all other officials concerned. In my Administration, these matters were almost invariably brought before the National Security Council.

Economic Considerations

Economic strength is a basic requirement for successful military operations—both in peace and war. This must be a fundamental concern of the President. Pre-war Japan is a good example of the potential danger of violating economic requirements. In the interwar period, it began feverishly to expand its military forces. At the same time, the Japanese war lords were spending so heavily and consuming vital materials so rapidly that they were plunging their country into acute economic difficulty. I have always believed that one of the reasons for the timing of their attack at Pearl Harbor was the knowledge that their economy could no longer meet their current demands without admitting bankruptcy before the world. They therefore had to attack promptly, to use what they then had, and to try, with the aid of surprise, to defeat America. From their standpoint and under the conditions of the moment, that military decision was probably the best one available to them—that is, to strive with the initial blow so to cripple their enemy that they could thereafter sustain and solidify their position. They miscalculated. They should have known that, in a long war, against a resolute and aroused United States, they would not be able to support the kind and scale of military organization they required. It was too much for the economy of their empire.

Our own experience in World War II emphasizes the importance of economic considerations and shows what can be done to keep the economy going well and national morale sustained at a high pitch in the event of a prolonged war. We started World War II with little in military strength. Since we lost a large part of our fleet at Pearl Harbor and were sadly unprepared otherwise, the marvel of the war was that the nation's morale and production were equal to the task—in two simultaneous war theaters and while providing mountainous supplies to the Soviets—of mounting the tremendous attacks that did so much to bring the military power of the Axis nations to final destruction.

In the postwar world, we cannot count on time for producing the machinery necessary for victory after sustaining a serious surprise attack, but must maintain a high degree of readiness. Accordingly, following the armistice in Korea we decided to avoid the traditional postwar disintegration of security forces, and instituted the concept of a military establishment designed and supported for the long pull. One result of this shift of approach was to engage the President, continuously and directly, in the security decisions required in a dangerous nuclear-armed world.

Foreign Relations

Moreover, because security must, for the free world, be a collective as well as an individual nation's effort, the President's conduct of foreign relations inevitably involves security matters. Because dealings with other nations are part of the shifting security mosaic, the President must work intimately and continuously with his Secretary of State to assess events and policies abroad and to give the direction that assures that our security policies will serve the higher national purpose.

We know from experience that the more complex and broad in scope the responsibilities of an individual, the more capable—and often larger—must be his supporting organization. A partial analogy may be helpful in visualizing the Commander-in-Chief's need for organizational support. Numbers of Americans have some knowledge of a theater headquarters in a war situation. The functions of the Supreme Commander in any theater involve the use of conventional general and special staffs, as well as various special groups for the administration of conquered areas and sometimes for necessary supply to civilian populations. Theater commanders in World War II had hundreds of officers on their staffs, all of whom had just one responsibility—that of giving to their Commander-in-Chief the knowledge and conclusions on which to make proper decisions. The staff then had to broaden the Commander-in-Chief's decisions into plans and see that the plans were executed by all concerned in a coordinated fashion.

In speaking of assistance for the theater commander in the field, I am not referring to the old-time Council of War; as far as I know, none of these has been held in the American Army since the Civil War. (A well-known example occurred at the Battle of Gettysburg, when the Union Corps Commanders were asked for their votes as to whether the Union forces should stay in position or retire.) I am referring, rather, to informed and well-considered counsel by responsible staff subordinates working, in the aggregate, across the entire span of their commander's responsibilities.

A President needs this kind of organized advice far more than a wartime theater commander. Beyond indispensable military counsel, he needs also the political opinions of his Secretary of State and factual information from such specialists as the Chairman of the Atomic Energy Commission, the Director of the United States Information Agency, and the Director of the Central Intelligence Agency. Remembering that the security of the United States is, in the long run, not merely a matter of military power in being, but rather the product of the over-all moral, economic, political, and military strength of the nation, he must also have among his advisers, for example, the Secretary of the Treasury, the Director of the Budget, and others.

However, the President himself can by no means give his attention solely to problems of defense. Other duties make their demands. He is the ceremonial head of the nation. He is responsible for the execution of the laws, whether they require such dramatic action as was taken in Little Rock in 1957, or any other. He must guide and shape the domestic legislative program. He is head of a political party, and is largely responsible for national morale in times of crisis.

In most instances, conflicting considerations arise from these multiple responsibilities. When the Korean Armistice was signed only a few months after I entered the Presidency, I was urgently advised that the military budget be promptly reduced to what was called "peace-time" proportions. One prominent senator, anticipating the war's end, argued long and bitterly for an immediate cutback in military costs of 60 to 70 per cent. He believed that the economy demanded such a cut and predicted that if this was not accomplished at once the Republicans would be repudiated in the 1954 elections. On the other hand, I believed that America had paid a terrible price for its traditional unpreparedness. Even the cause of the Korean War was to be found, I thought, in our inexcusable weakness.

So it was determined that, for the first time in its history, the United States should be adequately prepared for battle, and if this caused difficulties in the economy and reacted adversely on Republican fortunes, we would, nevertheless, have to pay the price. I did strive, of course, to gain public approval for this national about-face, but there was no concealing the rift in governmental thinking caused thereby.

National Security Council

With all these domestic as well as national security responsibilities to carry on simultaneously, it is of overriding importance to conserve the President's time. All of the supporting organizations he sets up must make their contribution in this regard.

This means that the advice reaching him must be of the highest quality. It is by no means sufficient merely to place before him, periodically, a mass of undigested information and the unilateral opinions of various assistants. All information should be as complete as possible and should be organized, analyzed, and carefully examined by experts. This should be accomplished by preliminary joint staff study to make certain that no significant item of intelligence is overlooked. The presentation of all this in orderly and succinct fashion to the President is, in itself, the result of good planning. Thereafter, conflicting conclusions among principal subordinates must be debated, never concealed.

All this means that staff assistance must be carefully organized. This was accomplished in the 1950's through the National Security Council and its supporting bodies.

Organization cannot make a genius out of a dunce; neither can it make decisions for its head. The Executive Department is not a legislature or a committee thereof. It is one man— with properly organized subordinates. Important national decisions must be made by the head; any attempt to use a voting system would be futile because a single man, the head, carries all the responsibility. Reliance on unanimity would bring inaction, futility, and frustration. Indeed, in devising a national security policy and program it is rare to find those who spend the money and those who provide it in the same camp. If the Secretary of Defense and the Secretary of the Treasury are strong-minded men, there constantly arises a need for Presidential decisions, based on his higher view and wider range of responsibility. This difference in viewpoint was invariably brought to the fore in my Presidency, particularly when the annual Mutual Security Bill came up for discussion. To the Treasury Department, these programs were "giveaway"; to the State and Defense departments, they were essential components of our national security policies.

In the National Security Council meetings during my Presidency, there would normally be present the Vice President, the Secretary of State, the Secretary of the Treasury, the Secretary of Defense, the Attorney General, the Budget Director, the head of Civil Defense, the Chairman of the Joint Chiefs of Staff, the Director of Central Intelligence, and others with specialized knowledge concerning the subject under study. My Special Assistant for National Security Affairs represented the Planning Board, which, as a subordinate of the Council, had already examined the problem exhaustively. Whether the problem was a long-range American policy concerning Central America or a matter for more immediate decision, such as going to the assistance of Lebanon or defending Quemoy and Matsu—all factors were dealt with through full debate.

The National Security Council was not expected, of course, to make decisions; a vote was never taken among its members. Even during those periods when illness or other causes prevented my presence in a meeting, its conclusions were invariably brought to me for final action. Its functions were to debate and discuss. It comprised strong men charged with important responsibilities; opposing views were expressed forthrightly and with the confidence that they would be weighed dispassionately. Afterward, whether the problem was one of long-term policy or an emergency situation, timely decisions had to be forthcoming.

With the National Security Council serving in this way, a President is never surprised; he is always ready to do his part. To my mind the secret of a sound, satisfactory decision made on an emergency basis has always been that the responsible official has been "living with the problem" before it becomes acute. Failure to use, on a continuing basis, the National Security Council, or some similar advisory body, entails losing the capacity to make emergency decisions based on depth of understanding and perspective—that is, on a clear comprehension of the issues involved, the risks, the advantages to be gained, and the effects of this particular action on the abiding and diverse security interests of the United States.

I remember several times when, after having such problems presented to me, I preferred to take a different course than that almost unanimously proposed. Sometimes the matter under discussion was one in which my own experience had a bearing, or in which I felt I was able to take a broader view than that suggested. One example of this took place early in my first administration. It involved the basic character of our future defense establishment—a transformation that came to be called the "New Look." Essentially, it was a decision to avoid primary dependence on numerical strength of military forces, as in the past, and to turn more to the sophisticated weapons then emerging—missiles, high performance planes, nuclear weapons, and various other scientifically advanced systems—as the basis of military organization and planning. Many of my advisers were fearful of such a solution, but the determining factors for me were two: the deterrent effect of such a system and the knowledge that a free country could not always be fully mobilized.

Even in this kind of case, when their advice is overruled, I believe that subordinates act most effectively and confidently when they are free to express their views face-to-face with the President and know that he has not missed implications they consider important. At the very least, this kind of discussion never failed to give me a deeper understanding of questions. In several instances, I might add, such deliberations persuaded me to reverse some of my preconceived notions. As early as 1954, for example, I had concluded that the American contingent in NATO should immediately be substantially reduced. After long discussions with the State and Defense departments and the CIA, however, I had to change my mind.

Though the methods used by a President are personal and responsibility for basic decision rests on him individually, it is clear that any President needs an intelligently conceived organization to assist him. Badly informed critics, however, sometimes argue that an organized advisory staff tends to insulate the leader from his subordinates and from real knowledge of his problems. This is exactly contrary to the truth. Among the statements attributed to Napoleon (and every soldier seemingly likes to call upon Napoleon as his own authority for a belief) is one that I particularly like: "The genius in war is the man that does a sensible thing when everybody around him is going somewhat crazy." The capacity to be sensible on a continuing basis and across a wide spectrum of problems involves self-preparation, including constant access to sound information and continuous study.

Good organization helps the President to do the sensible things. If the resulting action is lacking in sensationalism or contrived drama, it is also more likely to lead to success, and success is the only objective of war—just as it is of proper readiness and deterrence of war at the least over-all cost to the nation. Thus, costly or dangerous adventures, damaging reversals, or catastrophe will be avoided. A President cannot make mistakes and throw the blame on others. Where he stands, at the summit of responsibility, the thinking through of vital factors becomes essential. He must have the organization to help him with this task.

The complexity and importance of the issues with which the President must deal emphasize the necessity for coordination, not only in policy making but also in policy implementation. On one occasion, I recall, the Secretary of Agriculture saw an opportunity to reduce the amount of wheat in our surplus and at the same time to render assistance to a needy nation, India. He took the matter up with an official in the State Department who, seeing no implications other than that this would be a helpful action, agreed that we should send a million tons of wheat to India. The result was that the Prime Minister of Burma, when visiting me later in Washington remarked, "Mr. President, we are Buddhists and, therefore, we do not complain about things; but you have just ruined our rice sales to India. We would like to know what you are going to do to give us some relief in this situation."

We had failed to make sure of coordination in implementation. We developed a staff to help in this matter, the Operations Coordinating Board, and in the course of time made much improvement in this necessary function—traditionally a weak area in the government.

Mobilizing National Support

Turning to the future, several additional points deserve special mention. The first of these is the necessity for the President to give continuing attention to national morale. In part this is because he is not only the Commander-in-Chief, but also a politician. Even more important, he knows that if our country is to be counted upon in international affairs, he must have strong public support. His task is not to seek public favor or to follow public opinion; rather, it is to give the nation a clear understanding of the particular foreign problems confronting it, so that the people as a whole will support his decisions. In an increasingly complicated world, this is an increasingly difficult task. One of the important reasons for using an advisory body of the stature of the National Security Council is the fact that the public, knowing the quality of the advice, will be apt to develop a strong feeling of confidence in the adequacy of the nation's security.

To illustrate a President's proper concern about opinion and morale, we need only look at some of the protests over American policy in Viet-Nam. Some people, either through misguided conviction or deliberate intent, oppose the President in carrying out his constitutional duty of conducting the foreign relations of the United States. While I believe that every citizen has the right to communicate his views on such matters to the President, publicly opposing him in critical situations of this kind presents to the world a picture of a divided America. Long-range policy and the history of past operations in foreign relations are always, in my opinion, proper subjects for open and free debate, but I, for one, will never publicly oppose or criticize my Commander-in-Chief while we are in a state of crisis.

We have seen uselessly publicized riots in universities by exhibitionists voicing catcalls of "Get out of Viet-Nam." Such events are not important so long as they are mere incidents created by immature individuals; but, if they were to become widespread, they could damage the best interests of the United States. One of the heavy burdens resting on the President is to find ways to make certain that the requirements for the nation's security are met without damage to the country's morale. When the country's security is involved, he deserves the assistance of the nation's publicity media.

A second point that deserves special attention in the future is the question of how extensive and detailed a role the President should personally play in the planning and executing of national security policies. Revolutionary developments in communications have made it possible for the President to be involved in security problems in an intimate way and on an everyday basis, but there is a line he should not overstep. To succeed in his monumental tasks, the President must, like any other commander or high executive, determine the character of the decisions reserved to him and the kind of information and help he needs or wants. Any President who might be tempted to involve himself too deeply in the details that seem constantly to force themselves on his attention—details that should best be left to a proper subordinate—would find it difficult to absorb the basic information and understanding that he must have in order to solve the great and central security problem: "How to keep the military, moral, and economic strength of the nation adequate at all times—in times of peace to be satisfactorily prepared and in time of war, if we should again meet such a tragedy, to deal with it."

This necessity of every superior doing his own job and insisting that every subordinate do his will constantly increase in importance. "Centralization," it has been said, "is the refuge of fear"—a statement I think is largely true. General George Marshall, who in many ways was the outstanding soldier this country has produced, believed and practiced this doctrine. Once I heard him say, "I have dozens of able officers who bring to me brilliantly analyzed problems, but who almost invariably want me to solve them. From them I need answers for their problems, not questions."

If this were true in his case, how much more true it will be in the future! Men will have to reach solutions in a matter of minutes, if not seconds, rather than in hours and days. Each direct subordinate of the Commander-in-Chief must be carefully selected, as far as possible tested, and then trusted.

The President's desk is the place where all important controversial questions finally meet. They must leave his desk as a single answer, in a form that can be easily understood, to be implemented by the responsible agencies. Regardless of organizational forms or mechanisms for insuring thorough analysis and appropriate recommendations and for overseeing coordinated implementation, close and cheerful cooperation among subordinates is essential. Efficiency can be helped by sound organization; but in its highest form it must also have the cooperation of men animated by a loyalty to their common chief. He must inspire such a loyalty. The more difficult and intricate the problem and the more demanding the conditions of work, the more necessary it is that the chief be their true leader, not merely their commander. In such a staff, differences are always objective and official, never personal.

As long as future Presidents have the judgment to select and support able assistants, the ability to organize and the wisdom to sort out common-sense solutions to problems on which their advisers will be legion, and the moral courage to make timely and clear decisions and stand by them in spite of criticism or persuasion, then our treasured system of self-government will never be lost or seriously threatened.

10. The Role of the Joint Chiefs of Staff in the National Security Structure*

LIEUTENANT GENERAL
ANDREW J. GOODPASTER

In examining the role of the Joint Chiefs of Staff in the national security structure, it is useful to focus upon national security policy, giving "policy" a good deal of operational depth. Policy is best thought of as guiding plans, preparations, deployments, operations, and actions of all kinds. With such reach and depth, the structure of policy extends, like a vast military iceberg, far beyond the surface layers that often tend to catch the eye. General Marshall's reminder that "man is made for action," cautions us that the work of the Joint Chiefs of Staff should always be measured in terms of the actions in which it finally results.

The role of the Joint Chiefs—what it is and what it should be—has two principal aspects, one downward and inward, the other upward and outward. In the first respect, the Joint Chiefs deliberate and debate as a corporate body to formulate their views and seek consensus; they employ and direct a capable professional staff of high capacity, the Joint Staff; they direct the unified and specified commands; and they supervise major defense agencies in the fields of intelligence,

* The views expressed in this essay are the author's own and do not necessarily represent those of the United States Government.

communication, and atomic activities. The outward and upward, or external, aspect of the role of the Joint Chiefs
responds to their designation as the chief military advisers to
the President, the National Security Council, and the Secretary of Defense. Looking further outward, they have a responsibility to the Congress and to the public, but these elements
of their role lie largely beyond the scope of the present
discussion. While the internal and external aspects may be
considered separately for purposes of analysis, they in fact
exist in intimate combination, and must of course be so
understood.

The Background

Historically, it could be argued that, to a degree—though only
to a moderate degree—the institution of the Joint Chiefs, like
the British Empire, was formed in a fit of absent-mindedness.
The first step was the constitution of the Joint Board in 1903,
with Army-Navy membership. That body had a very limited
role, concentrating on amphibious doctrine and joint plans of
a rather formalized kind, but giving little guidance or advice on
current security problems.

Three principal changes can be identified since that time.
The first change was from static planning to what may be
termed the dynamic direction of war, which became a major
role of the Joint Chiefs of Staff in World War II. The
wartime Joint Chiefs of Staff organization was formed almost
as a by-product of the creation of the Combined Chiefs of
Staff (the U.S. and British chiefs of staff working together) in
January, 1942. It is ruefully recalled by Americans that the
British came to the Arcadia Conference—a series of military
and political consultations held in Washington from December, 1941 (after Pearl Harbor), to January, 1942—prepared
with proposals, the well-reasoned and well-presented product
of prior work by their Chiefs of Staff Committee, to introduce
into the deliberations. They and their supporting staff, in the

words of American participants, "ran rings around us" in the caliber of the papers they had prepared, and in the depth and scope of the analyses they brought to the conference. As a result, the U.S. Chiefs decided that they must organize their own activity and its supporting structure more effectively. One story has it that they were spurred on by President Roosevelt, who was aware of the American disadvantage. In any case, the Chiefs quickly absorbed and vastly extended the functions of the old Joint Board. They undertook an increased role in the higher direction of the war, coordinating the operations of the Army, the Navy, and the Army Air Corps, and reporting directly on such matters to the President. They advised him regarding military strategy, military relations with our allies, the allocation of munitions and shipping, requirements of all kinds—including the manpower needs of the armed forces—and matters of joint Army-Navy policy.

As today, a flood of specific actions, decisions, and requests for recommendations in all these areas came to them. President Roosevelt thought it better not to attempt to formalize their activity, but to let them organize and operate as the war's needs dictated. Accordingly, they operated throughout the war without a formally approved directive or charter. As for organization, the Chiefs themselves were supported by a Joint Secretariat and a wide range of full-time or part-time standing committees—the Joint Staff planners, the Joint Intelligence Committee, and the Joint Logistics Committee being of key importance. These key groups were in turn assisted by two Plans Committees (War Plans and Logistic Plans) and by other committees in specific functional or technical fields.

Following the war, a second major change occurred. The National Security Act of 1947 formalized their status providing legislative underpinning for their continued operation. They were given a full-time Joint Staff. The National Security Council was formed, and the Chiefs were made advisers to it. The Act also created the office of Secretary of Defense, with general directive authority over what was designated the National Military Establishment. It is significant that, in the early years, reductions of the military budget and defense of these reductions against attack were perhaps the primary preoccupation of the Secretary of Defense and the office he established.

In 1949 and again in 1953, steps were taken by legislation and by executive order, which strengthened unification and furthered the trend toward integration, while making clear that the military departments or services were not to be fully merged. Along with these measures, however, came trends and actions that somewhat weakened and detracted from the role of the Chiefs as a body. For instance, despite statutory limitations on the role and authority of the Chairman (i.e., "he shall have no vote"), influence in high policy circles in many matters came to him at the expense of the Joint Chiefs of Staff as a body, and particularly at the expense of the service Chiefs as members. An action that made the military departments (that is to say, the Secretaries of the Army, Navy, and Air Force) the "Executive Agents" for the Joint Chiefs of Staff introduced an anomaly that fragmented and diluted the control of the Joint Chiefs of Staff over field operations and circumscribed the degree of unity of planning, of concept, and of operations that could be attained. The fact that the Chief of Naval Operations, the Chief of Staff of the Air Force, and the Commandant of the Marine Corps by statute exercised command functions contributed to this situation. (Although the Chief of Staff of the Army did not have command, his power of direction closely approximated that of his colleagues.)

Perhaps the most important of the unifying steps took place in 1958. This third major change could be termed a shift from partial to full unification. By legislation passed after sharp debate, the role of the Joint Chiefs of Staff was strengthened and the position of the Secretary of Defense clarified. (Such was the intent; in practice, it might be more accurate, as indicated below, to say that the role of the Joint Chiefs was clarified and that of the Secretary was strengthened.) The Chairman of the Joint Chiefs of Staff was given added authority for the management of the Joint Staff. The Joint Staff itself was authorized to be an operational staff, with typical staff divisions (Personnel, Intelligence, Operations, Logistics, Plans and Policy, and Communications), although it was specifically enjoined not to constitute an Armed Forces General Staff. Legal status was given to the unified and specified commands, and their commanders were given increased, more clear-cut command authority. Command authority was removed from the Chiefs who had it—the Chief of Naval Operations, the Chief of Staff of the Air Force, and the Commandant of the Marine Corps. It is probably of major significance to the subsequent role and problems of the Joint Chiefs of Staff that command authority was not vested in them as a body.

President Eisenhower's Special Message recommending these 1958 legislative changes to the Congress recognized that "separate ground, sea, and air warfare is gone forever." He continued:

> If ever again we should be involved in war, we will fight it in all elements with all Services as one single concentrated effort. Peacetime preparatory and organizational activity must conform to this fact. Strategic and tactical planning must be completely unified, combat forces organized into unified commands, each equipped with the most efficient weapons systems that science can develop, singly led and prepared to fight as one, regardless of service.*

The Act of 1958, in clarifying the authority of the Secretary of Defense, has had a result not anticipated or consciously intended, by those who participated in its formulation. With

---

* Dwight D. Eisenhower, "Message to Congress on Defense Reorganization," April 3, 1958, U.S. Congress, House: Communication from the President, Department of Defense Reorganization Bill of 1958. Document No. 371, 85th Cong. 2d Sess. (Washington, D.C.: GPO, 1958).

regard to operational planning and the military and tactical advice that is offered to decision makers, the intent of the legislation was to concentrate responsibility in the Joint Chiefs of Staff, thus ending the situation in which the individual services, acting separately, extended operational influence over field commands. The Secretary of Defense and his immediate office would exert policy direction and control. But in the application of the Act, a further shift has occurred, resulting in a more detailed treatment of a wider range of matters at the civilian level of the Office of the Secretary of Defense than was then foreseen. In addition to bringing to bear budgetary and foreign policy factors, this higher echelon also accomplishes detailed staff work on operational matters—such as the field operations of military forces (for example, in the Cuban crisis, in the Dominican Republic, and in Viet-Nam), the comparison of alternative weapon systems, tactical nuclear planning, military requirements for new weapons, and the use of a new missile such as the PERSHING. Many factors have contributed to this shift—the introduction of more rapid, high-volume communications and data-display systems, the development of new managerial techniques, and, out of concern over nuclear weapons and the dangers of escalation, an urge to exercise control in finer detail. Nevertheless, where the act visualized fixing the responsibility for military operational matters in the Joint Chiefs of Staff and assigning the conduct of combat operations to the unified commands, there has evolved in practice a sharing of the Joint Chiefs of Staff role and a retention of operational decision on a more centralized basis at the Secretary of Defense level of control than was anticipated in 1958.

The Environment

The national security environment within which this evolving organization has operated has itself been marked by ceaseless change in detail, though the major underlying characteristics have been consistent. While the details generally involve classi-fied matters, certain of the broad characteristics may be freely discussed. At least four broad characteristics of this national security environment condition the role of the Joint Chiefs of Staff: the importance, the dynamism, the complexity, and the political framework of national security affairs. A few words on each characteristic may give helpful perspective on the Joint Chiefs' role.

The first and overriding characteristic of national security affairs is their importance; in matters of security, the stakes are high. They concern the continued existence of the United States as a free nation, with free institutions. What is really involved is self-preservation, the first law of life. In this sense—and to this degree—military and security needs take priority over almost all other considerations. While these are not of themselves primary goals of a national society—as are the freedom and self-government, and the education, health, economic well-being, and the cultural and moral advance-ment of its people—without the protective shield of the power and readiness to defend ourselves, it is not likely that these others could be attained. Nor could we expect a world order favorable to such positive ends to be long preserved.

The quality of military leadership, adequacy of defense programs, readiness of forces, arrangements for command and control, and restrictions on the development and application of our forces (such as in the test-ban treaty) are all matters of the greatest sensitivity and importance. It is perhaps espe-cially appropriate to cite as authority an economist of the standing of Adam Smith, who tells us, in Book IV of *The Wealth of Nations*, on this point, that "defense is of much more importance than opulence." The magnitude of the stakes is also reflected in budgets of $50 billion a year for defense and in the 3 million men in uniform.

A second characteristic of national security affairs is that they take place in a dynamic environment and as a dynamic process. The principal changes are those arising from shifting international power relationships, from technology, from the creation of new nations, from the accession of new leaders in the major nations of the world, and from the initiation of new quarrels or the flare-up of old ones. There is truly no stopping place, nor any way to "hold everything"—frequently not even a pause to catch our breath. The world will not stop, and we cannot get off.

This dynamic process is marked by a constant conflict between the broad and the specific in our policy decisions. Shall our approach emphasize the formation of broad policy guidelines, or shall we concentrate on specific solutions to specific problems? Obviously, we must give attention to each, but the weighting is important. Broad policies have greater durability, but specific decisions give a tighter grip on day-to-day action. General principles, if they do not decide specific cases, certainly help to do so. There is a need for broad policies to give coherence and reach to our operations and to save us from the tendency toward weathervaning or "making policy off the cables." On the other hand, the pressures are heavy upon every administration, every national leader, to try to make a good showing on specific problems of the day as they arise, in order to project an image of leadership and to hold the focus of political power. The Joint Chiefs of Staff, like their superiors, must combine the search for broad policies, long in duration but loose in grip, with a fast-reacting concentration on the specific, hard issues that flow to them in an unending stream.

The national security environment is also a complex one, in which relationships are intricate, often unstable. Below the President, participation is widely diversified into strongholds vested with particular interests, values, and responsibilities. Viewing security problems from the White House, one has the ineluctable impression that only on the President's desk does everything come together. The big issues affecting national security arise, in particular, between the departments of Defense and State. Not only in dealing with security problems, but also in framing them, the military and the diplomatic approaches are inherently different. Still, it remains necessary to draw them into some coherent combination. There is nothing diplomatic about a machine gun, nor can an *aide mémoire* of itself stop subversive infiltration and terror; yet, in the modern world it is clear that both must be employed in some higher security context if security and safety are to be served. A diplomat's calling—reinforced by his training and his set of mind—leads him toward restraint in the exercise of force. He seeks to read the fine nuances of exchanges between nations, but such concern with signaling, once shooting starts, can impinge upon the effectiveness of military operations.

The interest of the State Department is to limit the scale and extent of violence, while that of the professional military man, once higher authority has decided to resort to force, is to seize and hold the initiative and to gain quick preponderance over the adversary, employing force decisively and aggressively to accomplish the mission with minimum loss of life and minimum risk to the United States. Paradoxically, however, the military often display a greater reluctance to threaten or to initiate the use of force than do their civilian colleagues— or at least the military often have a greater tendency to reserve the resort to force or the extension of guarantees that could involve force to matters more directly and vitally affecting the security of the nation.

Issues of this kind come to the desk of the President because easier problems are solved elsewhere—typically, by direct agreement at the departmental level, often monitored by a member of the President's staff. It is important that processes should exist by which those who hold major responsibility can bring their views effectively and responsibly to bear. The more mature and reliable the process, the higher the level of mutual confidence and restraint and the less the tendency to internecine warfare, bureaucratic fast practice, one-sided actions, and other unproductive enterprises that leave confusion and erratic action in their trail and that are of no assistance to the President in his search for a common security policy and effective lines of action. There is, on these grounds, a clear and continuing need for an established voice and role for the Joint Chiefs of Staff, with opportunity for mature deliberation within their own council and in higher councils of the government.

The final characteristic of the national security environment is the fundamental fact that the conduct of policy and action occurs within an over-all political framework. The framework is political both internationally and domestically. Internationally, it is evident that considerations of security guide both the foreign policy activities of peace and the warfare that continues foreign policy by other means. Domestically, those who hold high office are bound to weigh the impact of their policies, decisions, and actions on the American people and on their ability to muster public and Congressional support. There is nothing unworthy in itself about placing tight budgetary pressure on defense programs and operations—even though a favorite bit of Americana may pretend the opposite. It would be derelict to do otherwise. What is required is frank recognition of the interaction and importance of the financial *and* the military, avoiding alike the pretense that economic, financial, and budgetary pressures do not operate, and the denial of a military need in order to avoid its budgetary impact. President Eisenhower always regarded the Joint Chiefs of Staff as the "hinge" between the military establishment and higher civil authority. In the current idiom, they operate at the "interface" between a hierarchical military structure and the higher political stratum. The need for them to interpret the actions and needs of each to the other is obvious, as is the need for them to provide a link that channels responsiveness and valid professional advice from below and decisions that are clear and timely, as well as support (budgetary and otherwise) that is commensurate with national security requirements from above.

Professionalism

Underlying the role of the Joint Chiefs of Staff is the two-fold belief that the professional military can give the best military advice to higher authorities and provide the best planning and operational direction of unified military forces, and that the professional heads of the separate services, meeting together as a corporate body, comprise the best military source for this purpose. The first may seem self-evident, the second nearly so. But we should not be misled. There are important and difficult questions connected with each of them. For tests of their validity, and to emphasize the extent to which they are borne out in reality, it is necessary to examine the quality of the product the Joint Chiefs of Staff can provide, and the extent of acceptance of that product. In practice, these tests determine the role-in-fact of the Joint Chiefs of Staff. A few observations on each are in order.

For the capability—i.e., the "product"—of the Joint Chiefs of Staff to be of high quality, the Chiefs must lift themselves above pure service interests. A raw clash of service interests and narrow rivalry does not give rise to the best product from the standpoint of national security. To the extent that the Chiefs are unable to overcome the ever-present pull toward this kind of factionalism, the role of providing military advice, planning, and direction will tend to shift from them to others. Some of the changes introduced by the Act of 1958 clearly reflected a dissatisfaction at the higher levels of the government with the form and degree of service rivalry then manifest. The act took steps to eliminate such sterile rivalry. It created a chairman, with statutory powers, and emphasized corporate responsibility. It strengthened the role of the Vice-Chief in each service, to enable him to shoulder a larger part of the burden of service operations, thus clearing the agenda of the Chief and allowing him to spend more time on his corporate responsibility.

One of the results of vesting the civilian Secretary of Defense with unquestioned authority has been to assure that decisions can be made more readily in case the Chiefs are unable to reach agreement. In this connection, the Chairman has been given the statutory power to take disagreements to the Secretary of Defense in order to obtain decisions. Consequently, the Chiefs and the issues are no longer stymied or stultified by such disagreement.

The professional heads, the service Chiefs, are preeminent in their military qualifications. They provide responsibility; they know the feasibility and practicality of operations; they have the factual information; they are involved in the day-to-day activities of their services. At the same time, however, service outlook and service problems bear strongly upon them. The result of this interplay is highly dependent on the scope of these individuals' vision and on their urge to find and take constructive action. When they are successful, no other person or group can match them in depth and soundness of professional advice and action.

It seems inarguable that solutions to national security problems should reflect the military factors involved in them. If they do not, the odds are high that we will find ourselves in trouble—involved in problems of overcommitment, mistakes in timing, missed opportunities, and lack of orientation and objective in action and decision. The inevitable cost will be greater loss of life and greater risk of failure. The Chiefs should express these military factors; professional military men should enunciate them. To the old aphorism that "war is too important for generals" can be added that it is also too difficult for amateurs.

There is room for contributions to security policy from both the military and the civilian. The interface, however, is not only a hard one to delineate, it is also bound to be unstable as a result of changing, ever-present pressures from both sides. There is strength in a degree of instability of this kind, however, since it means that old policies and old methods are frequently challenged and re-examined in the light of new facts, new methods of analysis, new or wider application of computer techniques, and the like. This process, if kept within the bounds of constructive competition of insight and ideas and away from the slippery slope of mutual frustration, disparagement, and mistrust, can give vitality and fresh insights to the system.

These considerations suggest, then, that the proper contribution of the Joint Chiefs of Staff in national security affairs should be the maximum of which they are capable, determined on the standard of how the nation's security needs will best be served. Although this principle seems almost self-evident, it is remarkably difficult to apply in practice.

An organizational device that has been used to this end is to maintain the Joint Chiefs of Staff as a kind of "indigestible lump" in the defense structure. The organization chart shows that the Joint Chiefs of Staff with their supporting organization are maintained as a distinct entity that has not been homogenized, so to speak, into the over-all structure of the Office of the Secretary of Defense. This arrangement was considered with great thoroughness, and some intensity, in 1958. It was recognized then (as it is still) that certain values and certain problems attend this solution. Its proponents cited the need to protect the integrity of military advice and planning. They argued that military needs to carry out security objectives should be reported directly—without dilution or suppression through premature cuts by anonymous budgeteers or others—to the Secretary of Defense, the National Security Council, and the President. Its opponents argued that it would tend to perpetuate and continually to intensify what was noted as an attitude approaching hostility between the civilian echelon subordinate to the Secretary of Defense and the military organization of the Joint Chiefs of Staff. The manner of exercising the budget and comptroller functions in the Office of the Secretary of Defense, particularly in the late 1940's, had established an attitude of mistrust.

The military felt that statements of the budget-reducers had been invalid and incorrect to the point of lacking integrity, and that cuts harmful to national security were being made by anonymous men who did not take responsibility for the results of their actions. Leaks to the press denigrating military men worsened the relationship. The sight of a burgeoning civilian bureaucracy moving into functions with high professional military content gave added concern.

The civilians, on their side, felt that military men were more interested in self-seeking for their services, whether through attacking another service or joining in mutual log-rolling, than in getting the best defense for the funds provided or in tackling problems in a unified way. Leaks to the press from military sources were being used to support the special pleas of an interested service or to undercut the efforts of the Secretary of Defense. Moreover, the civilians regarded as job jealousy the resistance by the military to the extension of the civilian echelon into a wider range of defense functions.

Although some of the same charges, considerably muted, were still heard in 1958, concern over maintaining the integrity of military advice and planning carried the day; the separate arrangement was continued, but with the recognition that it imposed a special need for leadership at top civilian and military levels to keep mutual mistrust and hostility under control.

On cooler reflection, some would feel today that there is, in fact, a touch of inspiration in having a recognized entity thus identified with the basic function of combat which, as a capability for purposes of deterrence and as an engine of destruction in case of actual conflict, is the *raison d'être* of the whole defense establishment. This mode of organization simply recognizes the priority given by Adam Smith to defense over opulence. It recognizes the priority of security considerations—in their starkest terms, self-preservation—and is a special effort to make it unlikely that these security considerations will be silenced despite a big and complex

organization or that the needs of defense will be left un-
voiced.

In rebuttal, others argue that military men, when asked for
advice, have some tendency to exaggerate the requirements.
The point is, of course, one for debate, particularly at budget-
making time. The counterargument runs that it is worth some
price in extra insurance to know that there exists a body that
will not fail to analyze and to press home security interests,
since, in the interest of the nation, it is literally vital that
those security interests be given voice.

To summarize, it should be no surprise to find that there
derives from this organizational approach a dialectical process
between the Joint Chiefs of Staff and the civilian side of the
house. This may be healthy, or it may get out of hand; the
approach provides a trial of leadership, foreseen in 1958, for
both the high civilian and the high military echelon. Where
formerly it was heard that military leaders "should be kept
sullen but not mutinous," the importance and immediacy of
security today require a vigorous, candid relationship—not
only between principals, but between supporting staffs as
well.

It is important that the voice of the Chiefs be heard at the
council table. A failure to assure that the Chiefs are deliberately and systematically brought into the consultation process
and kept in it continuously, right up through the point of
decision, can lead into deep trouble in a world where "crisis
management" is tested repeatedly in every continent. They
must have a part in the orchestrated whole, and they must be
prepared to play it. It was such a need, one may believe, that
led to the famous letter of instructions to the Joint Chiefs of
Staff from President Kennedy following the Bay of Pigs—the
principles of which have since been reaffirmed by President
Johnson:

> I regard the Joint Chiefs of Staff as my principal military advisor
> responsible both for initiating advice to me and for responding
> to requests for advice. I expect their advice to come to me

direct and unfiltered. . . . I expect the Joint Chiefs of Staff
to present the military viewpoint in governmental councils in
such a way as to assure that military factors are clearly understood before decisions are reached. . . . While I look to the
Chiefs to present the military factor without reservation or
hesitation, I regard them to be more than military men and
expect their help in fitting military requirements into the over-
all context of any situation, recognizing that the most difficult
problem in Government is to combine all assets in a unified,
effective pattern.*

General Taylor has commented on the matter in these
terms:

Flexible and adequate policy making in times like these calls for
a sophisticated blending of all components of national strength—
political, economic, ideological, as well as military. It requires
the presence at the council table of men of broad experience
capable of weighing these disparate factors in achieving proper
balance. I do not share the view that each advisor should be a
specialist, bringing to the table a narrow, specialized view of
the problem, derived from the interests of the agency of government which he represents. President Kennedy solved any doubt
in the minds of the Joint Chiefs of Staff as to his views on the
subject when, in April, 1961, he wrote to them [as quoted
above].†

Advice: Substance and Procedure

To fulfill the responsibilities that derive from such a role and
place in the structure of government, the Joint Chiefs of Staff
accord highest priority to their joint duties—thus satisfying
one of the purposes of the 1958 legislation. The schedule of
meetings of the Joint Chiefs of Staff has been markedly
expanded in recent years. Since 1962 they have met three

* Cited in part by Maxwell D. Taylor, "Military Advice: Its Use in
Government," delivered at the annual meeting of the Fellows of the
American Bar Foundation, Chicago, Illinois, February 15, 1964. Quoted in
Vital Speeches, XXX, No. 11 (March 15, 1964), 339.

† *Loc. cit.*

times a week, with the Secretary of Defense present for at least part of the first meeting each week. In addition, representatives of the State Department—normally Assistant Secretaries, Ambassadors on home visits, or both—join with the Joint Chiefs of Staff once or twice each month to take up the problems of a specific area or a specific treaty organization. On occasion, other groups or individuals, often from the scientific community, meet with them in a similar manner. They regularly bring to their meetings staff officers and specialists who can contribute to the discussions or to the follow-up work. Through deliberations of this kind, frequent and searching, they keep themselves deeply and closely involved with the stream of evolving security affairs and defense problems.

In addition to their meetings, there is a considerable range of other techniques by which they can make decisions or by which their assistants or their staffs can take action in their behalf. Simpler issues and operational measures are dealt with by "telephone vote." Other matters are handled by a kind of "pocket veto" technique; the papers on them having been developed with staff-level coordination, they are issued with a statement that, unless objected to by a Service Chief before a specified date, they will be executed.

Other steps have been taken to speed and strengthen the operation. An extremely valuable procedure has been instituted that gives authority to the Chairman, to the Director of the Joint Staff, and to the Directors of major staff divisions (and their principal assistants) to issue instructions within the bounds of established policy and known positions of the Joint Chiefs of Staff, to coordinate on action papers presented to them by other elements of the Department of Defense (and other governmental offices and agencies), and to provide information directly to such offices to facilitate their work. This procedure has proved highly effective in extending the area of cooperative effort.

By means such as these, a widening range of time-tested

normal staff techniques has been applied to the specific relationships between the Organization of the Joint Chiefs of
Staff and the Office of the Secretary of Defense. Statistics
indicate that, during 1965, about one half of the total actions
taken by the Joint Chiefs of Staff organization were taken by
this technique, with obvious gains in speedier action and
closer staff understanding. In part, these actions represent a
saving of effort to the Chiefs on matters of detail, in part a
net increase in intercommunication, which improves information flow. In any case, these and similar processes clear away
many of the preparatory or implementing actions and permit
the Chiefs to focus their efforts on the more basic issues and
policy questions. With a flow of policy papers requiring attention of the Chiefs and their Operations Deputies running to
twenty to thirty a week (and perhaps an equal number of
operational and planning messages going out to the unified
and specified commands), it is apparent that such streamlin-
ing procedures provide the Joint Chiefs of Staff greater freedom to exercise initiative on important questions and to
enhance the quality of their contributions.

The Chiefs' basic contribution takes several forms. Fundamentally, they give advice; although sometimes oral and informal, this advice is more often provided in written form.
They also guide and direct the field commands, subject to the
authority and direction of the Secretary of Defense. Without
a doubt, the centerpiece of their written advice is a pair of
major plans prepared annually under their direction and with
their personal, lengthy participation, pencil in hand. These
are the Joint Strategic Objectives Plan and the Joint Strategic
Capabilities Plan—the "JSOP" and "JSCP."

The objectives plan looks three to ten years into the future,
undertaking to identify "reasonably attainable forces" against
a background of national security needs and to show in at
least broad policy terms the possible mode of employment of
those forces in behalf of our security interests—always in ways
consonant with sound military operations and with the politi-

cal realities of our international environment. The Strategic Capabilities Plan is, as its name implies, a plan which, for the current year, allocates existing forces and provides in broad policy terms how they would be employed in major conflict or applied to contingency situations if such were to arise.

The development of these plans is an arduous process, both in the preparation and in the deliberation on the many issues that they bring to the surface. Once prepared, the plans are used by the staff and by the Chiefs themselves as a basis for a kind of running comment they give on the flood of specific questions that arise through the year. As plans, they do not, of course, give pat or complete answers to the questions that arise; they do, however, provide coherence, depth, and a well-reasoned basis for such answers. In this way, they illustrate the issue of broad versus specific policy previously mentioned. An almost unbelievable amount of work goes into these plans; they do, however, have a sustained and continuing payoff, and they provide an ingenious and practical solution to the problem of giving broad guidance for an extended period of time. The plans are updated as necessary during the year to reflect significant changes that may occur in the never-static security situation of the United States or its allies.

A great many special studies are also prepared under the direction of the Chiefs, together with memoranda commenting on specific questions, often addressed to them by the Secretary of Defense. These studies and memoranda relate to every aspect of a multitude of military actions and activities. In crisis situations, they may carry recommendations on major security decisions, such as the "go" or "no-go" decision that determines whether to introduce U.S. forces into a threatened, friendly nation. In such decisions, the forces, the timing, the objectives, the risks, the restrictions to be observed must all be addressed—as they have been, for example, in relation to our assistance in Viet-Nam. Such memoranda giving comment, advice, and recommendations flow steadily from the Chiefs.

The Chairman of the Joint Chiefs of Staff attends meetings of the National Security Council, representing the Joint Chiefs of Staff. On occasion, all the Chiefs attend a particular National Security Council meeting—normally when items of major military importance are discussed. In addition, the Chiefs act through participation of the Chairman in high councils of government, such as the EXCOM (a select group of presidential advisers chosen to deal with a particular situation, such as the Cuban crisis in 1962); the Committee of Principals, concerned with disarmament; or the Senior Interdepartmental Group (SIG), established by President Johnson in 1966 with subordinate area groups (Interdepartmental Regional Groups, or IRG's) to coordinate U.S. activities abroad.

When he is invited, the Chairman also attends formal and informal meetings with the President. In addition, other military representatives of the Chiefs participate in numerous established planning groups with State Department and other executive branch officials. Of these groups, the IRG's show promise of playing a particularly important role, and military participation in these groups may be a milestone toward thoroughly reasoned and informed governmental action. In general, there seems to be a growing effort, over a wide range of problems, to provide for direct participation by military representatives in the planning and formulation of policy recommendations on politico-military questions involving foreign operations.

In such operations, the ability to act quickly is of tremendous importance. In fast-breaking problems, the opportunities to introduce their views when they can be effective are often open to the Chiefs only fleetingly. The pace of government action can be fast, particularly during crisis situations in which one government's speed of action gives it an advantage over an adversary. The Chiefs must, therefore, be ready, and their staff must be ready, to give their views at any time. This means that prior analysis must have covered a great range of potential problem areas. Even so, there is always a scramble. It is sad indeed to have a better recommendation that was ready too late achieve less effect than a good one ready in time would have had, simply because the stage that could have been influenced had passed.

The quality of the military answers is no less important than their timeliness. Nothing discredits a contribution from the Chiefs so much as a hint that service interest has won out over objectivity and may have biased the contribution they are making. In the arena where the clash of views is sharp, the allegation that one has catered to parochial interest is enough to kill. Within the Defense Department, log-rolling is not a technique that can be practiced effectively with a Secretary of Defense devoted to systems analysis. Nor is any purpose served by "waffling" to the Secretary to conceal a disagreement or to mean different things, or all things, to different people. That technique is disappearing, unlamented. Neither does undue concern over minutiae or over peripheral issues register effectively in the high councils of government, where time is precious and energy must be conserved for the national interest.

Within the Joint Chiefs arena, a number of factors press toward improved answers. Foremost, of course, is the breadth of view of the Chiefs themselves and the leadership of their Chairman. Second, better methods of preparing papers have been adopted, which make the Joint Staff officer responsible for the content of a paper as it comes to the Joint Chiefs, letting service staff officers argue, disagree, or attach dissents but not alter the substantive content unless the Joint Staff officer agrees with them. The result has been to get the issues sharply and clearly to the Chiefs. Third, Joint Staff members are participating more widely in committees and working groups, largely as a result of the procedure, mentioned earlier, of coordinating in accordance with normal staff practice. Consequently, the Chiefs now seldom find themselves confronted, at an eleventh hour, with something that could only be brought into line with their views by discarding the whole of the preparatory work.

Step by step with these innovations—aided by them, but indispensable to them—has been a noticeable growth in what might be termed the integrity, the sense of identity, of the Joint Staff. Its members increasingly take their joint assignment seriously; no longer are they spokesmen for the advantage of their particular service. The initiative for planning, the focus of operational matters, has indeed shifted to the Joint Staff. It is quite evident that the Chiefs respect and rely upon their objectivity, and look to them to put forward truly "joint" staff effort.

Finally, one of the steps pressing toward good solutions is the policy established by the Secretary of Defense that only he or the Deputy Secretary of Defense will overrule, disregard, or modify recommendations of the Joint Chiefs of Staff. Their views cannot be set aside by faceless individuals who do not carry top responsibility. This rule has exerted a most effective discipline throughout the Department of Defense. Its effect carries back to the Joint Chiefs of Staff themselves, who well recognize that they must pay in the coin of good workmanship if this rule, and opportunity, is to continue.

Evaluation

To what extent is the institution of the Joint Chiefs and its supporting organization able to provide a sound and timely product? One's judgment here is largely personal. My own is that the trend is favorable. Rivalry is restrained. The Chiefs themselves have shown determination to make the system work. Even recognizing that the conflict in Viet-Nam may have tended to suppress rivalry unnaturally, there are grounds for satisfaction. In part, these relate to the increased integrity and effectiveness of the Joint Staff, manifested in better papers, more drive, and a willingness and ability to tackle important questions. At the working level, coordination is improved. Timeliness of operation, too, has been improved, although perhaps not so much; it is still limited in particular by the entree that the Joint Staff is accorded in the early consideration of issues and throughout the preparation of papers. An interesting change has come in this regard. In times past, when Joint Staff people were a little loath to participate in the early stages of interdepartmental work, we were unaware of a latent problem. Now it is rising to the surface in the form of a repeated necessity to press hard to make sure that Joint Staff members are able to participate in the consideration of problems from the outset. While there may be instances of conspiratorial secrecy or deliberate intent to exclude military people from participation in security problems or to present them with a near *fait accompli* when it is too late for them to influence it, in general the difficulties are simply administrative lapses or a lag in adjusting procedures to keep pace with the maturing of the national security process and the development of more open, more rational methods of operation.

There is a fuller understanding of what information the Secretary of Defense and other higher authorities require to fulfill their heavy responsibilities. Equipped with this understanding, the Joint Chiefs of Staff and their supporting organization can be more responsive to these needs.

Great room for improvement (within the joint organization as in the government more broadly) certainly exists, and it challenges all who bear responsibility to identify and accelerate the measures that will achieve it. The Joint Chiefs of Staff system remains, at the top, a committee system. Valuable as it is to enhance deliberation and preclude rash action, there is still a kind of inherent attraction toward minutiae on occasion and an urge toward the watered-down or ambiguous (even though all the Chiefs remain keen and acutely sensitive on this point).

It is noticeable that the Chiefs are able to do best on large and complex matters for deliberation, on broad issues, and on key decisions, particularly those involving military plans and operations. They find more difficulty, as would be expected, on questions of programs, priorities, and resources that touch the Service budget.

Finally, it must be asked to what extent their product is reflected in the action taken by the government—whether the acceptance accorded their product corresponds to its validity, that is, whether the contribution of the Chiefs as it is "actualized" in governmental policy and action is the maximum of which they are capable. A current judgment must be largely personal. My own is that the trend is mixed, and that there remains an important, continuing task for the Chiefs and for the government to find ways of bringing their views most effectively to bear. Under our system, there are sharp limits on what the Chiefs themselves, or any military men, can and should do along these lines. Even if they find their advice unheeded or opportunity denied them to give professional direction as they think they should, these sharp limits still apply. Ultimately, of course, the matter is inescapably one for the over-all political process.

Prediction of future trends affecting the manner in which the contributions of the Chiefs are given and received is marked by uncertainty. In part, the trends respond to changing security threat and involvement, difficult to foresee in specific terms. When times are calm, threats less acute, and operational involvement limited in scale or immediacy, the emphasis tends toward multi-year programs and administration, in the day-to-day, "real-time" actions within the Pentagon. In a sense, plans and operational concepts then serve primarily to inform and support programs. But when actual conflict occurs, as in Korea or Viet-Nam, operational factors are brought to the fore, and programs take the supporting role. The techniques of generalship are called into day-to-day contest with the enemy. We must expect then that the role of

the Joint Chiefs of Staff—their product and its acceptance—
will tend to reflect the intensity of the troubles of the times
and to rise when troubles sharpen or deepen.

The role will also vary with a different type of factor. Each
new administration brings its own approach, its own style, to
the problem of correlating professional military judgment and
action with the exercise of over-all political authority and
responsibility. New men in key civilian posts will inevitably
limit their reliance on their military colleagues until they have
been able to assess, in practical action, the competence, integrity, and value systems of the men in uniform. It is also
characteristic of the first years of a new administration that
it occupies itself with carrying out the conceptions it brought
into office. An aura of activity exists as these conceptions are
applied to a wide range of activities. The military role is then
largely to adjust the military structure to these directions.
Later, as new problems emerge in the environment that has
been created, a role giving greater emphasis to study in depth
and to deliberation can be expected to recur.

The irresistible advance of technology has its impact on the
dialogue between the Joint Chiefs of Staff and higher authority. Each Chief of Staff, within his own service, must supervise and direct the adjustment of every activity to new weapons
and new equipment. The sheer mass of Service operations—
personnel, training, equipment, distribution, and maintenance—makes this adjustment an enormous task, each step of
which must be supported by funds and program decisions
involving the services and the Office of the Secretary of Defense, with advice from the Joint Chiefs of Staff for matters
having a strategic or operational impact. A curious dichotomy
sometimes results. On the one hand, the Chiefs press insis-
tently for the authorization to develop, procure, and deploy
the most advanced weapons and equipment. On the other,
because of the momentum of existing practice or weight of
habit, there is often resistance to giving up the old and

difficulty in reshaping operational concepts to take full advantage of the new. The new instruments of "strategic mobility"—giant long-range aircraft and fast-deployment logistic ships—provide fascinating examples of the scope of change required and the challenge to the Joint Chiefs of Staff to see that this potential is utilized effectively.

Numerous means are open to the Chiefs to bring their views effectively to bear and to make their maximum contribution to policy and security. One means available to them is periodically to take a long view of the trends behind and the trends ahead. Americans are probably overly addicted to actions for the moment. A contribution the Chiefs can make, as they look back over lifetimes spent in service to the nation's security and as they look at the forces they will leave to generations of successors concerned with the nation's defense, is to draw attention to the importance of longer-range security problems. In this field, they have unique capabilities not matched by those who pass more quickly across the security stage; and it is in the nation's well-being, in the deepest sense, for them to exercise these capabilities fully. In the same way, they can take a more comprehensive view, using their experience to draw together all facets of a problem and to make sure that solutions are not drawn up for one part of a problem to the detriment of the rest. They can also bring out squarely and carefully the whole truth of close decisions—the pros and cons, the strengths and weaknesses alike—in order to provide a balanced view, rather than a pitch for a particular service or another, narrower interest. Furthermore, they can emphasize the values that are to be gained, in operational situations such as Viet-Nam, by carving out as broad an operational task as possible, under clear and explicit objectives, and charging it to a field commander under a broad statement of mission. Where military operations impinge deeply on political questions, such delegation is, of course, more difficult to design. Nevertheless, such arrangements should remain a constant aim, for the military experience of the centuries shows that clear assignments of broad missions, with minimum withholding of decision-authority, are rewarded by increased effectiveness, more skillful operations, and quicker and surer success with less loss of life.

They can show by their breadth of understanding of the great issues that affect our people, by their dedication to enduring national values and their recognition of needs, by their awareness of the diplomatic and other processes that advance international well-being, and by the character of their military stewardship that they have a worthy and useful contribution to make in policy councils.

Finally, they can work from their side to remove mistrust between military and civilian and substitute cooperation and common purpose for antagonism wherever it exists. Anyone who has seen a unit come alive when teamwork and mutual respect replaced dissension and hostility will appreciate the continuing importance of such efforts.

Continued improvement in the product that the Chiefs offer—that is, in the quality of their advice and the skill of their direction of forces—will undoubtedly add to the acceptance accorded to it. But whereas the quality of the product is largely up to them, the determination of what is to be done with it involves, for them, a lesser role. They can, however, do what is theirs to do by making their presentations forthright, clear, and valid, in pointing out clearly the consequences of their proposals in containing aggression or would-be aggression, in deterring war or conducting it successfully if it occurs, in keeping resource costs to a minimum, and in saving the lives of Americans, in uniform and out.

The full test of acceptance is a complex and continuing one, but one worthy of the attention of the government and people. It embraces a sequence of questions: Whether the trends in our security are up or down, and in what respects; to what extent it lies within the power of the United States to influence these trends; and whether the product of the Joint Chiefs of Staff is being sufficiently or correctly used to achieve this influence. These are, of course, broad and intricate considerations not capable of simple, conclusive answers, and they are at least as much a responsibility of higher authority and of the citizenry at large as of the Joint Chiefs of Staff.

11. Military Advice in Decision-Making: Past and Prologue*

LIEUTENANT COLONEL JOHN W. SEIGLE

It has become common since the end of World War II to speak of the revolutionary changes in military policy that were initiated by that conflict. Rapid technological advances not only ushered in the age of the atom but also shrank the world dramatically in terms of travel or delivery time. Organizational changes created a single Department of Defense within which the military services competed for roles and missions as they had never done before. Annual appropriations for defense rose to a level that would have been considered impossible if suggested in the first half of the century, whether measured in dollars or as a percentage of the national product.

It has become common, too, to speak of military officers transcending the traditional bounds of their profession. Although the armed forces' interest in international politics, in economic problems, and in social forces is neither everywhere applauded nor everywhere evident, this interest marks a distinctive development of the past twenty years, in which military officers have heightened their awareness of a whole range of problems facing the society they serve. The members of that society, on the other hand, have become more inter-

---

* The views expressed in this essay are the author's own and do not necessarily represent those of the United States Government.

ested in the size and composition of the nation's armed forces than they ever were before except when the nation was engaged in a great war. The well-worn term "Cold War" indicates how much the situation has changed from the days in which peace and war were considered mutually exclusive conditions.

Finally, it has become common to debate (sporadically, at least) the proper role military leaders should play in advising politically responsible officials on the force structure—the level and composition of the armed forces—the United States should maintain. Debates on this subject prior to World War II occurred only within the military profession.

It has rarely been noted, however, that the current guidelines for a proper advisory role for military officers were forged before World War II and under circumstances radically different from those of the present. Rarer still has been the realization that these earlier rationales concerning the proper scope for military advice were the products as much of the political context in which they were developed as of the views of the military officers who developed them. Rarest of all has been the recognition that professional military desires and the political climate of that earlier era inadvertently combined to deflect these definitions of military advisory roles away from reality and into pretense.

In order to appreciate how this could have happened—and to demonstrate that it did—it will be useful to turn briefly back to the beginning of the present century, when the United States began to be a world power (although not necessarily to behave as one), when the Army and the Navy were creating the staffs to give advice to responsible political leaders, and when the service war colleges were beginning to pass to successive generations of officers explanations of their proper roles in American security. The purpose of this brief historical tour will be to examine some of the factors that shaped the military role perceptions, which, whether adequate or not, are still very much with us. Historical interpretation

alone will not suffice to inform us of the proper nature of
military advice, but it may help us understand how the
explanations still prevalent today came into existence. This
review will also permit us to suggest the general direction
which formulations more adequate to the present and future
should take.

Traditional Attitudes

The keystone of traditional American attitudes toward issues
of national security has been the sharp cleavage in thinking
between war and peace. De Tocqueville noted this in the
1830's, and nothing occurred until the middle of the present
century to change it. The semantic distinction between war
and peace was extended to a dichotomy in policy as well. War
signaled the interruption of political processes rather than, as
in Clausewitz' famous dictum, their continuation by other
means. Moral sensibilities forbade the use of coercive power
for any save moral, total ends. Wars that had been avoided at
all cost were, once they came, pursued with all vigor.*

Having separated war and peace so that the rationale of one
was excluded from that of the other, Americans proceeded to
reverse Clausewitz on another count. He had warned that
although war has its own grammar it does not thereby have its
own logic. The American tendency was to give it a logic of its
own—expeditious military victory, the precondition for a return to peace. This automatic wartime objective was accepted
by American military leaders as well as by the public and its
elected officials. In the 1950's, an emotion-laden debate
swirled around General MacArthur's apothegm, "There is no
substitute for victory," but, in 1931, when he was Chief of
Staff of the U.S. Army, not an eyebrow was raised when

---

* See Robert E. Osgood's *Limited War* (Chicago: University of Chicago
Press, 1957), Chap. 2. This description summarizes Osgood's conclusions
from an earlier work, *Ideals and Self Interest in America's Foreign Relations*
(Chicago: The University of Chicago Press, 1953).

MacArthur declared, "The objective of any warring nation is victory, immediate and complete."*

Military leaders generally accepted, too, the popularly held view that separated war and politics. Admiral Leahy summarized this attitude when he was Chief of Naval Operations: "When statesmanship has failed . . . and when the citizens of our country . . . have decided that war is necessary as a last resort, . . . then the responsibility of bringing the war to a close . . . rests with the armed forces. . . ."† It is needless to say, Leahy continued, that the people will expect the armed forces to secure military victory in order to attain the ends for which the nation went to war.‡

The effect of these areas of agreement was to make almost all questions of military advice questions of peacetime advice. During war, when the military were the accepted guardians of the nation, acceptance of their advice was limited only by the nation's ability to provide men and to produce the implements of war. In peacetime, however, popular attitudes were taken to require that force levels be reduced to a minimum. This minimum was influenced by the expectation that the citizenry could spring to arms when dangers threatened; it was further influenced by the latent fear that the regular military establishment, because of its virtual monopoly of the means of physical coercion, represented a potential challenge to the existing order. Military forces were regarded as surely unproductive and wasteful, probably immoral, and possibly dangerous to the fabric of society.

One effect of these prevailing popular attitudes was to set professional officers more apart from the rest of society than the members of any other group. ("Civil-military relations" is

---

* U.S. War Policy Commission, *Hearings* (Washington: GPO, 1931), p. 355. MacArthur's assertion was then considered so unexceptionable that it even went unchallenged (and was tacitly accepted) by Norman Thomas. See Thomas' testimony in *Ibid.*, pp. 722–27.

† U.S. Congress, House Committee on Naval Affairs, *Hearings, on H.R. 9218,* to Establish the Composition of the United States Navy . . . and for other Purposes, 75th Cong., 2d Sess. (Washington: GPO, 1938), p. 1940.

‡ *Loc. cit.*

a common term in American usage; there is no "civil-anything else relations" to parallel it.) This comparative isolation, in turn, meant that military efforts to evolve an acceptable rationale for advice had to take place without much participation by political leaders. Military leaders were naturally interested in seeing their advice lead to a force structure that seemed at least adequate to the tasks it might be called upon to perform. As advisers, they desired to be thought useful by the political leaders to whom their opinions were addressed. As citizens they consistently sought, to their credit, to ensure that their position remained subordinate to that of those who bore political responsibility.

The problem facing these military leaders was to reconcile simultaneously all three of these conditions—to be at once useful and subordinate while contributing to decisions to maintain adequate forces. There was theoretically no reason why military leaders should consider adequacy as part of their responsibility. There was, however, a very practical reason why they did so. It was they, after all, who would have to direct the forces in battle in war. Particularly in the earlier stages of a conflict, they would be required to use the force structure already in being. They had little desire to face a future filled with recriminations over who was responsible for having lost a war. The very indifference that characterized the attitude of most political leaders to the maintenance of adequate forces caused military leaders to accept this concern as their own. The importance of this reaction can hardly be overemphasized.

Devising a satisfactory rationale for advice-giving was not the only task confronting military leaders. Nor was it, in their view, the principal one. More than with anything else, they were concerned with developing a high level of professional competence within their services. In the Navy, this meant emphasizing the handling of fleets rather than the handling of ships. In the Army, it required acceptance of the proposition that the regular establishment could provide some unique service not performable by the minuteman. In both services, the self-image that answered these needs was that of a profession which possessed a homogeneous set of special skills gained through long study and practice and not, therefore, easily acquired by others (the militia) or by repetition of relatively simple procedures (sailing a ship).*

Given this combination of self-images and isolation from society, a rationale to explain the role of military advisers had to be developed in a context in which the over-all problem of security was frequently ignored by political leaders, while military leaders, on the other hand, assumed that it was only a complementary part of the narrow professional problem of developing a single set of skills.

Authoritative Guidance: The Extrapolation from Tactical Doctrine

One way in which all three of the criteria for military force structure advice might be satisfied would be for political leaders to determine the objectives of military policy—the territory and values to be protected—before turning to their military advisers for expert opinions on the means necessary to secure these given ends. Subordination and usefulness would thereby be guaranteed; the adequacy of the resulting force structure should be assured if the advice thus requested were followed. Military leaders recognized this potential means of resolution and eagerly sought its realization. As Admiral Dewey wrote to his civilian superiors in 1909, "What may be the facts determining the international relations only the Administration can know and until their knowledge is communicated to the Joint Board [of the Army and the Navy] it cannot intelligently make recommendations. . . ."†

* See Samuel P. Huntington, *The Soldier and the State* (Cambridge, Mass.: Harvard University Press, 1957), pp. 11–18, 195–97, 226–30.

† Letter, Dewey to Secretaries of War and Navy, February 21, 1909, in Joint Board Copy Book (July 17, 1903, to May 8, 1911), p. 326. National Archives.

Requests for definitive political guidance were not limited to isolated instances; they were made repeatedly throughout the decades prior to World War II.* Military leaders took the initiative in proposing new institutional machinery to provide political guidance for military planning and advice.†

Despite their frequency, pleas for definitive political guidance as the precondition to military advice went unanswered. Two basic reasons why political leaders did not respond during this period are that the United States itself was physically safe from attack and that these leaders were, by and large, determined to secure important external commitments (such as protection of the Philippines) as well as declaratory policies (the Open Door policy for China) by means that did not imply recourse to armed force. But there were other reasons, too, that continued to exist after the public and its elected leaders had ceased to be indifferent to peacetime issues of military force structure.

The military's effort to achieve a homogeneous and unique set of skills came from the deep-seated belief that the "science of war" could only be comprehended after diligent mastery of the timeless principles of war.‡ The ultimate purpose of such mastery was qualification for high command in war. Military educators actively sought an organizing concept that would lend itself to studies illuminating the principles of war and that would help officers better to prepare for high command.

---

* See Fred Greene, "The Military View of American National Policy, 1904–1940," *American Historical Review,* LXVI (January, 1961), 354–77.

† A 1911 initiative is described in Paul Y. Hammond, *Organizing for Defense* (Princeton: Princeton University Press, 1961), pp. 64–71; for developments in the interwar period, see Ernest R. May, "The Development of Political-Military Consultation in the United States," *Political Science Quarterly,* LXX (June, 1955), 161–80.

‡ Both services accepted uncritically the contentions of Jomini that meaningful principles existed and that they could be an adequate guide to action. The founders of both the Naval War College (Adm. Stephen B. Luce) and the Army War College (Gen. Tasker H. Bliss) referred to the "science of war" as that which could be understood by study, whereas the "art of war" was the skill in practical application that drew on this scientific knowledge. The similarity of views was not accidental: Bliss had been one of Luce's original assistants at the Naval War College.

By 1910, such an organizing concept had been developed at the Army Staff College (as it was then called) at Fort Leavenworth and adopted by both service war colleges. It has remained in use within the armed forces, virtually unchanged, to this day. It is a simple, straightforward, and sound doctrine for tactical decision-making. It stresses a maximum permissible freedom of action for subordinates once they have received from a superior officer a general statement of the objective to be attained. It adopts as a basic premise the expectation that, with a standardized frame of reference, the individual closest to the actual events will best be able to make sound decisions.*

The essence of this doctrine is contained in the "estimate of the situation." From a given or implied mission—the task to be accomplished—one methodically analyzes the situation and then deduces a decision. This process is obviously useful at subordinate levels in hierarchical institutions at all times. It could be used, although not without some difficulty, at even the very highest levels in wartime, as long as total military victory remained the automatic and accepted "national mission." It could not even begin to operate, however, unless a mission were provided or could be reasonably deduced from the situation and the known desires of superiors. It could

* In 1906, Major Eben Swift published *Field Orders, Messages and Reports* (U.S. War Department, Office of the Chief of Staff, Doc. No. 278; Washington: GPO, 1906), which presented the "five paragraph field order." Swift argued that the practice of Napoleon and Wellington—the issuance of minutely detailed orders to many echelons of subordinates—was not suitable to a highly professionalized army. Rather, he wrote, a high level of training should ensure that all hierarchical levels would act in concert, because each would know the problems facing the others. Swift's colleague, Captain Roger S. Fitch, contributed a second pamphlet, *Estimating Tactical Situations and Composing Field Orders* (Ft. Leavenworth: U.S. Army Staff College Press, 1909), which first presented the deductive mental process of the "estimate of the situation"—beginning with an assigned mission and reasoning to a logical decision. Swift became a director of the Army War College and introduced there the "applicatory system," as he called it, in 1908. The Naval War College adopted the same system without change in 1910. This deductive process for tactical decision-making was the only one used in the service schools prior to World War II. It is still the only process taught in some of them.

never be an adequate guide to military advice on force structure matters during peacetime unless political leaders were prepared to delineate the tasks the military should be prepared to accomplish in the event of war.

If political leaders would only define these objectives, the military profession could develop one doctrine that would be comprehensive and authoritative with respect to all military functions and, at the same time, satisfy the need for military advice to be subordinate and useful. These were the unrequited hopes of those who saw a potential resolution of their own problems in the hoped-for action of others. They did not, however, constitute the military leaders' only basis for military advice. When their calls for definitive guidance continued to go unanswered, they formulated advisory rationales that did not depend exclusively on such guidance. Two rationales, or models, of quite different kinds were developed. They are important because they exemplified the effort to define advisory roles without reference to the needs and interests of those being advised. They are also important because, since they did not depend on authoritative political guidance, they would continue to be advocated even when the military became aware of the unrealism of having ever expected such guidance. The first of these rationales may conveniently be called that of the "self-determinist." It emphasized independent, professional determinations of military force structure requirements. The second, that of the "subalterns," stressed loyal subordination.

"Self-Determinists" and "Subalterns"

"Self-determinists" equated military force with national security. Their function, as they saw it, was to inform political leaders of the forces necessary to achieve stated ends. In the absence of guidance, they assumed the national policies that their recommendations were designed to support. In their view, security could only be guaranteed by military means.

They rejected the proposition that diplomacy might reduce the need for armed forces; its efficacy, they said, rests solely upon its ability to call on force if necessary.* Their assessments consciously excluded considerations of what the nation might be able or willing to afford for defense. That was a task for political leaders. The military task was to determine what was necessary—the pure "military requirement"; statesmen were free to disregard military advice, but only at peril to the enumerated objectives.

One of the best examples of military advice based on a "self-determinist" rationale may be found in the pre-World War I Navy. The Navy's force planning staff of senior officers, the General Board of the Navy (GB), neatly summarized this position in a policy statement:

> It is not the province of the General Board to enter into political and economic considerations; but, it is its duty as a military board to advise clearly as to the strength necessary to meet contingencies, probable or possible, and to point out the naval forces which it deems indispensable to maintain the traditional policy of the United States . . . with or without the consent of those powers whose interests run in a contrary direction.†

These policies, assumed by the board as the basis for deductive determinations of force requirements, were the Monroe Doctrine and sole possession of the Panama Canal, protection of the Philippines, preservation of the "Open Door" in China, the avoidance of alliances, and exclusion of Asiatics from the United States.‡

* See, for example, Letter, General Board (GB) to Secretary of the Navy, September 21, 1921, Subj.: Limitation of Armaments. GB No. 438 (Serial No. 1088), Naval History Division, Washington: "Our diplomacy is effective almost in proportion to the possible effectiveness of our naval strategy. If statesmen make demands affecting Far Eastern questions, Japan asks herself what is the effectiveness of the [military] power that lies behind that demand."

† GB No. 420–22, April 21, 1909.

‡ GB No. 420–22, September 25, 1912. This list of assumed national objectives was begun in about 1909 and expanded to the aims stated here by 1912. It did not change thereafter, until after U.S. entry into World War I.

Army leaders during the interwar years, on the other hand, were avowedly "subaltern." They emphasized military subordination rather than military necessity. It was perfectly proper, they maintained, for political leaders to predetermine force levels based on economic considerations; the military advisers' task was to determine how these established levels could be made most efficient—to concentrate, that is, on questions of force composition. "It is not for military men to judge either the international situation or internal conditions," Chief of Staff Charles P. Summerall informed his principal assistants in 1929, "but it is for them to willingly accept the responsibilty of . . . a military establishment that incurs the minimum of expense."*

One might have wondered what this minimum might become. As Summerall wrote these words, the appropriations allowed an army strength of 118,750 men and 12,000 officers, as against the 280,000 men and over 17,000 officers permitted by the basic National Defense Act of 1920, then in effect. In a society that is often said to function largely on compromises resulting from countervailing power, it could prove fatal for the spokesmen for any interest to invite others to take advantage of popular demands to reduce the resources allocated to that interest. This, too, it will be noted, was a circumstance peculiar to the period in which only military leaders were considered to represent the interests of military security.

The army "subalterns" did not, in any event, continue to invite upon themselves decreasing force levels. Their stance was, like that of the "self-determinists," one of honest self-delusion. It represented what they thought military advisers should be, not what they were. "Self-determinists" did not really give independent advice, as they claimed, and "subalterns" did not remain unconcerned with the adequacy of force levels. Each group found itself impelled to maintain the pose of its proclaimed advisory rationale, while its actual

---

* Memo, Chief of Staff for Division Chiefs, August 8, 1929, Subj.: Survey of the Military Establishment. WPD 3345. National Archives.

behavior was permeated by considerations of feasibility and expediency.

The "self-determinist" Navy General Board, for example, referred repeatedly to its own 1903 goal of a 48-battleship fleet to be completed by 1920. The building program it recommended was claimed to be the result of a "mature and deliberate consideraton of all the elements" of foreign naval building and American interests.* Yet this program—as the board's own records reveal—was actually a drastic revision, reducing by 50 per cent the building rate recommended earlier in 1903. In February of that year, the board had recommended a 48-battleship force, to be completed in 1914 by laying down four new capital ships each year.† In October, after its initial recommendation had been pointedly ignored for many months, it blithely reduced this rate to two ships annually, making the new completion date 1919.‡ The board later changed this scheduled completion date arbitrarily and without explanation to 1920, in order to heighten the effect of comparisons with the German shipbuilding program aimed at completion in that year.§

Even the goal of 48 battleships was decided upon with primary attention to public appeal and political feasibility. Two General Board members recommended a program calling for one battleship for each state of the union. (Since battleships were named for states, the basis for this recommendation is not difficult to divine.) The board settled on a goal that was exactly twice the number of capital ships then in the fleet or already authorized.‖ Thereafter, it pursued this

* See Letter, GB to Secretary of the Navy, March 28, 1913, Subj.: Naval Policy. GB No. 446. This document is reproduced in "Report of the Secretary of the Navy" (*Annual Reports of the Navy Department, 1913*; Washington: GPO, 1914), pp. 30–34. This publication marked the first time since its creation in 1900 that any of the GB's recommendations were made public.

† GB No. 420–22 (Ser. No. 58), February 9, 1903.

‡ GB No. 420, October 17, 1903.

§ The change occurred in Letter, GB to Secretary of the Navy, September 25, 1912, Subj.: Building Program, 1914. GB No. 420–22.

‖ The GB deliberations, which lasted for less than an hour and a half, are summarized in Minutes of the GB (Letterpress), I, 235–38.

objective without significant change for almost fifteen years. International political developments that led naval officers to perceive differing potential enemies in different areas of the world were not reflected in the continuing recommendation for a fleet whose intended size had been in large part determined by an intuitive assessment of political feasibility.

The interwar Army, on the other hand, made repeated declarations of subordination, while it proposed a minimum force level—165,000 men and 14,000 officers—which it said should be adopted "at such time as the financial position of the government will warrant."* Army leaders gradually came to refer to this deferred goal as one that would enable the Army to acquit itself of all of its many responsibilities. In 1935, when the Congress finally authorized this force level, Chief of Staff MacArthur waxed ecstatic. Previous force-level ceilings, he said, had made Congress responsible for every defect traceable to inadequate force levels. Now these inadequacies had been corrected: "Congress has placed directly upon the shoulders of the Army itself full responsibility for the efficiency of the country's military defenses."†

When General MacArthur wrote these words, the 165,000-man army had been a constant eventual objective of army leaders for over thirteen years.‡ Senior army officers continued to assure its adequacy as late as the end of 1938.§ It remained unaffected by the Kellogg-Briand Pact outlawing war, by the Far Eastern crises (which continued to grow more acute after 1931), by the Austrian *Anschluss*, or the settle-

* See U.S. Congress, House, *History of Army Appropriations Estimates, 1928: Major Army Project No. 1*, Hearings before the Committee on Military Affairs, 69th Cong., 2d Sess. (Washington: GPO, 1927), Part 3 (CONFIDENTIAL), p. 160. A copy of these hearings, now declassified, is in the Records of the War Department General Staff, G-1/6379, in the World War II Records Division, National Archives. This document is cited below as *Major Army Project No. 1.*

† "Report of the Chief of Staff" (*Annual Reports of the War Department, 1935;* Washington: GPO, 1936), I, 42–43.

‡ *Major Army Project No. 1,* p. 120.

§ See "Report of the Chief of Staff" (*Annual Reports of the War Department, 1938;* Washington: GPO, 1939), I, 29.

ment at Munich. Yet as General George C. Marshall bluntly summed up this period, "As an army we were ineffective."*

Marshall's observation pertained to the claims of adequacy that his predecessors had made for the 165,000-man army, rather than to the actual purpose this proposed force level served. Although it was initially conceived purely as a statement of a well-balanced force composition within the Army, which would allow new kinds of units to be formed without reducing those already in existence, it came to be used as a countervailing pressure against the tendency to reduce army force levels progressively. It had absolutely nothing to do with an assessment of potential tasks involving foreign adversaries.†

Like the Navy's 48-battleship goal, the objective of a 165,000-man army was not based on detailed or skillful analysis. There was no operational reason why either should have been. Such analyses simply were not germane to acceptance or rejection. Political leaders viewed military strategy as an arcane art beyond the comprehension of civilians. Statesmen often disregarded the conclusions put forward by their military advisers, but they never asked for detailed elaboration of the reasoning that had produced those conclusions. The product of this combined deference and indifference was a situation in which the skill that mattered was the skill with which military advice—although dressed in the garb of objective analysis—was attuned to the political environment into which it was launched.

The Persistence of Traditional Rationales

In the decade following World War II, the several revolutionary changes affecting military policy and the military profession really did not touch these two traditional rationales

* *Biennial Report of the Chief of Staff, July 1, 1941* (Washington: GPO, 1941), p. 47.

† *Major Army Project No. 1*, pp. 119, 122–23, 125–59. It was army doctrine at the time this proposal originated (1922) that war and force planning should not be aimed at any particular potential adversary. This doctrine was abandoned by 1927, but the recommended force level remained unchanged.

for advice-giving. The explanations military leaders gave of their advisory roles tended to be either "self-determinist" or "subaltern." One military leader managed to be both, although not at the same time. He was a "subaltern" before the Korean War and a "self-determinist" afterward. Early in 1950, echoing statements he had made the previous year, the first Chairman of the Joint Chiefs of Staff told a congressional committee that since the strength of the nation rested on its industrial capacity military leaders should take care not to jeopardize that strength: "So if we [military advisers] came here and recommended to you a $30,000,000,000 or $40,000,000,000 budget for defense, I think we would be doing a disservice and that maybe you should get a new Chairman of the Joint Chiefs of Staff if I were the one who did it."* Three years later, as he was leaving office, General Bradley apparently decided that he had been wrong to accede to force levels that had been determined on grounds other than those of military necessity. He repudiated his earlier "subaltern" pronouncements and endorsed the other, equally traditional rationale for military advice: "We [the nation's military leaders] have no way of knowing what the country *will* afford or its economy *can* afford. Only the economic advisers . . . can make that estimate and that decision, and certainly our military recommendations on forces should not be curbed in any way by economic assumptions."†

These restatements of traditional positions (echoed by General Bradley's contemporaries) came at the same time as the profound changes noted at the beginning of this essay.‡

* U.S. Congress, Senate, *Department of Defense Appropriations for 1951*, Hearings before the Subcommittee of the Committee on Appropriations, 81st Cong., 2d Sess. (Washington: GPO, 1950), p. 73.

† Omar N. Bradley, "A Soldier's Farewell," *Saturday Evening Post*, August 22, 1953, pp. 63–64. (Emphasis in original.)

‡ An interesting variation on the "subaltern" rationale is given by Bradley's successor, Adm. Arthur W. Radford, in U.S. Congress, Senate, *Department of Defense Appropriations for 1955*, Hearings before the Subcommittee of the Committee on Appropriations, 83d Cong., 2d Sess. (Washington: GPO, 1954), pp. 83–84. For "self-determinist" statements, see Army Chief of Staff Matthew B. Ridgway's memoirs, *Soldier* (New York: Harper & Brothers,

But during the period in which these grounds for military advice were being reasserted, the phenonema that had brought them into being—the public's peacetime isolation of the military and the political leaders' indifference to peacetime problems of physical security—were beginning to disappear. This disappearance was, however, uneven and prolonged. Paradoxically, the first noticeable change that occurred was one that actually made the role of military advisers more difficult. It was the expectation by political leaders that their military advisers should be willing to endorse with pronouncements of adequacy whatever force structures had been decided upon through political processes. This expectation, apparent in both the Truman and Eisenhower administrations, made it as difficult for military officers to establish a firm basis for advice as it had been during the dark decades before World War II, although for quite different reasons.*

This newly manifested desire for military support on force structure proposals fortunately carried, as it were, the seeds of its own rectification. Military endorsements were wanted in order to assure other political leaders and interested citizens that the proposed force structure was sufficient for the protection of vital American interests and, at the same time, was only the minimum necessary for that purpose. This presumed not only that military officers were the only ones competent to declare when this optional condition was satisfied, but, more important, that complete security without wastefulness represented an attainable and definable condition. Both of these assumptions were challenged in the fifteen-year period

---

1956), pp. 287–88, 291–92, 345–46, and Air Force Chief of Staff Hoyt S. Vandenberg's classic formulation in U.S. Congress, Senate, *Department of Defense Appropriations for 1951*, Hearings before the Subcommittee of the Committee on Appropriations, 81st Cong., 2d Sess. (Washington: GPO, 1950), p. 226.

* Examples of this expectation abound in the three case studies of force-structure decisions analyzed in Warner R. Schilling, Paul Y. Hammond, and Glenn H. Snyder, *Strategy, Politics and Defense Budgets* (New York: Columbia University Press, 1962).

following World War II. The middle of the same period saw total military victory disappear as the automatically accepted national objective in any war. The United States came gradually to replace its absolutist perceptions with a more realistic view, in which security was recognized to be relative —in degree and with respect to other values.

The confluence of several factors contributed importantly to these postwar developments. Most obviously, the huge resource demands and the critical importance of military security in the Atomic Age caused individuals and groups who had earlier been indifferent to address security problems with great concern. The competition of the military services for strategic roles and the resources that these roles implied, when combined with the unknown character of atomic warfare, contributed further to the growing civilian willingness to venture into what had previously been a military preserve. As expert military opinions clashed, it was natural that military expertise should be questioned. As these opinions clashed over judgments to which military experience seemed only remotely applicable, the willingness to question the authority of military advice approached inevitably.

What came into question was not merely the wisdom of military recommendations, but the very foundation upon which those recommendations rested—the claim to sole possession of the ability to determine what forces were necessary for military security. As newly interested civilians probed these problems, they came anew to recognize that "minimum necessary military forces" is an indeterminate concept, unless security can either be achieved as an absolute condition or measured with reference to authoritatively defined political goals. Absolute security, if it was ever a realistic goal, became unattainable when the United States' atomic monopoly came to an end. Definitive guidance was, of course, precisely what military leaders had vainly called for in peacetime for many decades. In wartime, they had always had such a goal— expeditious total military victory. Then the Korean conflict saw even this certified objective disappear. Force structure determinations would henceforth be made without reference to an absolute goal under all conditions.

Awareness of the implications of these developments did not come suddenly. When it came, it was largely the gradual product of the minds and pens of unofficial and quasi-official civilians who began, in Colonel G. A. Lincoln's phrase, to "debouch into strategy."* Their explorations and explanations focused on four areas—a more realistic appraisal of the nature of the problem of security, a more sophisticated understanding of the needs and behavior of American political leaders, a more nearly complete critique of the traditional bases for military recommendations, and, finally, the development of a more satisfactory rationale for force structure advice.

National security, Arnold Wolfers reminded Americans, may realistically be sought in varying degrees, but not in totality. Since the resources devoted to the pursuit of security become automatically unavailable to satisfy other values, and *vice versa*, security must be considered in relation to all the other ends which the nation wishes to pursue.† Moreover, since nations determine their force levels in part according to the potential dangers perceived to exist from the forces of other nations, a present decision to obtain a certain military capability may itself cause another nation to react in such a way as to negate this capability. In short, an optimal military force structure cannot, because of the nature of things, be determined deductively using static considerations.

Heightened awareness of the dimensions of the security problem was paralleled by a more sophisticated understanding

---

* G. A. Lincoln and Richard G. Stilwell, "Scholar's Debouch into Strategy," *Military Review*, XL (July, 1960), pp. 59–70.

† Arnold Wolfers, " 'National Security' as an Ambiguous Symbol," *Political Science Quarterly*, LXVII (December, 1952), 481–502. Technically, an economy may devote more resources to national security (or any other objective) without reducing allocations to other objectives if it can increase efficiency or use idle resources. Still, the practical problem remains as stated as long as the security objective cannot be completely satisfied.

of the needs and resultant behavior of political leaders, particularly the President.* Practical statesmen must not only determine continuously which objectives receive what resources, they must also make their decisions stick. The American political system, characterized by divided institutions sharing power, induces in those with executive responsibility a decided tendency to attempt to keep the future open, to avoid pre-commitment to any course of action whenever possible, to defer decisions until it becomes necessary to make a choice in the light of conditions as they then exist, and to focus attention at least as much on the shifting sands of feasibility as on the abstract stars of desirability. Political leaders are no more likely, then, to define security aims without considering the implied means than they are likely to announce a new highway program with no idea of the costs of construction. Beyond this, transportation, education, and all other social needs must somehow be weighed in the same scales with military security. Workable allocations must be decided upon in this all-embracing matrix, simply because this is the nature both of the intellectual problem and of the political task. Again, there are very few occasions in which advice can be predicated upon definite ends that are to be completely achieved.

Civilian scholars, who began to pry into the framework for military advice as it pertains to this broadened context, found that the traditional military "requirements" approach (and the "priorities" approach, as well) was unrealistic in its deductive and definitive assumptions.† Some also concluded that the military profession had not adequately developed its ability to analyze strategic issues:

* The recent classic in this category is Richard E. Neustadt's *Presidential Power* (New York: John Wiley & Sons, Inc., 1960). Neustadt's thesis is instructive: A President must guard against becoming the captive of his subordinates, for they are prone to use his power for their purposes, and the purposes of none of them are the same as those of the President.

† See, for example, Malcolm W. Hoag, "Some Complexities in Military Planning," *World Politics*, XI (July, 1959), 553–61.

That is hardly surprising, since . . . [such a capability for analysis] . . . would have to follow the development of a theoretical framework which as yet can scarcely be said to exist. Creating the mere foundations of such a framework would require a huge enterprise of scholarship, and the military profession is not a scholarly calling—as its members would be the first to insist. . . . The scholar who on rare occasions appears within its ranks can expect but scant reward for the special talents he demonstrates. It is for quite different accomplishments that the silver stars which are the final accolade of success are bestowed.*

This omission would be of little moment, Bernard Brodie continued, if the timeless principles of war really did provide an adequate guide for detailed military assessments. These principles are, however, little more than skeletal truisms; they substitute slogans for analysis.†

The Development of a Better Framework for Advice

In commenting on the professional military preoccupation with tactical command, Brodie neglected to note how this predisposition had been reinforced by the traditional disinterest of political leaders in strategic issues—a disinterest now transformed into acute and continuous concern. Nor were military officers generally aware of this root cause of their attitudes. Lacking awareness of the profound change that had come over those to whom their advice was directed, military leaders did not examine the hidden postulate of their advisory rationales. But Brodie, among others, did recognize the need for some conceptual framework that would be more adequate as a basis for security planning and that would also allow recommendations to be weighed against each other. The development of a framework for the analysis of force structure problems, in his view, could best be provided by economic theory, particularly the concept of marginal utility.‡

* Bernard Brodie, "Strategy as a Science," *World Politics*, I (July, 1949), 467–68.
† *Ibid.*, pp. 468–75.
‡ *Ibid.*, pp. 474–88, *passim.*

His observation was remarkably prescient. A new framework for force structure advice was being developed, and it did use economic theory and economic reasoning for many of its central formulations. When political leaders began to find this new framework more attuned to their needs than the traditional forms of military advice, many senior officers were aghast. It seemed to some of them that a strange new jargon had been matched with mechanical computations in an unwarranted attempt to usurp military advisory functions.

Both adherents and antagonists tended to regard the newly articulated rationale as something completely different from all that had preceded it. The newcomers were, as Senator Henry M. Jackson has observed, "a bit brash, a bit disrespectful of established ways, a bit overconfident in their approaches, a bit skeptical of the lessons of experience."* Their jargon, so strange to military ears, prevented many officers from realizing that the basic approach of this framework for advice was to examine simultaneously the factors emphasized by "self-determinists" and "subalterns." The new approach seemed to many military leaders to present a challenge rather than to offer a sensible resolution of the advisory dilemmas with which military officers had wrestled unaided and unnoticed for so many decades.

The development of this newly articulated framework for advice began, for all practical purposes, with the World War II experiences of British and American "operational research" teams dealing with tactical problems. Unlike tactical military doctrine, however, the methods of this approach were gradually modified by its developers as they began to apply them to problems at the level of national strategy. Since the approach grew largely out of operations research it was perhaps inevitable that many of its critics—and not a few of its practi-

---

* Henry M. Jackson, "Executives, Experts and National Security," reprinted in U.S. Congress, Senate, *Administration of National Security*, Hearing before the Subcommittee on National Security Staffing and Operations of the Committee on Government Operations, 88th Cong., 2d Sess. (Washington: GPO, 1964), Part 9, p. 540.

tioners—should misconstrue its essence as a special case of the application of techniques rather than as an improved way of thinking about force-structure problems. The name it was given, systems analysis, contributed to the same misconception, for it sounded much like "systems engineering," "management analysis," and several other developing methodologies, which had sprung partially from the techniques of operations research.

This unfortunate concentration on techniques, many of which systems analysts abandoned in practice or used in only the very roughest way, caused some observers to fail to recognize that it was essentially a way of looking at security problems. Given a continuing dialogue between political leaders and their military advisers, it was a way that was superior to the traditional frameworks in which military leaders had tried (unsuccessfully) to cast their advice.

Systems analysis could not work without involvement on the part of political leaders; but the purely deductive advisory process based on definitive guidance and the traditional rationales of the "self-determinists" and "subalterns" could not function satisfactorily even when political leaders became attentive and involved. These traditional approaches, developed in part because of the indifference of political leaders in peacetime to force structure issues, lost whatever limited usefulness they may once have had when political leaders came to regard peacetime force structure as an issue of central importance. Systems analysis, on the other hand, would have been a grand irrelevancy had it been advanced in the earlier decades of this century.

There are two categories of reasons why systems analysis offers a better framework for military force structure advice for the present and future. First, it examines ends and means simultaneously, without treating either as necessarily fixed. It presents political decision-makers with elaborated choices of both ends and means rather than with unelaborated conclusions framed as recommendations. Second, in systems analysis, conditional objectives are associated with the costs of alternative means of satisfaction; condition resource allocations (either increases or decreases) are examined to assess the effect they might have on various capabilities.

As political leaders participate in this repetitive process, their military advisers learn which objectives those leaders are willing to consider in the light of their associated costs. As the returns to be expected from conditional resource adjustments are examined, responsible officials can judge whether the expected returns seem to indicate increasing or decreasing force levels or changes in composition. Political judgments can be made in the light of information specifically designed to improve the quality of those judgments.

In this respect, it will be noted, systems analysis does not assume responsibility for the adequacy of the force structure that is decided upon. It assumes only the task of informing responsible officials—to the extent it can do so—of the probable implications of their choices. (The decision-maker is even assisted when he knows the aspects of a problem in which analysis is unable to indicate these probable implications.) Systems analysis is completely dependent, if it is to be useful, on the interest manifested by the nation's political leaders, on their willingness to participate in this dialogue of refinement based on detailed but provisional analysis.

Having said all this, it is necessary to add several caveats, not as grace notes but because they are important. First, there is here no suggestion that systems analysts are inherently more "objective" than military advisers have traditionally been, or that these analysts do not sometimes become advocates for a given course of action. The distinction is one of method, not of intellect, ability, or detachment. Most men who are really involved in problems become advocates for a course of action they think to be superior to other alternatives. But the very approach of systems analysis acts as a partial corrective against abuse of this human tendency, for it rests basically upon demonstrating the reasoning behind a recommended course of action. It does not presume to justify conclusions on the grounds of expert reputation. This does not mean that intuitive judgment is rendered obsolete, or that analysis provides definitive answers to all problems. Indeed, analysts using the same general approach sometimes reach opposite conclusions.* The contention of this essay is not that systems analysis is a panacea or that analysts somehow avoid human foibles; it is simply that the approach is superior to those that military advisers have traditionally adopted.

If this interpretation is correct, a summary conclusion is in order. Both military and civilian leaders should profit from pondering the roots of the traditional forms of military advice. The willingness of political leaders to make their military advisers participants in a continuing dialogue is of such critical importance that both sets of officials should become acquainted with what has happened when such participation was denied. If military leaders were to examine the sources of their traditional advisory rationales, they should come to understand better how inadequate their traditional concept of military professionalism is when applied to today's problems of advice and how inappropriate are the equally traditional advisory formulations to the problems of the present and foreseeable future.

* A recent example is the continuing disagreement between the Navy and the Office of the Secretary of Defense over the wisdom of building nuclear ships. See U.S. Congress, Joint Committee on Atomic Energy, *Nuclear Propulsion for Naval Surface Vessels*, Hearings and Report, 88th Cong., 1st Sess. (Washington: GPO, 1963).

12. Security Decisions and Military Technology

JAMES ELIOT CROSS

It is almost a national article of faith for the American people that government offices are stolid and woefully old-fashioned. Those who have served in the government are equally convinced that all its offices are in a perpetual state of review and reorganization. It is, therefore, reassuring that one of the government's most complex and critically important decision-making tasks is performed by an office that is too young to have grown old-fashioned and that has enjoyed relative stability since its birth.

Defense Research and Engineering

The Office of the Director of Defense Research and Engineering was established in 1958. Since then, it has managed the vexingly complicated business of planning, developing, and, in large measure, selecting or at least setting the stage for the selection of the weapons systems that make up the nation's arsenal.

The introduction of the new office into the almost Byzantine structure of authority and prerogative under which the technical tasks of the armed services were handled was hotly, albeit discreetly, resented by many competent men who had worked long and hard under the pre-existing systems. During that time, and during the far greater transformations that accompanied the change of administration in 1961, the military research and development community found itself engulfed in new procedures. The corridors seemed crowded with men whose titles were unfamiliar and who were empowered and apparently determined to change long-standing practices. There was a strong and perhaps sometimes justified feeling that organizations that had evolved over the years to meet evident needs were being shaped to a procrustean uniformity for uniformity's sake alone.

Now, a few years later, it would be ridiculous to pretend that all misgivings about centralizing authority on technical matters had faded away. They have not. But there is wide and increasing agreement that something of this sort has been badly needed. It would be hard to find anyone who, looking at the requirements of military technology over the next decade, would argue against strong, technically knowledgeable authority near the top of the defense establishment.

Today's structure looks tidy and logical. The basic objective is to assure that the nation has the most appropriate and technically advanced weapons systems available to meet the threats that presently or foreseeably endanger us or our allies, and, further, that these systems are provided and maintained as economically as possible. Beyond this point, however, the tidiness and logic of the structure becomes perhaps a little deceptive, for the process of planning, developing, and selecting weapons of modern war can never be a wholly tidy and rational one. The decisions on what sorts of weapons systems are required, and the more immediately painful decisions on which of many competing systems are chosen for mass procurement, depend on the balancing of many factors, the majority of which are difficult to weigh and evaluate. It is this balancing process that almost invariably becomes untidy, and it is worth considering some of the main causes of this state.

Technical Innovation

We are naturally reluctant to have our military forces equipped with anything other than the most effective instruments of war that we can devise, and, as a technically advanced people, we have long been confident that we can give them the best. It follows that we feel frustrated and intellectually baffled when confronted by hostile forces whose organization and nature do not permit us to bring these supposedly superior weapons to bear. In recent years, this sensation has become all too familiar, and our sense of frustration forms part of an essentially political conundrum. We appreciate the folly of escalating a conflict by the use of possibly inappropriate weapons, but we feel somehow inept and consequently guilty at paying a price in blood and treasure, while not using all that we have in weapon capability.

Thus, the technical innovator is under constant pressure to come up with new devices, but at the same time he is constrained, for political considerations may set definite limits on the weapons acceptable for military operations. Since the nature and extent of political limits are difficult or virtually impossible to forecast in future situations, it is often hard to decide where to place the emphasis of the innovator's effort. On the one hand, he must provide strategic weapons of mass destruction that will never be brought into play so long as our potential enemies retain a shred of rationality. On the other hand, he must provide usable tools of war that enable us to meet any of a number of lesser forms of aggressive violence.

In reaching decisions on the design and selection of new weapons, the technical planner must lean heavily on the procurement and competent evaluation of intelligence. The probable value of any new offensive weapon depends directly on whether and how quickly a potential enemy will find a means to counter it. Similarly, sensible selections of weapons for the defensive arsenal should be based on the best possible forecasts of the offensive plans and capabilities of potentially hostile states.

The political expert may know quite accurately what objectives the enemy would like to achieve, and he can often provide a good estimate of the risks the enemy will be willing to run to attain them. It is the technical man who must say what the potential enemy is capable of developing, and here again this can often be done quite accurately. But an enemy capable of developing any one of a number of offensive systems is almost certainly incapable of developing many of them at the same time and must make his own selection based on his budget and the intelligence available to him. Our political, technical, and military experts must, therefore, reach some conclusions on the enemy's intentions within his capabilities, intentions that reflect both his concept of the most direct way toward his objectives and his estimates of what he will need to counter developments made by his opponent.

The move from the relatively straightforward task of gauging an opponent's capabilities to the far less certain one of gauging his intentions is always difficult, because the first is susceptible to some measure of factual proof while many intangibles go into any estimate of the latter. In gauging intentions, the military planner and his technical colleague are beset by uncertainties: Do they know enough of the enemy's capabilities to know all the options open to him and do they know enough of the enemy's pattern of thinking and of the constraints that are influencing him to forecast with acceptable reliability which of these he will choose when he does not yet know that himself, when in fact he has not yet been forced to make his choice because of his lead time factors. This naturally leads to a sort of qualitative arms race, in which the planners of each nation make the most of their technical capabilities while conjecturing about what the enemy thinks they think he thinks.

This problem, which in modified form, is familiar to every card player, is particularly tough in decisions on military technology. The lead time in developing many weapons systems can be as long as the systems' useful military life. We are all painfully aware of the seemingly interminable lags between the determination of requirements for a new weapon and the issue of the final product to a combat unit. Crash programs, established to make up for late starts, can reduce lead times dramatically and are properly hailed as sound achievements, but it must be remembered that such programs are grievously expensive, bleeding off funds and talent from competing and often important efforts. Like strong drink, these programs can serve a useful purpose when used in moderation. Overindulgence leads to chaos. Hence, there is unceasing pressure on technical planners to undertake at least the research and exploratory development work on weapons that are certain to be a full generation beyond those then in final development and sometimes two generations beyond those in current use. This is due in large part to fear that the enemy may be building into his systems devices that will reduce the effectiveness of our own, and the realization that ineffective, obsolete equipment will place our forces at a woeful disadvantage in any future conflict.

In a period of rapid technological advance such as the present, this puts the planners in an unending dilemma. They cannot plan and wait for revolutionary breakthroughs, but at the same time it is clearly too expensive to introduce frequent new models that are only marginal improvements over currently available materiel. Indeed, expense is not the only prohibitive consideration. The training and maintenance problems of a military unit using several successive and non-interchangeable models of a piece of basic equipment rapidly become insuperable. The planners are torn between a desire to freeze their designs and so achieve a marginal superiority in the short run and a temptation to wait just a few more months for the big improvement that may be just around the corner.

The Economics of Selection

In addition to the above, for better or for worse, a high proportion of the considerations weighed in reaching decisions on military hardware center in one way or another on costs. Even the richest nation in the world is finding the tools of modern war vexingly expensive, and the sheer dollar costs of current weapons systems dwarf anything conceived of as recently as the Korean War. Increasingly, we must make a choice between "desirable" weapons systems, and reaching this choice is itself an expensive business. We cannot sensibly decide on whether or not to develop and procure a given system until its potentialities and vulnerabilities are understood, and this is only possible when the initial research and exploratory development have been carried out. Hence, reasonably large sums are spent on the early development of many "concepts" that in all likelihood will never result in weapons production. Nevertheless, this is prudent, since exploratory research and advanced development on a future major weapons system account for perhaps a third to a half of the time required to produce it, but generally consume a quarter or less of the ultimate costs.

This investment greatly reduces delays in engineering development and production, if it is finally decided to buy the system. Alternatively, if the system is rejected, the effort can be stopped before work on these more expensive stages is begun.

Theory and practice sometimes diverge at this point, however, and the draconic selection that will terminate a program has often been too long deferred. Vice Admiral J. T. Hayward once quipped to the House Appropriations Committee that "Old development programs never die, they become weapons systems we can't buy." Unfortunately, there was almost as much truth as wit to his comment. To some degree, this is inevitable, for there is seldom a clear point in time when it is evident that a program should be terminated; even when it is in deep technical difficulties, there are always optimists with sound reasons for predicting early solutions to the problems. Even apart from such technical reservations and despite the best efforts of the men responsible, there are tremendous difficulties, political and otherwise, in shutting down a program that has already absorbed hundreds of thousands of man hours and where termination may bruise the economy of a whole city or region. It is to the credit of Secretary of Defense McNamara and his technical advisers that this painful step has been taken forthrightly in a number of cases since 1961, where the politically smoother course would have been to let work go forward or gradually taper off.

Direct costs are only a part of the mix of cost-related factors that demand painful selection decisions early in the development process. The truly hideous complexities of the construction, operation, and maintenance of many of the new developments have other ramifications. The officers and men who are to operate some of the new systems must begin specialized training a year or more before the weapon is deployed in their care. When this time is added on to months and even years of basic and advanced technical training, the total constitutes a disturbingly large percentage of an enlistment or even of a 20-year service career. The proportion of men in uniform who have the necessary intellect and temperament for technical training is always limited, and the time of these men is one of the most precious and easily wasted commodities we possess.

The pressures that work against the abandonment of a development program on which large amounts have already been spent is only one of a number of constraints that tend to influence technical planners. For example, the existence of large stockpiles of a given weapon may not reduce the initial research on new equipment that might possibly replace it, but, together with other factors, it can inhibit the more expensive development work on such equipment. Then, too, there is the inevitable human inertia that makes men reluctant to replace weapons that have proved their effectiveness in the past. This reluctance is at the root of the famous tendency of once successful armies to fight the next war with the weapons of the last. In another form, this inertia may prevent or delay examination of topics of new importance.

Today, in Viet-Nam, for example, we oppose an enemy that has infiltrated and intermingled with the population to an extent that renders almost meaningless the concept of a main line of resistance with relatively secure rear areas behind it. In the current situation, the control and care of the civilian population has taken on a criticality that we have perhaps been a little slow to appreciate. This calls for a greatly increased effort by the military in what is generally termed civic action, and it demands new accuracies in the use of weapons to prevent unintended and politically damaging civilian casualties.

Political Influences

As mentioned earlier, many political considerations influence and complicate the task of the technical planner. Our national arsenal is intended both to deter hostile action and to provide fighting power if deterrence fails and war does occur, but, in designing weapons systems, the relative emphasis on deterrent effect or optimum utility in action varies greatly with the political context in which a particular system will operate.

In developing weapons applicable to brushfire or limited wars, the planner hopes devoutly that potential enemies will be deterred, but, in a day when "wars of liberation" are avowed Communist doctrine, he realizes that optimum utility must be his primary goal. Here, his great uncertainty is the question already touched on of the limits that will be imposed in any given situation.

Domestic and, sometimes just as important, foreign re-actions to the use of more efficient means of killing or coercing human beings are understandably emotional and not always wholly rational. The brief introduction of non-lethal gas in Viet-Nam provides an example. It gave rise to a world-wide wave of anti-American editorials that to my recollection was marked by only one exception—an article in a London newspaper pointing up the paradox that, although mankind had for millennia sought a means of preventing or reducing loss of life in war, the first nation to take a positive step to-ward this goal was being roundly condemned.

Given the connotations of the word gas, some reaction of this sort was foreseeable, but with other weapons the situation is not likely to be clear-cut. Even the well-tuned antennae of experienced politicians may err, and the technical innovator may find the fruits of his labor rejected or held inactive for reasons quite unrelated to the quality of his work.

In developing strategic nuclear weapons applicable to the upper end of the spectrum of violence, political considera-tions are equally important but vastly different. Here the awesome aggregate energies involved reduce the relative im-portance of minor improvements in performance, and the primary emphasis lies on the deterrent effect of the system as a whole. Both political and technical experts are fully aware of the ghastly consequences of ever unleashing these energies, and so are their counterparts in the Soviet Union who control smaller but comparable forces themselves. While these forces remain in a balance that each side finds acceptable although hardly congenial, the essential political aim of avoiding a holocaust is achieved.

It would be comforting to enjoy the sense of security of a certainly effective striking force or a largely impenetrable defense, but there are cogent arguments against initiating a major effort in this direction. The cost would be astronomic, the chances of gaining a meaningful relative advantage would be negligible and the political effect would almost certainly be unsettling. Acquiring a significant, qualitatively new capability would demand a massive, extended, and highly conspicuous effort, and the opposition would appreciate its import fully and promptly. Since the Soviet Union, like the United States, has the technical and financial resources to mount an appropriate and timely responsive effort, the result would hardly be a quantum jump in the innovator's relative strength, but rather the start of a new and painfully expensive arms race, which would merely increase the already vast lead both countries hold over other aspiring nuclear powers.

Unless the technical nature of a major new strategic weapons innovation clearly indicates an intent to discourage or protect against adventures by third powers, such as China, its development and deployment by either the U.S. or the U.S.S.R. would give the other government justifiably serious misgivings about the motives, objectives, and even the good judgment of the developing power. These misgivings would, in all probability, create an atmosphere of political distrust and touchiness in turn creating dangers and problems far more serious than those the initiating power might hope to ease by the fleeting advantages of a brief head start in developing a new generation of weapons.

It follows that, for political reasons, the national leadership may quite logically elect not to develop completely and buy for production weapons systems that the scientific and engineering community has conceived and devised. Here again, the technical planner may feel frustrated in his desire to produce the best possible materiel, and he is likely to find vociferous support from many who feel that the greatest strength in mass destruction weapons provides the greatest safety, regardless of the potential enemy's capabilities. The natural and legitimate professional aspirations of the technical planner sometimes lead toward policies at variance with the political realities on which the national policy has to be based. At this writing, press reports indicate that a debate along these lines has been taking place in the Soviet Union on the creation of an extensive Anti-Ballistic Missile system, a step that would argue that the Soviets are either profoundly concerned by Chinese progress or have forgotten America's responsive capability.

While these matters are sometimes troubling, perhaps the most insidious problem that the technical planner faces is that of reconciling the technical opportunities created by his own research with the strategic requirements of his nation's situation. In short, to what extent is national strategy influenced by successful technology? There is no question that a nation, like a sensible man, should make the most of its strengths while minimizing the handicaps created by inherent weaknesses. It should also have a realistic appreciation of the limits that these weaknesses impose on its strategy and freedom of action. Nevertheless, this is different from allowing strategy to follow where technical strength leads; a tendency that becomes a strong temptation, when a nation possesses a particularly potent weapon applicable to only one sort of war. In considerable measure, we in the United States used this line of thinking during our period of nuclear monopoly. Our technological advantage in nuclear weapons and in long-range combat aircraft produced an unbalanced emphasis on strategic weapons and perhaps some self-deception as to their potential utility. While these were and are essential parts of the national arsenal, and our fixation regarding them apparently did us little harm in the circumstances of the 1950's, they were, as we have seen, signally ill-adapted to meet the problems of limited war that predictable political realities were even then beginning to force upon us.

Technical Goals

The technical demands of the next decade are hardly likely to be simpler than those of the past. But some of the main directions of our effort are foreseeable. One is in strategic weapons of mass destruction, where the need is to maintain, on an essentially relative basis, the awe-inspiring capability we now possess. As our potential enemies develop new and more sophisticated offensive techniques, these will call for equally or more sophisticated means of defense against them or, correspondingly, improved offensive techniques that will maintain our capability to deter. In crudest terms, our ability to kill vast numbers of human beings in any part of the world does not have to be enlarged, but, in the absence of far reaching disarmament agreements, it must be kept up.

For the technical planner, the very sophistication of these weapons systems creates special problems. They are costly both in construction and in the time and talent of the men who must design and man them, draining off assets and specialized manpower needed elsewhere, and they are relatively invisible, as they are not and, prayerfully, never will be used. Nevertheless, they are the shielding roof that provides ultimate protection for all our national activities, military and civilian.

The other direction of major effort over the next decade is clearly signaled by our experience in Viet-Nam. We must find more efficient ways of waging wars with limited political objectives, just as we must reconcile ourselves to the fact that low-key conflicts of this sort are in some measure a result of our success in deterring more open aggression.

The locale and the exact nature of such smaller-scale struggles cannot be fully foreseen. We only know for certain that, if they occur, we will have to send men and not just missiles to do the fighting. It follows that we will see an increased emphasis on the development of weapons that are simpler to move and maintain. As has been pointed out earlier, the complexity of many new weapons systems makes it difficult to find and train the men to use them. Equally important, the operation of such systems tends to be an all-or-nothing proposition, in which the equipment either functions as designed or does not work at all. Emergency repairs of the "bailing wire and friction tape" type, which could make much mechanical equipment function after a fashion, are rarely applicable to electronic black boxes. For small unit operations in the far corners of the world, increased reliability and simplicity of operation become highly important and respectable technological goals.

Relatedly, the likelihood that many future military operations will be both distant and tactically dispersed places particular importance on the continued improvement in the quality and reliability of communications. Command and control of operating forces are only as good as the links that tie them to their higher commands and to each other; in a period characterized by high military mobility and even higher political volatility, communications weaknesses may prove catastrophic.

The uncertain nature of future wars also makes it clear that we can neither justify nor afford to design and procure special weapons to meet each foreseeable contingency. Thus, we are forced to face the politically explosive question of compromising on ideal military hardware requirements so that several related needs may be met with the same piece of equipment, which will be adequate if not optimal for each of them. The well-worn jokes about standardizing on a single interservice belt buckle illustrate one aspect of this matter, but the furor over the TFX selection and the subsequent difficulties in developing this aircraft show that the problem is a good deal more than comic where major systems are involved. The development of acceptable multipurpose weaponry will call for a continuing technological effort of the highest order.

Finally, it seems clear that we must work hard to improve further our logistic capabilities. The appearance of the vast C-5A cargo aircraft and the versatile FDL cargo ship, both of which are expected in the next few years, will mark major steps in this direction, as will any breakthroughs that significantly increase our ability to cope with hostile submarine attacks. Present political trends make it likely that we will relinquish a number of our overseas bases in the not too distant future and the ability to deploy and supply men rapidly and over great distances will probably prove our greatest asset in deterring and, if need be, fighting the sorts of limited wars that appear all too possible in the years ahead.

In sum, our technological goal will not be to reduce the warrior's role in the waging of war by striving for some form of unthinking military automation, but rather to increase the warrior's perception and efficiency and to extend his capabilities in performing the tasks that are inescapably his.

13. Policy-Oriented Research: Contractors and Advisers*

LIEUTENANT COLONEL WILLIAM P. SNYDER

Social science research projects seldom become national news items. Even less frequently do they create a furor in the executive and legislative branches of the Federal Government. "Project Camelot" did both; more important, it provoked an angry reaction to U.S. policies from Latin America.

The controversy, which began the previous spring, was reported on July 8, 1965, by *The New York Times*, which wrote that "a study into the 'potential for internal war' in Latin America" had been "seized on by leftist newspapers [in Chile] as proof that a 'Pentagon plot' against constitutional government was afoot."† An embarrassed and irate American Ambassador, Ralph A. Dungan, who had not been informed of the project by the Department of State, had assured the Chilean Government that the study would be called off. The Department of Defense later announced that Camelot had "been reevaluated in the light of preliminary planning. . . . As currently designed, the project would not produce the

---

* The views expressed in this essay are the author's own and do not necessarily represent those of the United States Government.

† *The New York Times*, July 8, 1965, p. 11.

desired information and was therefore being terminated."* At the time of termination, one of the major unresolved issues facing Camelot's directors was selection of a country in which to conduct field research. Ironically, Chile was at no time a serious contender for this distinction.

Project Camelot, conceived early in 1964, was a response to the recommendations of several social science advisory groups that the research programs of the military departments give increased emphasis to the problem of insurgency in the developing countries of Asia, Africa, and Latin America. As initially envisaged by the Army's Office of the Chief of Research and Development (OCRD) and members of the staff of the Special Operations Research Office (SORO) of the American University, Camelot was to be a broad-gauged analysis of the problem of internal war. The project had two specific objectives: "The systematic identification of the forerunners of the breakdown of society"; and "the identification of actions that might forestall breakdown while at the same time not standing in the way of national development."†

Development of a research design, staff recruitment, and administrative planning proceeded during the latter half of 1964. For the first two tasks, SORO secured the assistance of qualified advisers from the academic community and the National Academy of Science. Concurrently, SORO and OCRD conducted informal briefings for interested government departments, including the Department of State and other agencies represented on the Foreign Area Research Coordination Group. Department of Defense approval of Camelot was obtained late in 1964, and funds were made available to the Army to support the project during Fiscal Year 1966. This ambitious and far-ranging research project

* *The New York Times*, July 9, 1965, p. 8.

† Subcommittee on International Organizations and Movements of the Committee on Foreign Affairs, House of Representatives, U.S. Congress, *Behavioral Sciences and the National Security* (Washington: GPO, 1966), p. 5. Hereafter cited as Fascell Subcommittee.

was scheduled for completion by the end of 1968, with estimates of the over-all cost ranging from $4 to $6 million.*

The Chilean incident triggered public discussion on two points of long-run significance: The possible implications for the academic community of research undertaken by its members for agencies of the federal government; and the propriety and implications of Department of Defense sponsorship of research related to foreign policies.† Subsequent decisions by the government clarified the second point: On July 23, the Department of State announced the "suspension" of an Army-sponsored research project scheduled for Brazil.‡ On August 2, President Johnson directed that "no Government sponsorship of foreign area research should be undertaken which . . . would adversely affect United States foreign relations . . . I am asking . . . [the Secretary of State] to establish effective procedures which will assure the propriety of Government sponsored social science research in the area of foreign policy."§

In addition to forcing changes in the machinery for coordination, Camelot prompted an informal review of service

* The data in this paragraph are drawn from the testimony of Lt. Gen. W. W. Dick, Jr., Chief of Research and Development, Department of the Army, before the Fascell Subcommittee, *op. cit.*, pp. 30 ff. Included among the thirty-three academic consultants on "the technical development of the research design for Project Camelot" were such prominent academicians as Dr. James S. Coleman (Johns Hopkins), Dr. Harry Eckstein (Princeton), Dr. S. N. Eisenstadt (Hebrew University), Dr. William Kornhauser (University of California), Dr. Thomas C. Schelling (Harvard), and Dr. Charles Wolf, Jr. (The RAND Corporation).

† At the 1965 convention of the American Political Science Association, held in Washington early in September, a special luncheon meeting was devoted to the Camelot affair. The discussion at that meeting appears in the November, 1965, issue of *Background: Journal of the International Studies Association*. In particular, see Kalman H. Silvert, "American Academic Ethics and Social Research Abroad: The Lessons of Project Camelot," and William R. Polk, "Problems of Government Utilization of Scholarly Research in International Affairs," in *Ibid.*, pp. 215–59, and Irving Louis Horowitz, "The Life and Death of Project Camelot," *Trans-action*, III, No. 1 (November-December, 1965), 3 ff.

‡ *The New York Times*, July 24, 1965, p. 7.

§ The full text of the directive appears in Fascell Subcommittee, *op. cit.*, p. 107.

department practices in regard to social science research projects conducted under their sponsorship. Specifically, questions were asked about the following: Should research be conducted in-house or under contract by a non-governmental agency, such as a university or non-profit corporation? What uses can and should be made of this type of research—can it, in fact, contribute to important substantive policy issues? Finally, how should the total research effort be coordinated among the many government agencies interested in the same general policy areas? This paper will seek to give tentative answers to these questions. Before turning to these questions, it may be useful to outline some of the more important dimensions of the Department of Defense's over-all research effort in the mid-1960's.

Financing Research

Total national expenditures for research and development in 1965 exceeded $20 billion: The federal government paid two thirds of this sum.* Because of the high cost of weapons development, the military departments are the major supporters within the government of research and development. In the period 1963–65, outlays by the services and defense agencies amounted to an average of $7.2 billion per year, approximately half of over-all federal research and development expenditures. Slightly less than one quarter of this $7.2 billion spent by the defense establishment is expended in-house; research and development projects undertaken for the military departments by extramural agencies—industrial firms, universities, and research institutions of one type or another—account for the remaining three quarters.

The research and development program of the military departments is, of course, heavily oriented toward the development of advanced military equipment. As the table below

* The statistical data in this section are drawn from National Science Foundation, *Federal Funds for Research, Development, and Other Scientific Activities*, XIV, Fiscal Years 1964, 1965, 1966 (Washington, D.C.: GPO, 1965).

indicates, only about 4 per cent of the money obligated by the military departments is devoted to basic research; of the remainder, some 21 per cent is spent on applied research and about 75 per cent finances the development of specific items of hardware. In terms of the type of scientific activity supported by defense outlays, 86 per cent of the research budget (excluding development expenditures) is spent on the physical sciences, and 5 per cent supports the life sciences. The remaining 9 per cent (about $161 million in Fiscal Year 1965) devoted by the military departments to what the National Science Foundation terms the "social, psychological, and other sciences"* represents slightly less than half of the over-all government effort in these scientific fields.

MILITARY RESEARCH AND DEVELOPMENT EXPENDITURES

By Type of Activity		By Scientific Area[a]	
Basic Research	4%	Physical Sciences ...	86%
Applied Research ..	21%	Life Sciences	5%
Development	75%	Social, Psychological, & Other Sciences .	9%

[a] Research expenditures only

Defense's predominance in the social, psychological, and other sciences is further underlined if its expenditures are compared with outlays in the same fields by other federal agencies concerned with foreign affairs:† In contrast to the

* The National Science Foundation defines these scientific fields as follows: "*Psychological sciences* deal with behavior, mental processes, and individual and group characteristics and abilities. *Social sciences* are directed toward an understanding of the behavior of social institutions and groups and of individuals as members of a group. These include sciences such as cultural anthropology, economics, history, political science, and sociology." *Other sciences* is the "category provided for reporting scientific research which cannot be readily classified under one of the above-named fields." The "other" category actually makes up the bulk of this three-part grouping. National Science Foundation, *Federal Funds for Research, Development, and Other Scientific Activities*, XIV, Fiscal Years 1964, 1965, 1966 (Washington, D.C.: GPO, 1965), 58–59.

† Included are Department of Defense, Department of State, Agency for International Development, United States Information Agency, Peace Corps, and U.S. Arms Control and Disarmament Agency.

$161 million obligated by the Department of Defense in Fiscal Year 1966, commitments by the Agency for International Development amounted to only $5.2 million, for the Arms Control and Disarmament Agency to about $4 million, and for the Department of State to only $125,000. (State's large in-house research effort, which is not reflected in these figures, tends to redress the balance somewhat.) In terms of the particular type of research activity and advice with which this paper is concerned—policy-oriented research,* included as part of the "social, psychological, and other sciences" category noted above—the amount underwritten by the military departments appears to constitute about the same share (94 per cent) of the total effort of the foreign affairs agencies, although precise data on policy-oriented research are not available.

In addition to leading in the financing of research and development, the military departments have pioneered new institutional arrangements for the conduct of research activities. Their principal innovation has been the non-profit research corporation, organized to perform research under contract from a sponsoring government agency. The first non-profit organization, The RAND Corporation, was established by the Air Force in 1946.† According to its charter, RAND was to provide " . . . a continuing program to assist the Air Force in improving its efficiency and effectiveness by furnishing information and independent, objective advice derived from selected research and analysis of airpower problems of

---

* "Policy-oriented research" refers to the broad spectrum of research and analysis related to defense policies and programs. The term is more inclusive than "strategic studies," used by the military departments to refer to research related to force structure, deployments, and weapons systems. Included under the broader category of "policy-oriented research" are studies of the strategic and other implications of hardware and scientific processes, as well as research related to management, organization, personnel, and administration.

† Initially a division of Douglas Aircraft Corporation, RAND separated from Douglas in 1948 and became an independent organization. See Gene M. Lyons and Louis Morton, *Schools for Strategy: Education and Research in National Security Affairs* (New York: Frederick A. Praeger, 1965), pp. 247–52.

interest to the Air Force."* By this arrangement, it was hoped that military security and academic freedom could be combined, thereby permitting the Air Force to secure objective advice from highly qualified civilian scientists.

Stimulated primarily by the success of The RAND experiment, which many observers felt had contributed importantly to the Air Force's dominant role in U.S. defense policies during the 1950's, the other military departments moved to establish similar research organizations. The result of these initiatives was the following list of major non-profit corporations performing policy-oriented research:†

Affiliated Research Organization	Sponsor
Institute of Defense Analysis	Office of the Secretary of Defense
Human Resources Research Office (George Washington University)	Department of the Army
Center for Research in Social Systems (CRESS)—Originally called Special Operations Research Office (SORO) (American University)	
Research Analysis Corporation	
Center for Naval Analysis (Franklin Institute)	Department of the Navy
The RAND Corporation	Department of the Air Force

This picture of the institutional arrangements through which research is conducted for the defense establishment needs qualification in four respects. First, since we are con-

* Ibid., p. 246.

† National Science Foundation, op. cit., pp. 69–70. Additional material on these organizations is contained in Military Operations Subcommittee of the Committee on Government Operations, House of Representatives, Systems Development and Management: Hearings before a Subcommittee of the Committee on Government Operations, Eighty-seventh Congress, Second Session (Washington: GPO, 1962), Parts 3–5 (hereafter cited as Military Operations Subcommittee); Lyons and Morton, op. cit., pp. 231–64, and James L. Trainor, "Government Use of Non-Profit Companies," Harvard Business Review, May–June, 1966, pp. 38 ff.

cerned primarily with policy-oriented research, we have omitted the numerous non-profit corporations or university centers whose work is primarily scientific and technical (e.g., Lincoln Laboratory, managed for the Air Force by Massachusetts Institute of Technology) or managerial (e.g., Aerospace Corporation, affiliated with the Air Force) in character. Second, there are numerous non-affiliated research organizations—Hudson Institute and Stanford Research Institute are prominent examples—which also provide policy-oriented research for the military departments. Third, the distinction between in-house and extramural research facilities is not absolute. The service departments detail qualified military officers to work with the staffs of their affiliated research organizations; conversely, employees of affiliated research corporations frequently assist on in-house research projects, particularly those undertaken by *ad hoc* groups. Finally, many of the affiliated organizations now accept projects from more than a single agency. As an example, in recent years The RAND Corporation, in addition to its work for the Air Force, has conducted research for the National Science Foundation, the National Institutes of Health, and the Office of the Secretary of Defense, as well as for various private foundations.*

To summarize, some two thirds of all research and development conducted in the United States is financed by the federal government. About half of this over-all federally financed effort, in turn, is supported by the military services. Although military support for research in the social, psychological, and other sciences is relatively limited within this total, it nevertheless comprises almost half of the over-all federal effort in these fields. When compared only with the agencies of government concerned with foreign affairs, the military services are overwhelmingly dominant in the effort in the social, psychological, and other sciences, conducting in excess of 90 per cent of such research. Even in terms of the more limited category of policy-oriented research, the defense

* Military Operations Subcommittee, *op. cit.*, p. 926.

effort appears to be more than 90 per cent of the total under-taken by all departments concerned with foreign affairs. Of the policy-oriented research undertaken by the military de-partments, an estimated two thirds is performed by the non-profit research corporations, several of which are affiliated with one of the services.

Conducting Research

Before turning to the first of the three questions posed above —should research be conducted in-house or by extramural organizations—it will be useful to outline the changing pattern of research undertaken by the military departments. As noted, the impetus behind the sponsorship of external research organizations was the rapidity of technological change in the post–World War II era. With new scientific and engineering advancements becoming available for incor-poration into military weapons systems, the best thinking of highly qualified people was needed, not only to design and engineer new weapons but also to determine the implications of these advanced systems for national strategies and for service budgets and force structures. In considerable part, personnel qualified to work on these problems were not available to or within the services. Employment in the mili-tary bureaucracies had little attraction for scientific and tech-nical personnel with advanced degrees. Salary was also a deterrent: Government pay scales could not compete with those in the private sector of the economy.* Development of military personnel selected from the officer corps was at best a palliative, because of the long period of time needed to acquire the requisite skills. A second reason for using external organizations was the services' need for another point of view, with perhaps a greater degree of objectivity in staff planning and decision making. The services' awareness of this need stemmed from criticism during the 1950's of their narrow-

* Bureau of the Budget, *Report to the President on Government Contract-ing for Research and Development* (Washington: GPO, 1962), pp. 47–68.

gauged parochialism and limited perspective on national problems. At least initially, non-profit research organizations were an obvious method of overcoming these deficiencies. Despite improvements in the conditions of government employment and in the training of uniformed personnel during the 1950's and 1960's, the Department of Defense's need for expertise, objectivity, and staff augmentation continues to dictate the use of extramural contractors.

Within the growing over-all defense research effort, the services have given increased emphasis in recent years to policy-oriented research. Four factors have contributed to the growth of this form of research. First, policy-oriented research has proven extremely valuable to the military departments. Beginning with the various operations-research groups established during World War II and moving to the many important contributions of RAND and other non-profit corporations, its usefulness has been repeatedly demonstrated.* Second, the interaction between the military departments and the outside research organizations has stimulated additional interest in policy-oriented research. One of the most important products of analysis is the delineation of additional areas requiring examination. Often at the urging of the affiliated organizations, the questions raised in research studies became the object of subsequent analyses. The process, in short, has been self-breeding, with research generating the need for still more research.

A third reason for the growth of policy-oriented research lies in the change in decision-making procedures in the top echelons of the Department of Defense. Increased centralization of authority in the Office of the Secretary of Defense, particularly in regard to resource management, is one important aspect of Secretary McNamara's widely publicized management revolution in the Pentagon. Accompanying this

* See P. M. S. Blackett, *Studies of War* (New York: Hill and Wang, Inc., 1962); Saul Friedman, "The RAND Corporation and Our Policy Makers," *Atlantic*, September, 1963; and Joseph Kraft, "RAND: Arsenal for Ideas," *Harper's*, July, 1960. See below, pp. 299–303.

centralization has been a change in decision-making styles. Mr. McNamara and most of his key civilian aides are deeply committed to what might be described as "decision rationalism." That approach involves a thorough, analytic examination of the issues involved and of the implications of the various alternative solutions to the problem. They have insisted that issues be fully explored, if possible in quantitative fashion, so that military and political judgment can focus on those portions of the problem that are properly matters for judgment.*

This change in decision-making style in the Department of Defense has had two important consequences. One is the sharp increase in the *quantity* of research and analysis required of the military departments. Some of the increase has been directed by higher authority, in the form of required studies on specific questions. One example is the series of studies initiated by the Secretary of Defense on strategic airlift and rapid deployment, which culminated in the decision to develop and procure the C-5A transport.† Although civilian leaders were initially responsible for this additional work load, senior military officers have been placing increased emphasis on extended analysis and are therefore contributing to the increased research task. Where it is widely realized that program proposals and policy initiatives have little or no prospect of surviving at higher levels unless they are justified by detailed analysis and research, lower staff echelons have also added to the quantity of research activity. A second consequence of the change in defense decision-making style is the requirement that the objectivity and quality of staff analysis and research in the military departments be improved. High quality research, in short, is very much in style; partly as a

---

* The basic references on the change in decision-making style are Charles J. Hitch and Roland N. McKean, *The Economics of Defense in the Nuclear Age* (Cambridge, Mass.: Harvard University Press, 1960) and William W. Kaufmann, *The McNamara Strategy* (New York: Harper & Row, 1964).

† The process is recounted in "Systems Analysis by Land, Air, and Sea" in Daniel Seligman, "McNamara's Management Revolution," *Fortune,* July, 1965.

consequence, the services have turned increasingly to the extramural organizations for assistance.

The fourth factor contributing to the growth of policy-oriented research has been the emergence in the 1960's of a new range of substantive defense issues. From 1945 to 1960, the military departments were centrally concerned with developing and refining a strategy of deterrence appropriate to the bipolar power configuration of the postwar world. By the mid-1960's, a similar process was well begun in response to a new range of substantive defense problems. Thus, one important new research task centers on the dispersion of nuclear weapons and the impact of dispersion on alliance policies and on arms-control measures. Communist China, with its growing nuclear capability and potential for involvement elsewhere in Asia, is a second area of interest. Triggered by the conflict in Viet-Nam, with its large scale U.S. involvement, defense policy makers also became increasingly concerned with the prospect of similar military operations in other geographic regions of the world. This third area of concern stimulated new research designed to explore the many dimensions of social and political change in the developing countries. Project Camelot, of course, was prompted by just these considerations and, despite its ambitious scope, was only one of the many research projects aimed at a better understanding of the problems connected with military operations in the developing areas.

These four factors have combined to place considerable pressure on lower-level staff sections in the military departments. To meet the need for more and better policy-oriented research, the services have turned increasingly to the extramural research organizations—not only to obtain the services of personnel qualified to perform the types of analysis required, but also to avoid depleting staff resources already strained by a demanding Secretary of Defense and, more recently, by the increased work load stemming from the U.S. build-up in Viet-Nam. A recent research project, based on extensive and systematic interrogation of prisoners, was directed toward gaining a better understanding of Viet-Cong motivation and of the "methods by which the Communists gain . . . the allegiance and control . . . [of] Vietcong troops." The results of the study have been termed "invaluable" for current U.S. operations in Viet-Nam. In response to sharp Congressional criticism for having the study done by an outside agency, a Defense witness told a House investigating committee that the need for expertise in the behavioral sciences and in the skills pertaining to the particular country and culture justified the use of a non-profit research organization.*

The services' quest for outside help has been facilitated by the ease and flexibility of the administrative procedures governing research projects. The contractual arrangements under which extramural research is conducted are relatively simple. This is especially the case with the affiliated corporations. Contracts are normally long-term—five years is common—and they establish a monetary ceiling on the amount of research to be conducted within the period. The specific research tasks, however, are left open for negotiation between the two parties. In addition, there is a high degree of decentralization in the over-all policy-oriented research effort. The services are given considerable discretion in selecting issues for research. Even greater latitude is permitted in deciding how specific projects will be accomplished. Put in other terms, although a study may be directed by the Office of the Secretary of Defense, the decision as to how and where to do the research is effectively taken in the service department staff. Consultation with academic experts and representatives of outside contractors on these procedural questions is encouraged. There is no great concern over the possibility of overlapping or duplication of effort. Indeed, some duplication may even be encouraged, on the theory that separate ap-

* Fascell Subcommittee, op. cit., pp. 73, 79, 81, 92–93.

proaches contribute to the formulation of additional policy alternatives.

Not only has the amount of work done by affiliated research organizations risen, but so also has that accomplished by the non-affiliated groups. Data on the strength of this trend are not available; it is relatively clear, however, that a growing volume of contract research is being undertaken by university centers, profit research organizations, and research staffs of large industrial concerns.* Two conditions have contributed to this broadening of the research support complex. First, recent organizational changes in the services and Department of Defense have created new agencies, commands, and staff sections. Faced with new problems and lacking established contacts with the affiliated contractors, these new organizations have sought support from other sources. Second, the affiliated research organizations have neither desired nor been able to keep pace with the demands from the services for additional research support. Projects proposed by the services, in fact, have often been refused because of the lack of staff resources, particularly because of the lack of personnel qualified to work on new substantive areas. The RAND Corporation, for example, has only recently begun to acquire the staff necessary to tackle major research projects on the developing areas. Hence, if the services wanted the research done, they had to obtain support from other sources.

To recapitulate, three major trends have appeared in recent years. First, the military departments have undertaken a growing volume of policy-oriented research. Second, the share of policy-oriented research conducted by extramural organizations has increased. Finally, the extramural support complex has become more extensive, and now extends beyond the

* A crude picture of the trend may be gained from an analysis of a partial inventory of government-sponsored research covering the period October, 1964–March, 1965. The inventory covered 179 separate projects and 49 related studies, and was concerned primarily with foreign area research. A total of 8 in-house organizations and 219 outside contractors were involved; only 38 of the non-government contractors were affiliated research organizations; 78 of the contractors were foreign firms.

affiliated organizations to include university centers, profit research organizations, and industrial concerns. The first two trends are primarily the result of a new decision-making style in the Department of Defense and of several new substantive defense problems. The third trend is due in part to the limitations, particularly in personnel resources, of the affiliated research organizations. Our projections for the next decade include a further growth in policy-oriented research and continued reliance on extramural research organizations, although the affiliated organizations, because of their established reputations, financial resources, and close contacts in the defense establishment, may be expected to recapture some of their former pre-eminence.

Utilization of Research

At first glance, it would appear that the question of the uses made of policy-oriented research would be relatively simple to answer. Certainly, the results of policy-oriented research are widely distributed. The memoranda prepared by contractors, as well as the results of in-house studies, are made available in multiple copies—in some cases from 500 to 2,000 or more—for distribution to those offices within the sponsoring agency that might be interested in the results. Copies are also provided to other agencies of government, in the case of classified reports, subject to security regulations. Unclassified contractor publications are normally provided to public institutions upon request. The RAND Corporation, in fact, maintains some 41 public and university depositories for its more than 1,500 unclassified memoranda.*

These procedures generally insure that research reports are made available to all potential users. Except for the staff sections immediately responsible for the research, and possibly a few other agencies interested in the same problem, the difficulty is mainly how to avoid being swamped by an endless

* Military Operations Subcommittee, *op. cit.*, p. 927.

stream of reports.* Partly to overcome this situation, and also to insure that the results of research are readily available to future consumers, the services established several document centers. These centers served as research and study depositories, providing the traditional bibliographic, abstracting, storage, and retrieval services common to libraries everywhere. In 1952, the service technical report collections were merged into a single facility, which is now known as the Defense Documentation Center. Partly automated, the Center plans to develop a fully integrated information storage and retrieval system for scientific and technical reports. A more recent and specialized endeavor, applicable to the particular type of research of interest here, is the Cultural Information Analysis Center, managed under contract for the Army by SORO (now redesignated CRESS).

Granted the widespread availability of policy-oriented research, what uses are made of its findings? Are they, as many allege, lost in the shuffle of the everyday actions of a busy staff section? Or are they, as still other observers claim, the source of important new ideas, including most of the major innovations in postwar U.S. defense policies?

Several examples suggest that extramural policy-oriented research can have a great and immediate impact. One is the strategic air base study prepared for the Air Force in 1954 by The RAND Corporation, which resulted in major changes in location, employment concepts, and force structure in the Strategic Air Command.† A more recent case is Research Analysis Corporation's "gold flow" studies. By critically re-examining the balance of payments implications of certain overseas military deployments, the study led to a reconsidera-

---

* The enormity of this problem can hardly be exaggerated. Knowledge of previous studies on any particular subject is passed from action officer to action officer, part of the folklore of the job. Filing practices are equally haphazard. In any particular staff section, there are usually two or three self-appointed critics, who establish an informal "best-seller" list of recent studies, which becomes, in effect, "must" reading for their colleagues.

† *Selection and Use of Strategic Air Bases*, RAND Report R-266, April, 1954. (For official use only.)

tion of a series of proposed overseas troop withdrawals and financial restrictions on personnel stationed overseas, actions that would have had a marginal effect on the U.S. balance-of-payments position, but a considerable impact on our overseas military posture. Other examples, perhaps even more consequential in terms of their impact on national policies, are provided by the work of Albert Wohlstetter and Herman Kahn in the fields of deterrence theory and civil defense.*

Granting the exceptional instances noted above, it is likely that research normally plays a less important role in the policy process. One reason is that much of the policy-oriented research provided under contract is not keyed to the policy process; rather, it simply provides information, as opposed to policy alternatives, for the policy makers. While analyses of this type often contribute importantly to the development of the alternatives considered in a particular decision, it is claiming too much to say that the research is consistently influential in policy decisions. A second explanation of the relatively modest impact of policy-oriented research is the nature of knowledge itself: Knowledge—i.e., facts, concepts, and theories—generally accumulates slowly, rather than by repeated quantum jumps. The development of modern economic theory provides an example. The process was a slow accretion of facts and a gradual refinement of concepts and theory. Occasionally, it is true, a Keynes appeared on the scene and succeeded in integrating seemingly unrelated notions, temporarily ordering the discipline for a subsequent period of accretion. But economic knowledge emerged in small bits and pieces; the efforts of many economists over several centuries brought the discipline to its present condition. A similar process is at work in terms of the kinds of knowledge advanced by policy-oriented research. This research contributes to the stock of information and enhances

* Albert Wohlstetter, "The Delicate Balance of Terror," *Foreign Affairs*, January, 1959, pp. 211–34; Herman Kahn, *On Thermonuclear War* (Princeton: Princeton University Press, 1961), and *Thinking About the Unthinkable* (New York: Horizon Press, 1962).

the understanding of policy makers, but the instances in which it makes a direct and immediate contribution to policy decisions are necessarily limited.

In assessing the contribution to national policy of policy-oriented research, the impact of several recent trends should also be noted. The growing in-house capability for policy-oriented research within the Department of Defense is of most immediate importance. By the mid-1960's, this capability had become available to all the services, the Joint Chiefs of Staff, and the Office of the Secretary of Defense. The major in-house groups include elements of the Office of the Assistant Secretary of Defense for Systems Analysis—a predominantly civilian group under Assistant Secretary Alain C. Enthoven—and four groups largely military in composition—the Special Studies Group of the Joint Staff and staff sections in each of the service departments. Although there is no pretense that in-house resources match those of the established contractors, the quality and capacity of these service research organizations are impressive. The result has not only been an enhanced ability to conduct studies, but also an improved capability to define tasks appropriate for extramural research and to evaluate research done under contract.

The second development has been an across-the-board improvement in the educational qualifications of military officers. Since World War II, all of the services have undertaken extensive programs of graduate schooling. Although the main thrust of service graduate education programs has been in the scientific and technical areas, there are, nevertheless, a substantial number of officers who have received training in the social sciences.* By the mid-1960's, recipients of this

---

* At the end of 1965, approximately 19 per cent of the Army officer corps held advanced degrees: 495 officers with the Ph.D., 8,180 with the M.A., and 9,698 officers with professional degrees. The number of officers holding M.A. and Ph.D. degrees has approximately doubled in the last decade. In addition, holders of advanced degrees are concentrated among career officers, mainly majors and above. As an example, approximately 49 percent of the officers selected for attendance at the 1966 class at the Army War College—a highly select group, destined for critical command and staff assignments—have been

academic training had begun to occupy, in fairly substantial numbers, the staff positions in which this educational experience was directly applicable to the task of conducting or evaluating policy-oriented research.

In addition to a greater capability to evaluate research performed by extramural contractors, the defense establishment has also devised some highly informal, but nevertheless effective, techniques to exploit the resources of affiliated research organizations. Many staff sections, particularly those involved in the preparation of annual planning documents (e.g., Joint Strategic Objectives Plan, Joint Long Range Strategic Study), attempt to arrange research contracts covering the spectrum of questions the staff expects to encounter in the immediate future. Then, when questions arise related to the issues under research, the staff seeks information, advice, and, in time of crisis, consultative assistance from the contractor personnel employed on the project. The contract is, in effect, a retainer, covering the special expertise and assistance of the contractor. The completed research may be an incidental by-product of the process; it may not be published and "approved" until months after the data and ideas it generates have made a contribution to decisions and judgments.

A second technique is the employment of contract research to assist the agency or department in advancing a particularly favored policy alternative. If the research supports the agency's position, the military sponsor then possesses not only a useful analysis of the problem, but may also enjoy the benefits of the contractor's prestige and reputation as it seeks concurrences on the proposal. The importance of this tech-

---

awarded the M.A. degree. The Army's graduate school is keyed to filling 5,420 positions requiring advanced education. Although precise data are not available, it appears that about 40 per cent of these assignments require advanced education in the social, psychological, and other sciences; some 20 per cent require training in the social sciences. The annual input into graduate-level programs has been running between 800–900 officers in recent years. The graduate education programs of the Navy and Air Force are roughly similar to that of the Army. For a journalistic treatment, see Charles J. V. Murphy, "The New Multi-Purpose U.S. Army," *Fortune*, May, 1966, pp. 123 ff.

nique may well be declining: The improved capability to evaluate research, plus a reasonably accurate knowledge of the staff resources available to the various research organizations, helps to offset the halo effect of a contractor's reputation. In short, research is increasingly judged in terms of the quality of the analysis.

The emergence of the procedures just described has given rise in some quarters to the criticism that extramural research creates experts who, although outside the formal structure of government, through persistence and personal contacts, are able to have their policy recommendations adopted. In considering this issue, it is useful at the outset to note that the American political system, both in its diffuseness and openness, provides numerous opportunities of this type. An agile expert can often "end run" the bureaucracy, approaching top policy makers directly to urge upon them the adoption of specific policies. Knowledgeable outsiders may also be recruited into top policy-making positions, from which they can impose a particular policy on the bureaucracy. There are numerous instances in which these situations have occurred—fortunately, some would argue—and they will undoubtedly continue to occur in the future. Parenthetically, it might be noted that the recruitment of outside experts into top-level policy positions is likely to increase in the future: One of the by-products of the vast extramural research program is the development of a corps of analysts—an elite specializing in research on public policies, and circulating among the universities, government, and extramural research organizations.*

* Examples are Charles J. Hitch, formerly of RAND, later Department of Defense Comptroller, and now a Vice-President of the University of California; Dr. Alain C. Enthoven, who after several years at RAND, joined the Department of Defense in 1961 and was appointed Assistant Secretary of Defense (Systems Analysis) in 1965; Henry S. Rowen, who followed much the same pattern as Enthoven until 1965, when he was appointed Assistant Director, Bureau of the Budget; Dr. William Niskanen, who after working for Enthoven in Defense joined the Institute for Defense Analysis; Dr. Jack Stockfisch, who has been a teacher, a RAND consultant, a systems analyst at Department of Defense, and a Deputy Assistant Secretary of the Treasury, and is currently on the staff at the Army's Combat Developments Experi-

Apart from those situations made possible by the very nature of American government, the opportunities for an outside defense adviser to exercise power without formal responsibility are numerous. In addition to his analytic and substantive competence, the non-governmental expert normally enjoys the advantage of a greater degree of permanence in his position, as contrasted to the relatively rapid turnover of officers in the service staffs. There are, however, numerous checks on the outside adviser. The most important is the nature of the policy process itself—ironically, the same process that creates the opportunity to influence policy. Policy making within the American executive branch is a complex phenomenon of consensus building throughout a large organization. Policy execution, as all competent executives are aware, depends importantly on the consensus created during the decision-making process. The sheer intricacy of the process and the time delay it involves thus limit the opportunities to exercise influence. The increasing competence of the services to evaluate research results enhances the effectiveness of this safeguard. Indeed, the greater difficulty, in all probability, is to insure that policy innovations from outside the formal structure of government survive the exigencies of the policy process.

Coordinating and Using Research in the Future

Whether externally conducted policy-oriented research will continue to contribute in a significant way to the formulation of defense policies is not entirely clear. One important reason to expect a decline in its importance is the growing awareness within the defense establishment of the limitations inherent in the research performed by extramural organizations. This

mental Center; and Dr. Martin C. McGuire, formerly of Defense and now with the Department of Commerce. Col. Robert H. Pursley, USAF, with a Ph.D. in Economics, who taught at the Air Force Academy and worked as a systems analyst at the Department of Defense and also on the inter-governmental supersonic transport (SST) committee, is one of the few military officers who can be included in this group.

awareness stems from the improved ability of the defense bureaucracy to evaluate research, which, in turn, is one of the benefits of the higher educational qualifications of civil servants and military officers. And some of the work of the extramural contractors is now clearly recognized as second-rate. Contributing to the low calibre of some research is the inability of extramural organizations to use up-to-date data and to consider fully the implications of research for related programs and policies. Such deficiencies are not, of course, entirely the fault of the contractor: Security restrictions sometimes prevent release of relevant data and full discussion of issues related to research under contract. Nevertheless, the work of organizations formerly praised for their objectivity and competence is increasingly criticized for failing to examine the problem in all its complexity and depth.

Along with a better understanding of the limitations inherent in contract research, there is growing confidence that high quality policy-oriented research can be performed in-house. "We can do it better here—so why bother with an outside contractor?" is a frequently heard evaluation of the research alternatives. There is considerable justification for this view. Military officers with the requisite analytical skills are available in larger numbers. Improvements in civil service salary scales have increasingly made government employment financially competitive with opportunities in the private sector. When coupled with highly aggressive personnel recruiting, emphasizing the opportunities to work on important national problems, the result is often a research staff of very high caliber. Finally, many senior analysts within the government are satisfied that much of the impartiality and freedom of action characteristic of the extramural research organizations can be attained within the government itself.*

* One of the in-house staffs that performs consistently high quality work is the Office of Systems Analysis, headed by Dr. Alain C. Enthoven (Assistant Secretary of Defense, Systems Analysis). The elan and enthusiasm of this carefully picked group are outstanding, and Enthoven is highly praised for creating the environment needed for high quality analytical work.

Because the Department of Defense has become capable of performing better quality research, it should not be concluded that the extramural organizations will fall into disuse. On the contrary, the research task will undoubtedly continue to expand in scope and complexity. What is more likely is that fewer of the highly important projects will be farmed out in the future. A steady diet of routine, flavored with only bits and pieces of the important projects, may make research for the Department of Defense less attractive for outside contractors than formerly.

Turning to our third area of concern—coordination of the policy-oriented research effort—it is possible to suggest at least some of the problems that will emerge in the decade ahead. Prior to the Camelot incident, the coordination task was rather narrowly conceived, with only two basic dimensions: coordination with the contractor, concerned principally with constructing the research design and establishing a meaningful dialogue between the research team and the initiating staff agency; and coordination to avoid unnecessary duplication of research effort, not only within the sponsoring department but also throughout the foreign affairs sector of government. The latter dimension, it was generally recognized, contributed also to the usefulness of the various research studies.

The second is necessarily the more complex of the two dimensions, frequently involving several departments and an even greater number of interested agencies, bureaus, and staff sections. To achieve the desired coordination, a fairly elaborate structure of committees and boards has been established. At the lowest level, the services appoint advisory boards for each major extramural contract. In the Army staff, for example, the Project Advisory Group (PAG) coordinates the project within the Army and provides guidance for the contractor. At the departmental level, each of the services has some form of policy committee to give direction to the department's over-all research program. There is, finally, the

Foreign Area Research Coordination Group (FAR), charged with interdepartmental coordination. Chaired by an official from the Bureau of Intelligence and Research of the Department of State, the FAR contains among its members representatives of each of the departments concerned with foreign affairs. The FAR was not established until 1964, however, and its authority is limited to recommendations to the agency sponsoring research.*

In the wake of Camclot, another dimension has been added to the coordination problem. This dimension concerns subject matter—what problems can be researched, as well as how and where. Prior to Camelot, there was only limited control of this aspect of the research effort. This control, moreover, was exercised by the services; the Department of Defense permitted a high degree of decentralization in decisions pertaining to research. Following President Johnson's directive of August 2, 1965, however, the policy-oriented research effort of the services has been subject to closer supervision by the Department of Defense. More important, the Department of State has been given authority to review for political sensitivity all government-sponsored research proposals in the social and behavioral sciences relating to foreign policies.

There was considerable speculation late in 1965 about the long-term consequences of the Johnson directive. Not surprisingly, the most frequent prediction was for a sharply diminished research role for the Department of Defense, in particular for the Army, which has been concerned more than the other services with foreign area research.† On the basis of incomplete information covering the months immediately following the directive, it appears that the State Department intends not to restrict others' efforts unduly, but to use its mandate, in a statesmanly way, to improve coordination of the over-all foreign research effort and to facilitate the work of

* See Fascell Subcommittee, *op. cit.*, pp. 197–202.

† Government expenditures for research "in the social sciences related to foreign areas and international affairs" were estimated to be $31 million in 1964, with an additional $61 million in progress. *Ibid.*, p. 198.

agencies undertaking research on sensitive subjects and areas.*

Given the trends in policy-oriented research—an increasing amount of research, new substantive areas of interest to the Defense Department, and continued use of extramural research organizations—the coordination task will certainly increase in complexity and magnitude. Whatever the particular devices and guidelines used in the future, the interests of all concerned should be preserved. For the Department of Defense, these interests are that a policy-oriented research program of broad scope and high quality be maintained as a contributor to a viable military strategy; for the Department of State, that a vital research program by the military departments be available as a supplement to its own miniscule research program. The national interest in an expanded policy-oriented research effort is also clear: Defense and foreign policies that will deal effectively with the problems of the 1970's and 1980's will require the best data and ideas that the social and behavioral sciences can generate.

* The State Department has established the Foreign Affairs Research Council, chaired by the Director of the Bureau of Intelligence and Research, to accomplish this review function. On State's plans for handling this task see Thomas L. Hughes, "Scholars and Foreign Policy: Varieties of Research Experience," *Background: Journal of the International Studies Association,* IX, No. 3 (November, 1965), 191–214, and Anthony Cowdy, "The Camelot Capers," *The Washington Post,* May 19, 1966, p. G10.

14. New Approaches to Defense Decision-Making*

COLONEL WESLEY W. POSVAR

The era of nuclear weapons is well understood to be a revolution in the nature of conflict. Less well understood is a similar revolution in the form of methods and concepts for the management of military force. The management revolution occurred largely as a response to the weapons revolution, induced by the need for both economy and rationality in a strategic environment of chaos and potential doom.

Albert Einstein, the dismayed founder of modern nuclear science, perceived that "our world is threatened by a crisis whose extent seems to escape those within whose power it is to make major decisions for good or evil. The unleashed power of the atom," he said, "has changed everything except our ways of thinking. Thus we are drifting toward a catastrophe beyond comparison. We shall require a substantially new manner of thinking if mankind is to survive."†

Although he undoubtedly had more altruistic improvements in mind, the new methods and concepts for the management of military force do constitute a "new manner of

* This essay is based on portions of the book, *Strategy Expertise*, by Wesley W. Posvar. Copyright © 1967 by Wesley W. Posvar. Used by permission of The Viking Press, Inc. The views expressed in this essay are the author's own and do not necessarily represent those of the United States Government.

† Quoted by Hans Helmut Kirst, *The Seventh Day* (New York: Ace Books, 1959), p. 6.

thinking," an attempt to fulfill the need Einstein expressed. The process of making decisions for national defense has been broadened in novel institutional and methodological ways. The process takes place both inside and outside government. Legions of analysts conduct myriad studies of weapon systems and force requirements. Groups of advisers weigh the issues of war and peace and probe the meaning of those issues to a greater depth than was ever possible through the old-fashioned intuitions of battlefield commanders and political leaders. This whole development—comprised of the methods, the concepts, and the advances in strategic doctrine and theory—can be characterized as "strategy expertise." It is treated here as a development of great importance in itself, one that was jointly created and is jointly employed by military professionals and civil servants inside government and by private experts and scholars outside government. The development thus transcends the jurisdictional doubts and quarrels that often divide these elements.

There are many critics—and they would surely include Einstein if he were alive today—who deplore the fact that these intellectual energies are devoted, essentially, to the preservation of military security through the manipulation of the very military instruments that constitute the hazard. Yet there has been no other possible way to provide security. The nation-state system is a reality. Any scheme for security on a planet that contains nuclear weapons is imperfect, even inherently dangerous.

Nevertheless, it is the world's great good fortune that the United States as a mature power with unusually moderate objectives was the first to acquire the responsibility of nuclear weapons. Moreover, it is the search for restraint in the exercise of nuclear power that makes the strategic task complicated. If atomic weapons had first become available to a totalitarian state, there might have been little need for the development of strategy expertise.

Origins

There are three intellectual sources of today's strategy expertise. The first is the body of military literature produced by
the old professionals. Besides Clausewitz, the notables included Jomini, a contemporary of Clausewitz in the late
eighteenth and early nineteenth centuries, and the more
recent naval strategist Mahan and air strategist Douhet.
These writers all made distinctive contributions to strategic
theory. Both Clausewitz and Jomini undertook to analyze the
phenomenon of war and its attendant practices in the context
of the new era, opened by Napoleon, in which powerful
European states invested all their honor and all their young
manhood, mobilized by the *levée en masse*, in their contests
with one another. Mahan related the employment of sea-
power to the strength and prestige of nations in the broad
sweep of history. Douhet developed doctrines for using air
weapons to attack industrial centers remote from surface
armies and for committing all available forces to a strategic
offensive at the outset of war.

In general, the military origin of strategy expertise was
limited to such writings.* Beyond them, relatively little had
appeared in the way of original, analytical military thought
before World War II. Strategic theory was, therefore, remarkable for its sparseness. Most military writers had tended
to adhere closely to the ideas of these classicists and to distill
those ideas into simplified forms, such as the so-called principles of war. The field of military planning, which in the
present day is so closely identified with the formulation of
strategic theory, was limited mainly to problems of mobilization and to determining the initial deployments of forces in
the event of war. Examples were the German Schlieffen Plan

* See Edward Mead Earle, *Makers of Modern Strategy* (Princeton: Prince-
ton University Press, 1943), Chaps. 4, 5, 17, and 20; Bernard W. Brodie,
Strategy in the Missile Age (Princeton: Princeton University Press, 1959),
Chap. 3.

and the French Plan XVII before World War I. The interactions of military forces that would take place after their
collision in the field were not an object of detailed planning.
Such unforeseeable events were left, necessarily, to the initiative of the commander. In general, then, it seems not unfair
to say that historically the military profession was uninter-
ested in theory and generally unconcerned with searching for
new ways to improve its efficiency as an instrument of the
state.

The civilian academic community provided the next source
of strategy expertise.* In the 1930's, the topic of war became
an object of attention at several important academic centers.
At the University of Chicago, Quincy Wright, professor of
international relations, conducted a major research project
called The Study of War.† This study undertook to survey
warfare throughout history, to examine its characteristics and
to identify its causes. At the Yale Institute of International
Studies, the nation's need for military security was examined
candidly and treated as an essential element of foreign policy
—an uncommon approach for those times. A number of
important books were produced there by a group of scholars,
of whom Nicholas J. Spykman and Arnold Wolfers were the
most prominent.‡ In New York City, the New School for
Social Research, a center for prominent refugee scholars from
Europe, organized a faculty seminar that treated war as a
contemporary social phenomenon.§ At the Institute for

* The general content of the next paragraphs follows Gene M. Lyons and
Louis Morton, Schools for Strategy (New York: Frederick A. Praeger, 1965),
Chap. 2.

† The result was a published work of impressive scholarship, a major influence on the students who participated in its preparation and upon numerous
others who have used it since. Quincy Wright, The Study of War (Chicago:
University of Chicago Press, 1942). Harold Lasswell produced his important
World Politics and Personal Insecurity (New York: McGraw-Hill, 1935), as a
consequence of studies begun in connection with Wright's project at Chicago.

‡ For example, see Nicholas J. Spykman, America's Strategy in World
Politics (New York: Harcourt, Brace, 1942), and Arnold Wolfers, Britain and
France Between Two Wars (New York: Harcourt, Brace, 1940).

§ The product was a volume titled War in Our Times, eds., Hans Speier and
Alfred Kählir (New York: W. W. Norton, 1939).

Advanced Study in Princeton, Edward Mead Earle established a faculty seminar in military affairs.*

All these scholarly ventures had a common source in the study and teaching of international relations at the university level. Thus, these efforts represented a major development in the academic discipline of international relations, an initial departure from the traditional emphasis on international law, international organization, and diplomacy as the generally accepted bases of international order. The significance of that departure may be difficult to appreciate now that three decades have intervened, but it cannot be overstressed. Disenchantment with the failure of the League of Nations and the dismal failure of utopian schemes such as the Kellogg-Briand Peace Pact outlawing war had begun to chill the hopes and disturb the basic assumptions of professors specializing in international relations. The problem of war, it appeared, was not to be solved solely by legal devices; more realistic and penetrating insights into the very nature of war were required.

Nevertheless, scholarly interest in war remained at a fairly abstract level during the 1930's. Not until World War II did scholars plunge themselves into an active strategic role, accepting the cruel character of the international environment as something to be accommodated to if it could not be changed. Only after 1945 did many scholars become willing to concentrate on the problem of improving the efficiency of military force as an instrument of the state.

The third intellectual origin of current strategy expertise is less easy to trace. It may be described loosely as "scientific," for it grew out of the technological enterprises of World War II. An aspect of that war quite without historic precedent was the mobilization of a large part of the scientific establish-

* This led to the brilliant collection of historical essays, *Makers of Modern Strategy* (important military thinkers from Machiavelli to Hitler). This volume, appearing as it did during World War II, served as a historical capstone, a definitive evaluation of three centuries of strategic development, just at the time when warfare was making its most radical break with the past and entering the nuclear era.

ments of belligerent nations, including tens of thousands of their best technical minds. The amazing collection of talent assembled in the Manhattan Project for the development of the atomic bomb is the best example of such activity, but only an example.

Among the welter of scientific activities in World War II, there appeared one specialty particularly relevant to the appearance of strategy expertise. This specialty eventually developed and merged with the military and academic antecedents already described. It began with the ad hoc efforts of scientists to improve the operational efficiency of military forces in combat. These efforts acquired the label "operational research," later called "operations research" or "operations analysis."*

Individuals or teams of scientifically trained analysts observed combat operations, gathered statistics, and, through mathematical analysis, endeavored to develop more efficient procedures and doctrines for the employment of forces. For instance, using data about the interceptions of enemy submarines and shipping losses to those submarines, they were able to recommend a more productive search pattern for antisubmarine vessels. In air operations, they treated such questions as the preferred size and shape of bomber formations and the best routes for penetration of enemy territory. In general, they developed a methodology and set of skills that were remarkably useful in their applications to military problems.

Developments in Analysis

In the postwar period, other methods and techniques were soon added to the repertoire of the military analysts. Some of them were derived from major theoretical advances. High-

* Having begun in Great Britain, operations research was quickly taken up in the United States and applied throughout the combat arms in all theaters. A thorough technical account of the early development of operations analysis by the U.S. is provided by Philip M. Morse and G. E. Kimball, *Methods of Operations Research* (New York: Technology Press and John Wiley, 1958).

speed computers came into prominent use, and the science of linear and dynamic programming was advanced. Not only war-game playing, but also game theory, soon came to be prominent objects of attention of the strategy experts, under the impulse provided by the theoretical formulations of John von Neumann and Oskar Morgenstern.* In game playing, two branches of effort, both experimental, appeared. One employs "rigid" games, which have fixed rules and procedures, and very often are based upon complicated mathematical models of war. Thus, a series of wars can be "fought" in a computer to test the effectiveness of a given weapon under varying assumptions about enemy attack plans. "Non-rigid" games involve role-playing by individuals, who simulate decision-makers in conflict situations. These games can provide experience to the players for dealing with several kinds of abstract problems: Judging relationships between different instruments of their own action; judging the effects of counteraction by an antagonist; and sensing the nature of uncertainties and unknowns in a conflict environment. Such games are therefore valuable for teaching students of foreign policy. They are also useful for preparing real decision-makers to cope with anticipated international crises with scenarios set in trouble-spots like Viet-Nam and the Congo. The utility of games, however, does not extend to discovering answers to policy problems or revealing desirable courses of action, as wishful proponents are sometimes tempted to claim. For decision-makers, there can be no substitute for reality.

The Economic Mode of Decision-Making. Bernard Brodie anticipated the future shape of strategic analysis in 1949, when he pointed out that the methods of economics had great promise for application to a new science of strategy. Both fields, he asserted, are basically concerned with the

---

* John von Neumann and Oskar Morgenstern, *Theory of Games and Economic Behavior* (Princeton: Princeton University Press, 1947). For a historical survey, see Clayton J. Thomas, "Military Gaming," in Russell L. Ackoff (ed.), *Progress in Operational Research*, Vol. I (New York: John Wiley & Sons, 1961), Chap. 10.

problems of allocating scarce resources in order to achieve stated aims.* Since that time, economists have taken the lead, not only in theory, but also in applications.

For example, at The RAND Corporation, procedures were developed for thorough measuring of the costs of new weapon systems.† These procedures took account not only of the obvious costs of procurement, but also of indirect costs like installations and supply, as well as future costs like fuel and personnel pay. Simple as it seems, The RAND costing technique was a breakthrough in determining price tags for multibillion dollar programs that had previously been undertaken without any reasonable conception of what their ultimate costs might be.

From the efforts of the early strategic economists, there followed directly a complete overhaul of budgeting and weapons selection procedures in the Department of Defense. When he moved from The RAND Corporation to become Comptroller of the Department of Defense in 1961, Charles J. Hitch exercised a historic opportunity to translate theory into practice.‡ Under Hitch's leadership, the whole defense budget-formulation procedure was pulled together, costing methods were streamlined, and the planning and programming cycle extended five years into the future. While the budget submission to Congress is required to be organized in functional funding categories, such as personnel pay, construction, and aircraft procurement, these categories did not lend themselves to evaluating program decisions. So a system

* Bernard Brodie, "Strategy as a Science," *World Politics*, I (1948–49), 467–88.

† Charles J. Hitch, David Novick, and associated economists at RAND developed and refined these techniques and proposals, which were later implemented under Hitch's leadership as Assistant Secretary of Defense, Comptroller. Key RAND publications were David Novick, *Efficiency and Economy in Government Through New Budgeting and Accounting Procedures*, The RAND Corporation, Report R-254, Santa Monica, Feb. 1, 1954; and Charles J. Hitch and Roland N. McKean, *The Economics of Defense in the Nuclear Age*, R-346, The RAND Corporation (Cambridge, Mass.: Harvard University Press, 1960).

‡ Charles J. Hitch, *Decision-Making for Defense* (Berkeley: University of California Press, 1965).

was introduced for identifying the costs of individual programs and program "packages," grouping together the costs of forces according to mission, like strategic war forces and transport forces. All these improvements enabled decisions about major weapon systems to be made more rationally, better matched to their mission. They clarified the strategic choices that had been implicit in earlier budget decisions—for example, the fact that to withhold funds from an air base hardening program is to reduce the "strike-second" capacity for nuclear retaliation, and, therefore, to reduce the stability of the deterrent posture.

Nevertheless, the costing of defense programs remains a complex procedure. There are many imponderables, such as the safety of crews, the morale of civilians, and the good will of allies, that are true values, even though they do not carry dollar signs. The decision-maker must assign them some weight when he makes his choices. There are also many technical problems in costing. For example, if an attack carrier with its air group is compared with a land-based air group, what portion of the land base costs are chargeable to that group when the base may have many other tenants? The answer may determine which of the air groups looks cheaper. Another difficult area is that of "residual" costs. Suppose there are two weapons with the same basic mission, a cheaper one with a five-year life expectancy, and a more expensive one that will not require replacement for ten years. How should they be reflected in a five-year budget? Should the cost of the latter weapon be discounted to show its residual value after five years? Or will it be obsolete then, in any case? This, and countless similar questions, are matters of opinion for the decision-maker.

Systems Analysis. The cardinal development in the new methodology for defense decision-making is really elementary in concept—an amalgamation of all these analytical methods in the procedure called "systems analysis." In a technical sense, systems analysis means the investigation and comparison of the effectiveness and costs of alternative means (systems) of accomplishing a stated objective. More broadly, it deals with the whole process of allocating defense resources. From another standpoint, systems analysis can be regarded as the product that emerges when experts from various disciplines are brought close together under favorable circumstances of organization and communication—experts who share attention to common tasks. It is a process whereby the whole is made to exceed the sum of its parts. In the words of one of its pioneers, systems analysis "permits the judgments of experts in many fields to be combined to yield results that transcend any individual's judgment."*

Systems analysis has been made a central element of the defense decision-making apparatus, along with the streamlined costing and budgeting procedures that were introduced in 1962 by the Defense Comptroller. In 1965, systems analysis was institutionalized in the office of the new Assistant Secretary of Defense (Systems Analysis), where studies are made of the cost and effectiveness of major prospective programs, such as the B-70, the Polaris submarine, the multipurpose F-111, and the nuclear-powered aircraft carrier. The first incumbent, Alain C. Enthoven, also devotes a major share of his efforts to fostering the use of better analytical techniques throughout subordinate staffs of the armed services.

To the uninitiated, systems analysis still conjures up an atmosphere of the occult. By mysterious mathematical processes, it is supposed that the practitioners of systems analysis produce solutions of remarkable advantage to their client, but quite beyond his capacity for comprehension. Granted that many of the computations involved are complex and require

* F. R. Collbohm, "Project RAND," an address before the Scientific Advisory Board (Santa Monica: The RAND Corporation, March, 1955), P-707, p. 5. An excellent introduction to the techniques is provided by Herman Kahn and Irwin Mann, "Techniques of Systems Analysis," RM-1829-1, The RAND Corporation, Santa Monica, June, 1957; and "Ten Common Pitfalls," RM-1937, The RAND Corporation, Santa Monica, July 17, 1957.

advanced training, it is still important to realize that systems analysis rests on simple logic and on the scientific method of diligently collecting, testing, and comparing data. It is, in this sense, operations research expanded to solve larger-scale problems.

Some of the best results of this kind of analysis can be shown to derive from nothing more mysterious than common sense. The classic example cited is that of the new operations researcher reporting to duty in the field, and at once encountering a long delay in the mess line waiting for soldiers to wash and rinse their mess kits. There were two tubs for washing and two for rinsing. He quickly observed that it took the average soldier three times as long to wash as to rinse. Applying his analytical powers to this problem, he produced the recommendation that, instead of two tubs for washing and two for rinsing, there should be three for washing and one for rinsing. Lo and behold, the delay in the mess line was eliminated. An equally simple analysis resulted in a World War II decision to increase the size of shipping convoys. Observations showed that the number of ships lost per convoy remained fairly constant, whether the convoy was large or small. By increasing the size of convoys, then, total losses were reduced.*

Moreover, even the most complicated analyses are built on an elementary concept, that of marginal comparison. This means that alternative weapon systems are compared on the basis of the marginal increases, or the increments, in effectiveness that can be obtained by adding a given amount of resources to each. A very large program, in which a huge investment has already been made, may show only a modest increase in effectiveness when added funds are funneled into it. In this case, the program is well along in the stage of "diminishing returns."

The marginal concept may be illustrated in a simple numerical example. Suppose there is a force of 300 missiles,

* Morse and Kimball, *op. cit.*, pp. 3–6.

each with a 30 per cent probability of target destruction, aimed at 100 different targets. Using a simple binomial equation, it can be calculated that such a force, on the average, would destroy 67 of these targets. If the force were increased to 600 missiles, the same calculation would show 88 targets destroyed. This is an increase, or marginal effectiveness, of only 21, due to diminishing returns. Similarly, a force of 645 missiles can be calculated to destroy an average of 90 targets. At this level, an additional 45 missiles (marginal cost) would eliminate only two additional targets (marginal effectiveness).

These figures do not constitute an argument against adding missiles to the force. The extra targets destroyed may well be worth the extra cost, high as it is. But the figures do prompt the analyst to search for alternatives and to examine their marginal effectiveness, too. Perhaps, for the same investment, it will be found more productive to purchase manned bombers, electronic aids for the existing missile force itself, or something else.

At the national level, then, the kind of problem treated by systems analysts often consists of comparing major program alternatives, in what is called the "cost-effectiveness study." The computations may require banks of computers, miles of digits, and formidable mathematical models. The important judgments, however (as well as the big mistakes), are not esoteric perceptions, but applications of basic economics. Systems analysis means, simply, that, for a given expenditure of resources, the performances of alternative systems are carefully compared, whether in combat, in the laboratory, or on paper. The systems in competition may be alternative small arms for Viet-Nam or alternative Intercontinental Ballistic Missiles. Conversely, the military task may be assumed as a constant—such as the destruction of a target system—and the cheaper way to carry out the task is selected between such alternatives as B-52 bombers or Minuteman missiles. (It would be erroneous, of course, to seek "least cost" and "most effectiveness" simultaneously. One or the other quality must be held constant for the sake of comparison.) Systems analysis also means searching for new alternatives in the broadest possible context. Before funds are committed to one mission, it is desirable to look at all other possible missions. Perhaps the over-all defense posture can be improved more by leaving the offensive forces unimproved and adding instead to air defense forces or to limited war forces.

A notable example of the broad kind of investigation is The RAND Report R-266, *The Selection and Use of Strategic Air Bases*, completed in 1954. After lengthy study, that report recommended reliance on lightly-manned and pre-stocked bases overseas, to be used for rapid forward staging of bombers in the event of war. The resultant saving in construction costs of the previously planned, more elaborate bases was $1 billion. More significant, however, was the fact that the study inevitably dealt with general strategic issues—the extent and dependability of U.S. alliances, assumptions about the political circumstances in which war might begin, and the nature of the strategy of deterrence. It also led to collateral studies of programs for airborne alert, base hardening, early warning, bomb-detonation alarm, and others.* R-266, therefore, became far more than a technical project. It employed extensive logistic analysis, but it also required the best judgment of economists and political scientists.

Systems analysis at the national level is, therefore, more dependent on good reasoning and reliable data—always fortified by common sense—than on obscure mathematical formulations. The outcomes are usually forthright and easily comprehensible: The B-70 is a more costly method of delivering nuclear weapons in retaliation than other available aircraft and missiles; a civilian shelter program, at initial levels of expenditure, is a better investment for saving lives in the

* The RAND Corporation, the First Fifteen Years (Santa Monica: The RAND Corporation, 1963), p. 16; and E. S. Quade (ed.), *Analysis for Military Decisions* (Santa Monica: The RAND Corporation, November, 1964), Chap. 3.

event of nuclear attack than an Anti-Ballistic Missile; a more productive way to apply resources to aircraft carrier forces is to buy more carriers and fewer aircraft than originally programed. This latter finding relies on more rapid shifting of aircraft, as they are needed, back and forth between previously deployed carriers.

The incisive reasoning that is required in systems analysis is most usefully applied to the definition and demarcation of the problem under study itself. The study may be too narrow, and thus exclude useful considerations, or it may be too broad, and thus be inconclusive. It may pertain to the wrong period; it may suffer from an orthodox bias or an excess of zeal for change. One analyst recounts his own experience in the early postwar design of strategic bombers to be used in the middle 1950's. He expended much effort in investigating the problem of tail turret design for effective aiming of machine guns at attacking fighters. He then suddenly realized that by the time these bombers were in service, air-to-air missiles would have made his guns obsolete. He had been studying the wrong problem.* (The bombers, by the way, were built with tail turrets.)

One of the most beneficial results of the introduction of systems analysis at the national policy level, therefore, has been to draw widespread attention to the importance of judgment in defining a study. Underlying assumptions, previously taken for granted, are now thought through and made more explicit. If they are not, the result can be embarrassing. The systems analysts in the Office of the Secretary of Defense spend much of their time probing for errors in the definition and scope of studies made by lower agencies. Does an Air Force justification for air-to-surface weapons take account of the availability of artillery? Does an Army study of intratheater airlift requirements assume such short legs of resupply and such limited airstrip availability that it erroneously slants

---

* Quade, *op. cit.*, p. 301. For an extensive discussion of technical errors, see Chap. 16. See also Kahn and Mann, "Ten Common Pitfalls," *op. cit.*, and Hitch and McKean, *op. cit.*, Chaps. 9–11.

the findings against larger Air Force transport aircraft? Conversely, the service staffs probe for loopholes in Defense analyses. Does a Defense study of, say, the numerical need for ICBM's, base its results on a too benign intelligence estimate of enemy forces? In this manner, the whole nature of the defense policy dialogue in the Pentagon is changing. The new goal of partisanship is to produce red faces on those whose errors of judgment are uncovered. This seems to be a somewhat more productive way to channel strategic debates than in former times, when assumptions were too often implicit, data were inaccessible or concealed, and budgetary disputes were won or lost in back-room compromises or in bombastic confrontations.

Some critics, nevertheless, point out the deleterious effects of all these methodological changes on the corporate well-being of the defense establishment. They complain of overcentralization of decisions and warn against undermining of military professionalism. Whether the critics are right or wrong in their general accusations, most of those who can remember how the system of defense decision-making worked earlier take a temperate, if not an enthusiastic, view of the changes in methodology. Those earlier years were characterized by an exaltation of "pure" military requirements, the hidden roll-back of expenditures, and the "cost-squeeze" and consequent cancellation of programs that had been initiated without knowledge of whether there might be room for them in subsequent defense budgets.

Estimates of the savings effected by the new procedures run into many billions of dollars. One high official affirms that the United States has been able, so far, to fight a major war in Southeast Asia while maintaining its strategic posture and also avoiding general mobilization only because of the economies obtained by the new defense budgeting and analytical procedures. Whether or not his claim is extravagant, it should be acknowledged that management efficiency and good military professionalism ought to be natural companions. Ultimately, there is reason to expect that most of the present frictions in defense administration will dissipate of their own accord, when wider acceptance and use of the new management tools improve the quality of the output and, consequently, strengthen the position of the military staffs.

Development of Concepts and Theory

Looking beyond the methodological successes and the dollar savings provided by strategy expertise, one finds another kind of contribution of immeasurable but probably even greater value to the nation. This is in the abstract realm of theory, concept, and doctrine.

From 1956 to 1959, for example, The RAND Corporation conducted, on its own initiative, a study of civil defense in the United States. Although there was no conclusive result in the form of a national program for civil defense, it increased national leaders' awareness of the possible effects of nuclear war, and it undoubtedly improved the climate for acceptance of realistic security programs in general.

Albert Wohlstetter's article, "The Delicate Balance of Terror,"* which had considerable public impact, was the unclassified outcropping of a series of vitally important studies that revealed the technical problems of maintaining an effective posture of deterrence. As a consequence of these and other efforts, concepts of deterrence have become more sophisticated, able to distinguish between the forces required for first- and second-strike, and able to treat deterrence by strategic forces of threats other than all-out war. These phrases may not presently stimulate much excitement, but it is useful to recall the comparative lack of understanding of such matters a few years ago. (Wohlstetter, for example, earlier encountered resistance in official circles to the notion that to suffer a surprise attack might make a decisive differ-

* Albert Wohlstetter, "The Delicate Balance of Terror," *Foreign Affairs*, Vol. XXXVII, No. 2 (January, 1959), and "Scientists, Seers, and Strategists," *Foreign Affairs*, Vol. XLI, No. 3 (April, 1963).

ence in the ability of United States strategic forces to strike back.)

Some of the major new landmarks in the development of military thought have appeared as published books. William Kaufmann's *Military Policy and National Security** raised vital questions about the efficacy of deterrence as conceived in the mid-1950's; Samuel P. Huntington's *The Soldier and the State†* provoked a thoughtful public discussion about the proper role of the military profession in this country's government; Thomas C. Schelling's *The Strategy of Conflict‡* opened a new vista for studying relations and communications between military antagonists. Any bibliography in this area contains many other examples of great merit.

In considering all of these contributions together, it appears that a new body of strategic theory is beginning to take shape. It draws upon game theory, theories of bargaining and communication, and certain propositions of economics, such as the duopolistic competition of firms.§ The new theory illuminates the nature of modern conflict. It contributes to refinement of the policy of deterrence of nuclear war. It fosters better understanding of the nature of nuclear stability. And it opens the way for arms control, explained as a "shared interest" between adversaries in such goals as accident prevention and, if war should occur, damage limitation.¶ (They are goals

* William W. Kaufmann, *Military Policy and National Security* (Princeton: Princeton University Press, 1956).

† Samuel P. Huntington, *The Soldier and the State: The Theory and Politics of Civil-Military Relations* (Cambridge, Mass.: The Belknap Press, 1957).

‡ Thomas C. Schelling, *The Strategy of Conflict* (Cambridge, Mass.: Harvard University Press, 1960).

§ The pioneering work was Schelling, *The Strategy of Conflict.* See also Kenneth Boulding, *Conflict and Defense* (New York: Harper and Brothers, 1962); Anatol Rapoport, *Fights, Games and Debates* (Ann Arbor: University of Michigan Press, 1960); Klaus Knorr and Thornton Read, *Limited Strategic War* (New York: Frederick A. Praeger, 1962).

¶ Representative of the arms control literature are Donald G. Brennan (ed.), *Arms Control, Disarmament, and National Security* (New York: George Braziller, 1961); and Thomas C. Schelling and Morton H. Halperin, *Strategy and Arms Control* (New York: The Twentieth Century Fund, 1961).

that may require, paradoxically, increased defense expenditures.) The jargon of the new body of theory has grown to include such terms as escalation, intra-war communication, city hostages, crisis management, and limited strategic war—some of them simplistic notions, all of them representative of earnest efforts somehow to improve national security in a setting of unprecedented international insecurity.

In the domain of strategic theory, then, there occurs the full blending of the sources of strategy expertise. The earliest source, the ideas of military writers like Clausewitz and Mahan, has direct relevance as a preface to the newer concepts of strategy. The same is true of the academic source, the prewar studies of international politics that now acquire special urgency in the environment of nuclear weaponry. And the scientific source—operations research expanded into systems analysis—provides a methodological framework upon which new theory can be built.

Limitations

The new approaches to defense decision-making were described as productive of greater efficiency and actual monetary savings. There can be no question that the policy of the United States is deeply affected when many prominent officials in the Joint Staff, in the Office of the Secretary of Defense, in the Department of State, and even in the White House spend hours absorbing the ideas of strategic thinkers by reading their reports and books—and without the distractions of office politics and personalities that usually accompany officials' involvement in such subjects. The policy revolution, then, is proving to be a potent response to the nuclear weapons revolution.

One is left feeling some uneasiness, nonetheless, regarding the new approaches to defense decision-making. One cause for concern is the fact that strategy analysts are subject to the impulse to "optimize" their sphere of investigation—reaching to the ultimate scope, the whole of national policy and international security. They enter the obscure realm where the ends and means of high policy are weighed and mingled through political judgment, where objectives and criteria for strategic programs shape as well as reflect the strategic environment of the future. Their impulse toward generalization is not undesirable in itself; it stems from a natural striving for the broadest possible studies, encompassing as many relevant assumptions as possible.

The concern, then, lies in whether the governmental system and its leaders have the capacity fully to understand and to incorporate this expertise into the decision-making process in a politically responsible manner. To be more specific, systems analysis has been successively expanded to incorporate more uncertainties, incommensurables, and unknowns. When it is necessary for analysts to make assumptions about who might deliberately launch a general war, which countries might acquire (or even which should acquire) independent atomic forces, or which economic and political factors will decide the future alignment of underdeveloped countries, they have arrived at the highest level of policy. Expert advisers may also be impelled to consider the whole scope of policy, because they often feel better equipped to do so than the government officials whom they advise. The danger is that the top government official may be limited in his ability to comprehend an analytical study that is implanted with policy assumptions; he is certainly limited in the time he has available for reasoned contemplation of the complex issues involved in such a study.

Another difficulty of defense decision-making is even more profound. Strategy expertise has developed better ways to handle the unknown. Through statistical techniques and decision-making methods, the government is now aided in dealing with the uncertainties of the present and future in research, development, and long-range planning activities.

The arena of international conflict, however, is an amorphous
sphere of unpredictable, unaccountable, and incomprehen-
sibly complex human initiatives. Despite successes in coping
with uncertainties, therefore, strategy expertise is destined to
remain "suboptimal"—inadequate—in relation to the broad
creative challenges of strategy. For there is obviously a difference between anticipation and creativity, between exercising
prudent choice in respect to the future and employing imagination. The great initiatives of international politics arise
from the womb of change. The economic mode of selecting
courses of action among definable alternatives, however,
represents a commitment to the kind of alternative that can
be defined.

Bernard Brodie pointed out that systems analysis pertains
not so much to the fine determination of the highest point of
a curve, as to ascertaining whether it is acceptable to be on
that particular curve at all.* Creativity is the discovery of
altogether new curves. Strategy analysts may assist in discovering them, but they are not able to furnish marvelous techniques for doing so. The decision to send a manned expedition to the moon was a creative decision, right or wrong, and
one which would not meet the test of any normal economic
criteria.

In a deeper philosophical sense, the future is not only
unknown but unknowable. This fact presents a particular
hazard for creativity in national policy—the temptation to
pursue utopian solutions. To be able to visualize a resolution
of the problems raised by the existence of nuclear weapons is
to be deceived by one's own desire. Hegel, who made the
highest claims for historical inevitability, nevertheless denied
the possibility of insight coming to the aid of those who
attempt to set the course of history: "Philosophy always

---

* Bernard Brodie, "The Scientific Strategists," in *Administration of National Security* (Selected Papers by the Subcommittee on National Security
Staffing and Operations of the Committee on Government Operations, U.S.
Congress, Senate [Washington, D.C.: Government Printing Office, 1962]),
p. 198.

arrives too late for that. . . . The owl of Minerva begins its flight when dusk is falling."*

The breadth of judgment, then, that is needed to transcend the limits of analysis and methodology must reside in the decision-maker himself. Otherwise, he would be no more than the efficient manipulator of power. He would be limited to mechanical perceptions of international conflict, bound by techniques and procedures, and constrained from the creative search for new solutions. He would lack the understanding of the real stakes of conflict, the values inherent in the political system that he serves. The wisdom that is required to strike a balance between resolution and restraint in the use of nuclear power would be wanting.

* Quoted in Carl J. Friedrich, *The Philosophy of Hegel* (New York: Random House, 1954), p. 227.

Contributors

GEN. CHARLES H. BONESTEEL, III, is Commanding General of the United States Eighth Army in Korea. He has served as Special Assistant to Ambassador Harriman, then heading the Marshall Plan in Europe; as a deputy to Ambassador Spofford with the NATO Council Deputies; as Defense Member of the Planning Board of the NSC; and as Special Assistant (Policy) to the Chairman of the JCS. He has commanded the 24th Infantry Division and the VII Corps and has served as Director of Special Studies in the Office of the Chief of Staff, USA. He has also been Senior USA Member of the Military Staff Committee of the U.N. Gen. Bonesteel is a graduate of the USMA, the National War College, and Oxford University.

JAMES ELIOT CROSS, author of *Conflict in the Shadows: The Nature and Politics of Guerrilla War*, is a Professorial Lecturer in the School of International Service, American University, and Secretary of the Institute for Defense Analyses where, from 1963–64, he was Acting Director of the Economic and Political Studies Division. A graduate of Yale University, he holds an LL.B. from the University of Virginia and has served as a Research Assistant to George F. Kennan at the Institute for Advanced Study, Princeton University; as a staff member of the Gaither Committee; and as a Special Assistant to the Secretary of the Navy.

GEN. DWIGHT D. EISENHOWER, 34th President of the United States, is the author of *Crusade in Europe, Mandate for Change*, and *Waging Peace: The White House Years, 1956–61*. Among his many assignments, he has served as Allied Commander in Chief during World War II; as Commander of U.S. occupation forces in Germany; as Chief of Staff of the U.S. Army; and as Supreme Commander, Allied Powers Europe. Gen. Eisenhower served as President of Columbia

333

University from 1948–52 and is the recipient of honorary degrees from numerous institutions in this country and abroad.

LT. COL. ROBERT G. GARD, JR., is Military Assistant to the Secretary of Defense. He was formerly Special Assistant to the Assistant Secretary of Defense, International Security Affairs (ASD–ISA), and Chief of the NATO Branch of the European–Western Hemisphere Division of the Policy Planning Staff in the Office of the ASD–ISA. He earlier commanded the 5th Battalion (Airborne) 81st Artillery, 8th Infantry Division. He is a graduate of the USMA, where he taught from 1957–60, and holds an M.P.A. and Ph.D. from Harvard University.

COL. ROBERT NEVILLE GINSBURGH, who has recently been selected to become a Brigadier General, is a member of the Chairman's Staff Group in the Office of the Chairman of the JCS. A contributor to numerous journals, he is the author of *U.S. Military Strategy in the Sixties.* He has been a member of the State Department's Policy Planning Council, Assistant Executive to two USAF Chiefs of Staff, and Legislative Liaison Officer in the Office of the Secretary of the Air Force. From 1955–58, he was a Plans Officer of the Allied Air Forces Southern Europe. Col. Ginsburgh holds a B.S. from the USMA, where he was an Assistant Professor, and an M.A., M.P.A., and Ph.D. from Harvard.

LT. GEN. ANDREW J. GOODPASTER, Director of Army Studies, was formerly Director of the Joint Staff. He earlier served as Special Assistant to the Chairman, JCS. Other posts have included Commanding General of the 8th Infantry Division in Europe; Defense Liaison Officer and Staff Secretary to the President of the United States (1954–61); and Special Assistant to the Chief of Staff, SHAPE (1950–54). He holds a B.S. from the USMA and an M.A., M.S.E., and Ph.D. from Princeton. He has recently been named the next Commandant of the National War College.

LT. COL. PAUL F. GORMAN is Commanding Officer of the 1st Battalion, 26th Infantry, 1st Infantry Division, now stationed in Vietnam. He has served as Deputy Secretary to the General Staff, Seventh Army, and in the International Policy Division of the Plans Directorate of the Army General Staff. He is a graduate of the USMA, where he later served as an Assistant Professor, and holds an M.P.A. from Harvard.

COL. AMOS A. JORDAN, JR., Professor of Social Sciences at the USMA, is a graduate of that institution and of Oxford University and holds a

Ph.D. from Columbia University. He is the author of *Foreign Aid and the Defense of Southeast Asia*, and a contributor to *Contemporary Foreign Governments, Southeast Asia: Problems of United States Policy, Economics of National Security*, and numerous journals. Among his many politico-military assignments, Col. Jordan has served as Director, Near East and South Asia Region, in the Office of the Assistant Secretary of Defense; as Special Political Adviser to the U.S. Ambassador to India; and as Economic and Fiscal Policy Adviser in the U.S. Economic Mission to Korea.

LT. COL. ROGER H. NYE is an Associate Professor at the USMA. He has served in a variety of military assignments, including Battalion Executive Officer and S-3, Reconnaissance Squadron, 24th Division, in Germany. A graduate of the USMA, he holds an M.P.A. from Princeton and is currently a doctoral candidate at Columbia.

LT. COL. GEORGE K. OSBORN, III, is a Senior Investigator (Research and Analysis) in the Advanced Projects Agency Field Unit in Vietnam. He earned his B.A., M.A., and Ph.D. at Stanford University and has been an Assistant Professor at the USMA. Lt. Col. Osborn has also served as Assistant Executive Officer, J-3 (Plans, Policies, and Operations), U.S. European Command.

COL. WESLEY W. POSVAR is the editor of *American Defense Policy* and a contributor to numerous periodicals. A graduate of the USMA and the Air Tactical School, he holds a B.A. from Oxford University and an M.A., M.P.A., and Ph.D. from Harvard. Col. Posvar is Professor of Political Science at the USAF Academy and Chairman of the Department of Political Science. He has been a Littauer Fellow at Harvard and a Research Fellow at the MIT Center for International Studies. He has recently been chosen to be Chancellor of the University of Pittsburgh.

RUTH B. RUSSELL, Research Associate in the School of International Affairs, Columbia University, is the author of *A History of the United Nations Charter: Role of the United States, 1941–45; U.N. Experience with Military Forces: Political and Legal Aspects;* and *The U.N. and U.S. Security Policy*, and has contributed to numerous scholarly journals. She has been a member of the Senior Research Staff, Foreign Policy Studies, of the Brookings Institution; an Assistant to the Special Assistant for Postwar Planning, in the State Department; and a member of the Secretariat of the Bretton Woods International Monetary Conference. Miss Russell holds a B.S. and M.A. from the University of California at Berkeley.

LT. COL. JOHN W. SEIGLE is presently with the U.S. Army in Vietnam. His earlier assignments included Tank Company Commander, 1st Armored Division and Assistant Operations Officer, CCA, 3rd Armored Division. He is a graduate of the USMA, where he was an Assistant Professor from 1963–65. Lt. Col. Seigle was a Littauer Fellow and Teaching Fellow in Government at Harvard University and he holds an M.P.A. and Ph.D. from that institution.

LT. COL. WILLIAM P. SNYDER is the author of *The Politics of British Defense Policy: 1945–62* and *Casebook in Military Systems Analysis*, and a contributor to *A Modern Design for Defense Decision: A McNamara-Hitch-Enthoven Anthology.* He served as an Assistant Professor in the Department of Social Sciences at the USMA, from which he holds a B.S. degree, and is currently a student at the U.S. Army Command and General Staff College. Lt. Col. Snyder earned his Ph.D. at Princeton University.

GEN. ROBERT JEFFERSON WOOD, RET., was Director of Military Assistance in the Office of the Secretary of Defense just prior to his retirement in 1965. His long career has included service as Deputy Defense Adviser to the U.S. Ambassador to NATO; Commanding General of the AAA and Guided Missile Center at Ft. Bliss, Texas; Deputy Chief in the Office of the Chief of Research and Development in the Department of the Army; and Commanding General of the U.S. Army Air Defense Command in Colorado Springs. Gen. Wood is a graduate of the USMA and the National War College.